D1341875

Assessing Quality of Life in Alzheimer's Disease

Steven M. Albert, Ph.D., M.Sc. is Assistant Professor of Neuropsychology (Neurology) and Public Health (Sociomedical Sciences) at Columbia University. His research examines the quality of life impact of cognitive deficit in both clinical settings and in population-based research. He leads the Outcomes Division of the Gertrude H. Sergievsky Center at the College of Physicians and Surgeons at Columbia University and directs the MPH Program in Aging and Public Health at the Joseph L. Mailman School of Public Health. Recent projects include a study of the quality of life of people with advanced dementia and an analysis of the risk of medical service use associated with Alzheimer's disease. He is currently completing research on determinants of self-reported functional ability among older adults in different sociocultural groups.

Rebecca G. Logsdon, Ph.D., is Research Associate Professor in the Department of Psychosocial and Community Health, University of Washington School of Nursing. She is a clinical psychologist specializing in gerontology, and has been affiliated with the University of Washington Geriatric and Family Services Clinic and Alzheimer's Disease Research Center for over 13 years. Her research focuses on maximizing functioning and improving quality of life for individuals with dementia and their caregivers. Recent projects involve assessment and treatment of depression, anxiety, and agitation by teaching family caregivers problem-solving strategies and identifying and implementing meaningful activities and pleasant events. Dr. Logsdon is principal investigator of a National Institute of Aging longitudinal investigation of quality of life of individuals with Alzheimer's disease and their caregivers.

Assessing Quality of Life in Alzheimer's Disease

Steven M. Albert, PhD, MSc
Rebecca G. Logsdon, PhD

Editors

 Springer Publishing Company

The bulk of the material in this volume was originally published as a special issue of the *Journal of Mental Health and Aging* (Volume 5, Number 1, 1999).

Springer Publishing Company, Inc.
536 Broadway
New York, NY 10012-3955

Acquisitions Editor: Bill Tucker
Production Editor: Helen Song
Cover design by James Scotto-Lavino

00 01 02 03 04 / 5 4 3 2 1

Library of Congress Cataloging-in-Publication-Data

Assessing quality of life in Alzheimer's disease / Steven M. Albert and Rebecca
  G. Logsdon, editors
        p.   cm.
  Includes bibliographical references and index.
  ISBN 0-8261-1333-8
  1. Alzheimer's disease--Patients--Care. 2. Quality of life. I. Albert, Steven
M. (Steven Mark), 1956- II. Logsdon, Rebecca G.

RC523 .A83 2000
362.1'96831—dc21

                                                                99-088404

Printed in the United States of America

Contents

Contributors

Robert Abrams, M.D.
Weill Medical College of
  Cornell University
New York, New York

Steven M. Albert, Ph.D., M.Sc.
Gertrude H. Sergievsky Center
Columbia University
New York, New York

Karen Bell, M.D.
Columbia University
New York, New York

Betty S. Black, Ph.D.
Johns Hopkins University
Baltimore, Maryland

Meryl Brod, Ph.D.
Lewin Group
San Francisco, California

Lois Camberg, Ph.D.
West Roxbury/Brockton Veterans
  Administration Medical Center
Bedford, Massachusetts

Caridad Castillo-Castanada, B.A.
Columbia University
New York, New York

Laura E. Gibbons, Ph.D.
University of Washington
Seattle, Washington

Richard J. Harvey, M.D., FRCP
Institute of Neurology,
  The National Hospital
Queen Square, London

Douglas Holmes, Ph.D.
Hebrew Home for the Aged at
  Riverdale
New York, New York

Ann C. Hurley, R.N., D.N.Sc.
E.N. Rogers Memorial
  Veterans Hospital and
  Northeastern University
Bedford, Massachusetts

Diane M. Jacobs, Ph.D.
Columbia University
New York, New York

Bruce Jennings, M.A.
The Hastings Center
Garrison, New York

Judith D. Kasper, Ph.D.
Johns Hopkins University
Baltimore, Maryland

Leah Kleinman, Ph.D.
Johns Hopkins University
Baltimore, Maryland

M. Powell Lawton, Ph.D.
Polisher Institute
The Philadelphia Geriatric Center
Philadelphia, Pennsylvania

Rebecca G. Logsdon, Ph.D.
University of Washington
Seattle, Washington
Johns Hopkins University

Susan M. McCurry, Ph.D.
University of Washington
Seattle, Washington

Carol Merchant, M.D., M.P.H.
Columbia University
New York, New York

Donald L. Patrick, Ph.D.
University of Washington
Seattle, Washington

Margaret Perkinson, Ph.D.
The Philadelphia Geriatric Center
Philadelphia, Pennsylvania

Peter V. Rabins, M.D.
Johns Hopkins University
Baltimore, Maryland

Martin N. Rossor, M.D., F.R.C.P.
Institute of Neurology,
   The National Hospital
Queen Square, London

Katy Ruckdeschel, Ph.D.
The Philadelphia Geriatric Center
Philadelphia, Pennsylvania

Laura Sands, Ph.D.
University of California
   San Francisco
San Francisco, California

Mary Sano, Ph.D.
Gertrude H. Sergievsky Center
Columbia University
New York, New York

Mario Schittini, M.D.. M.P.H.
Columbia University
New York, New York

Caroline E. Selai, Ph.D.
Institute of Neurology,
   The National Hospital
Queen Square, London

Joyce Simard, M.S.W.
CareMatrix
Needham, Massachusetts

Scott Small, M.D.
Columbia University
New York, New York

Yaakov Stern, Ph.D.
Columbia University
New York, New York

Anita L. Stewart, Ph.D.
University of California
   San Francisco
San Francisco, California

Linda Teri, Ph.D.
University of Washington
Seattle, Washington

Jeanne Teresi, Ed.D., Ph.D.
Hebres Home for the Aged
   Research Division
Riverdale, New York

Rochelle Tractenberg, Ph.D.
University of California San Diego
La Jolla, California

Michael R. Trimble, M.D., F.R.C.P.
Institute of Neurology,
   The National Hospital
Queen Square, London

Kimberly Van Haitsma, Ph.D.
The Philadelphia Geriatric Center
Philadelphia, Pennsylvania

Ladislav Volicer, M.D.
E.N. Rogers Memorial Veterans
   Hospital-GRECC
Bedfords, Massachusetts

Peter J. Whitehouse, M.D., Ph.D.
The Alzheimer's Center
University Hospitals Cleveland
Cleveland, Ohio

Introduction

Assessing Quality of Life in Alzheimer's Disease: Conceptual and Methodological Issues

Rebecca G. Logsdon and Steven M. Albert

Quality of life (QOL) is an elusive concept that has been defined in a variety of ways, depending on the context in which it is used and on the conceptual orientation of the investigator (c.f. McSweeny & Creer, 1995). Medically oriented definitions of QOL include physical, social, and role functioning; mental heath; and perception of health (Cella, 1992; Wilson & Cleary, 1995). From a bioethical view, QOL has been defined as the essential conditions beyond mere survival that are needed for individuals to have experiences that provide meaning and joy to their time (Post & Whitehouse, 1995; Roy, 1992). Lawton (1983, 1991) provides a theoretical framework for QOL in older adults that includes four domains: behavioral competence (the ability to function in adaptive and socially appropriate ways), objective environment (everything that exists externally of the individual, including both physical and interpersonal factors), psychological well-being (mental health and emotional status), and the individual's subjective perception of and satisfaction with his or her overall quality of life. In a review of quality of life research in frail older adults, Birren and Deutchman (1991) describe quality of life as a multidimensional construct, including social, environmental, health, spiritual, and emotional states. Whitehouse and Rabins (1992) add work and hobby activities, cognitive ability, economic success, and subjective well-being to the list, and point out that, ultimately, quality of life is determined by the individual's own assessment of the relative importance of each of these factors. A report of the Institute of Medicine (IOM, 1986) echoes these views of quality of life, describing QOL in chronically ill older adults as a sense of well-being, satisfaction with life, and self-esteem, that is achieved through the care received, the accomplishment of desired goals, and the ability to exercise a satisfactory degree of control over one's life.

QOL has been identified as an important outcome variable with diseases as diverse as mental illness, cardiovascular disease, cancer, and asthma (Guyatt, Feeny, & Patrick, 1993; Parmenter, 1994; Patrick & Bergner, 1990; Romney, Brown, & Fry, 1994; Wilson & Cleary, 1995). Contents of QOL assessments are as diverse as the diseases themselves, including specific health-related outcomes (such as physical symptoms of a specific illness), functional assessments (e.g., ability to dress oneself), psychosocial outcomes (such as depression or relationships with family), and economic outcomes (such as return to employment after an illness). QOL assessments also include multiple perspectives—the patient, a family member, a health care provider, or society as a whole (Pearlman & Jonsen, 1985). Finally, both objective factors (overtly measurable characteristics) and subjective reports (individual perceptions and interpretations) have been used to a greater or lesser extent in defining QOL across investigations (McSweeny & Creer, 1995).

Thus, there is tremendous diversity in how QOL is defined and measured, who is asked about QOL, and why QOL is evaluated. Despite this, as researchers become more aware of the issues involved in assessing QOL, some areas of agreement appear to have emerged. Common threads include the acknowledgment that assessment of QOL involves both a subjective global rating by the individual, as well as more specific ratings of physical, psychological, and social variables, and the recognition that the exact nature of the assessment of QOL depends on the group being evaluated and the purpose of the evaluation. The importance of the individual's personal sense of satisfaction with various areas of life is recognized by all, as are the contributions of physical comfort, emotional well-being, and interpersonal connections.

Assessing QOL in Alzheimer's Disease (AD) poses unique challenges that have only recently been addressed. First, QOL assessment is difficult because affected individuals eventually lose the ability to comprehend questions or communicate their own subjective states. As a result, researchers must carefully evaluate the cognitive and communicative abilities of individuals before assuming they can respond appropriately to QOL assessments. Mildly affected individuals can often respond to carefully designed instruments, but it remains unclear when, in the course of dementing illness, individuals are no longer able to provide reliable reports. For more severely affected individuals, researchers must rely on proxy reports or behavioral observations, which introduce additional difficulties.

A second challenge involves the residential status of the individual being assessed. Through the course of the disease, individuals may move from independent living, to assisted living, to institutional settings. Different living situations offer radically different environments, with different opportunities and challenges to QOL; these must be considered in any adequate measurement system. A related challenge is to find indicators of quality in individuals whose daily lives are quite restricted by care environments.

Finally, QOL assessment efforts have been hampered by a widespread sense that cognitive impairment undercuts the basis of personal identity and, for this reason, makes QOL assessment beside the point. Some bioethicists have gone so far as to say that "the severely demented . . . approach more closely the condition of animals than normal adult humans in their psychological capacities" (Buchanan & Brock, 1989).

Reasons for measuring QOL in people with AD, however, are now quite clear. First, therapies for AD have become increasingly available; QOL indicators are required to determine if therapies have intended effects and may help clarify the route by which these treatments have their effect. For example, suppose a therapy delays functional decline without a clear benefit in patient cognitive performance, as was the case in the recent selegiline and alpha-tocopherol trial (Sano, Ernesto, Thomas, et al., 1996). QOL measures might identify alterations in mood, engagement in activities, self-awareness, response to the environment, and other allied indicators that would shed light on this finding by identifying areas of improvement that impact functioning but are not assessed by traditional cognitive tests.

Second, QOL assessments may provide a measure of "consumer satisfaction" with treatment. QOL assessment offers a mechanism for individuals to weigh costs and benefits of treatment and to rate the overall impact of treatment on their lives. Researchers are increasingly concerned with "clinical significance;" QOL assessments may be the most effective way of obtaining this information, since they provide a mechanism for individuals and their caregivers to express whether an intervention made an important difference in the patient's life.

Third, patients with comparable levels of cognitive deficit show great variability in some indicators of QOL, including affective expression and participation in activities. QOL measures may provide an opportunity to refine measures of disease severity, and may sharpen the ability of these measures to predict time to disease end points.

Finally, QOL measures can be used to assess how disabling a disease state is, and how much benefit individuals and society can expect to gain from slowing progression or delaying onset. Judgments of quality of life at different stages of chronic illness have been used to evaluate the relative utility of treatments (Sano, Albert, Trachtenberg, et al., 1998). One goal of treatment of AD is to preserve the functioning of the affected individual for as long as possible, and to shorten the length of time of severe impairment. Individuals indicate that they prefer to live longer in a milder stage of dementia than in a more advanced stage, and even mild advances in treatments for early-stage AD would likely yield major cost savings in a cost-effectiveness model, by delaying the need for the most intensive level of care (Albert & Sano, 1997).

This volume provides an overview of both conceptual and practical issues in the measurement of QOL in AD. Three papers explore the use of self-report measures for individuals with mild to moderate cognitive impairment (Brod, Logsdon, Selai), three rely on proxy assessment (Rabins, Albert, Sano), and two on behavioral observation of indicators of QOL (Lawton, Volicer). Teresi and colleagues discuss difficulties of assessing depression and other subjective states in individuals with impaired cognition and communication ability, and provide recommendations for such assessments. Simard discusses an innovative approach to improving QOL in individuals with mild cognitive impairment who reside in assisted living facilities. A final paper sets QOL investigation and dementia in a philosophical context (Jennings). In his conclusion, Whitehouse reviews the current state of the art of QOL assessment in AD and provides recommendations for future research.

This volume is intended to provide a foundation for ongoing work in QOL assessment in AD. Many questions are raised; few are completely answered. Both ethical and conceptual issues about what should rightfully be included in the assessment of QOL in Alzheimer's disease are identified. Methodological issues, including use of self-report, proxy report, and direct observation (as well as establishment of reliability and validity of QOL measures), and the use of these measures with individuals who have differing degrees of cognitive impairment are discussed. Solutions are proposed, and some are empirically tested, but it is clear that this line of research is in its infancy and will benefit from ongoing dialogue and collaboration among investigators, clinicians, and philosophers. The ultimate goal of this volume is to facilitate such collaborations, and to develop a network of researchers who rigorously tackle these important issues.

REFERENCES

Albert, S. M., & Sano, M. (1997). Eliciting utilities for states of dementia. Paper presented at the meeting of the International Psychogeriatrics Association, Jerusalem, Israel.

Buchanan, A. E., & Brock, D. W. (1989). *Deciding for others: The ethics of surrogate decision making.* Cambridge, England: Cambridge University Press.

Cella, D. F. (1992). Quality of life: The concept. *Journal of Palliative Care, 8*(3), 8-13.

Birren, J. E., & Deutchman, D.E. (1991). Concepts and content of quality of life in the later years: An overview. In J. E. Birren, J. E. Lubben, J. C. Rowe, & D. E. Deutchman (Eds.), *The concept and measurement of quality of life in the frail elderly.* New York: Academic Press, Inc., pp. 344-360.

Guyatt, G. H., Feeny, D. H., & Patrick, D. L. (1993). Measuring health-related quality of life. *Annals of Internal Medicine, 118,* 622-629.

Institute of Medicine (1986). *Improving the quality of care in nursing homes.* Washington, DC: National Academy Press.

Lawton, M. P. (1983). The dimensions of well-being. *Experimental Aging Research, 9*(2), 65-72.

Lawton, M. P. (1991). A multidimensional view of quality of life in frail elders. In J. E. Birren, J. E. Lubben, J. C. Rowe, & D. E. Deutchman (Eds.), *The concept and measurement of quality of life in the frail elderly* (pp. 4-27). New York: Academic Press, Inc.

McSweeny, A. J., & Creer, T. L. (1995). Health-related quality of life assessment in medical care. *Disease-a-Month, XLI,* 11-71.

Parmenter, T. R. (1994). Quality of life as a concept and measurable entity. *Social Indicators Research, 33,* 9-46.

Patrick, D. L., & Bergner, M. (1990). Measurement of health status in the 1990s. *Annual Review of Public Health, 11,* 165-183.

Pearlman, R. A., & Jonsen, A. (1985). The use of quality-of-life considerations in medical decision making. *Journal of the American Geriatrics Society, 33,* 344-352.

Post, S. G., & Whitehouse, P. J. (1995). Fairhill Guidelines on ethics of the care of people with Alzheimer's disease: A clinical summary. *Journal of the American Geriatrics Society, 43,* 1423-1429.

Romney, D. M., Brown, R. I., & Fry, P. S. (1994). Improving quality of life: Prescriptions for change. *Social Indicators Research, 33,* 237-272.

Roy, D. J. (1992). Measurement in the service of compassion. *Journal of Palliative Care, 8*(3), 3-4.

Sano, M., Ernesto, C., Thomas, R. G., Klauber, M. R., Schafer, K., Grundman, M., Woodbury, P., Growdon, J., Cotman, C. W., Pfieffer, E., Schneider, L. S., & Thal, L. J. (1997). A controlled trial of selegiline, alpha-tocopherol, or both as a treatment for Alzheimer's disease. *New England Journal of Medicine, 336,* 1216-1222.

Sano, M., Albert, S. M., Trachtenberg, R., & Schittini, M. (1998). Assessing quality of life in Alzheimer's disease: Ratings by members of the ADCS. *Neurology, 50* (suppl. 4), A301.

Whitehouse, P. J., & Rabins, P. V. (1992). Quality of life and dementia (editorial). *Alzheimer Disease and Associated Disorders, 6,* 135-137.

Wilson, I. B., & Cleary, P. D. (1995). Linking clinical variables with health-related quality of life: A conceptual model of patient outcomes. *Journal of the American Medical Association, 273,* 59-65.

Part I

Self-Report Measures
of
Quality of Life

1

Conceptualization of Quality of Life in Dementia

Meryl Brod, Anita L. Stewart, and Laura Sands

C onsideration of the concept of quality of life (QOL) in dementias of the Alzheimer's or vascular type is a relatively new phenomenon. Only 10 years ago, the issue was whether demented patients could even experience quality of life. In 1992, editorials were being written calling for attention to the topic (Whitehouse & Rabins, 1992). As recently as 1994, Lawton wrote "Quality of life is a concept much in the forefront of gerontological research but is neglected for the most part in patients with Alzheimer disease." Fortunately, in the last several years the field has progressed sufficiently to where we now ask questions such as "What is the best way to measure QOL in dementia?" and "How does QOL change as the disease progresses?" We are thus at the beginning of a new era in conceptualizing and assessing the QOL of persons with dementia. It is an exciting time when both researchers and clinicians are learning to speak the language of dementia and are interacting more directly with persons with dementia as well as their caregivers. This changing approach is occurring at the same time that, in the larger field of quality of life research, conceptualizations of QOL are being refined and sharpened so that clear distinctions between global, health-related, and disease-specific QOL can be appreciated. Dementia is now being acknowledged as another chronic condition for which a disease-specific QOL focus is needed (Rabins & Kasper, 1997). Such efforts will enable research on questions about the effect of treatments, interventions, patient characteristics, and life circumstances on the QOL of persons with dementia.

It is the goal of this paper to: (1) briefly review what is currently known about conceptualizing dementia-specific QOL, (2) present a model for conceptualizing QOL in this population, (3) offer preliminary support for this model with data from the Dementia Quality of Life scale (D-QOL), a patient-focused measure of QOL based on this conceptualization, and (4) contribute to the discussion of how best to 'think and talk about' QOL for persons with dementia.

3

PRIOR EFFORTS AT CONCEPTUALIZING QOL
IN DEMENTIA

Whereas over 20,000 articles have appeared in Medline since 1980 with 'quality of life' as a keyword, this number drops dramatically to 151 when the keywords of dementia or Alzheimer's are used in addition. One hundred thirty-two (87%) of these were published between 1990 and mid-1998. Of these, only 25 have the words 'quality of life' in the title, and of these 25, three are editorials and four are related to other forms of dementia (AIDS, cancer). A closer inspection of the larger literature of 151 articles reveals that the majority of these publications only briefly mention QOL as an area that needs to be explored or note that it is likely to be affected by the intervention under discussion. Many of the remaining publications which focus directly on quality of life assess only one aspect of QOL, for example, depression, functioning, or behaviors. In all but a very few, QOL is assessed by proxy, clinical rating, or observation. This paper is not intended to be a comprehensive review of this literature, rather, we will cite issues raised by these publications.

ISSUES IN CONCEPTUALIZING QUALITY OF LIFE
FOR DEMENTED PERSONS

To adequately conceptualize QOL, two steps are essential. First, one must adequately define the phenomenon. Second, a model depicting the elements of the conceptual framework and their interrelationships must be elucidated.

Definition. Quality of life for persons with dementia has been defined in many ways, but most notably, it has not been defined at all (Lawton, 1997). Historically, definitions of QOL in dementia have relied on generic definitions taken from the field of general quality of life, which are then superimposed on dementia. The traditional components of quality of life include physical, mental, and spiritual health, cognitive abilities, family and social relations, work and hobby activities, economic success, and—a critical element—subjective well-being. Unfortunately, when dementia-specific definitions based on these domains have been offered, they tend to be derived from assumptions about the demented person's QOL by the caregiver or health care professional (Albert, 1997; DeJong, Osterland, & Roy, 1989). Definitions have largely ignored the point of view of those very persons whose QOL is being evaluated (Cotrell & Schulz, 1993). Thus, the definition and operationalization of QOL for dementia have been inconsistent and no commonly accepted standard has evolved (Howard & Rockwood, 1995).

Is QOL a unidimensional or a multidimensional construct for demented persons? Quality of life as defined by Lawton (1991) is "the multidimensional evaluation, by both interpersonal and social-normative criteria, of the person-environment system of the individual." This generic definition can be made more relevant for a particular reference group by determining which domains are most salient for that population. Lawton (1997) has suggested five concepts that are relevant to persons with dementia, including self-esteem, satisfaction with health care, spare time, meaningful time use, and social engagement.

However, most studies of QOL in dementia use a single construct to assess QOL. For the most part these have been objective indicators such as problematic behaviors or daily activities. Perhaps even more troublesome in the quest for an adequate definition of QOL in dementia is that the objective events for which the data are collected are themselves often only proxy indicators of QOL. For example, the number of pleasant events (Teri & Logsdon, 1991) has been used as a surrogate measure of QOL (Albert, 1997). Yet, the authors of the instrument suggest that the reason to measure pleasant events is to help generate a strategy to improve well-being through the development of individualized, appropriate programs (Teri & Logsdon, 1991). It is understandable that because of issues of recall, comprehension and anosognosia in dementia patients, it is the observable domains which have been most often assessed. However, this approach has further clouded the definition of QOL for dementia by precluding development of definitions that include subjective components (Stewart, Sherbourne, & Brod, 1996), as well as development of multidimensional instruments for dementia patients that tap a broad range of domains of QOL (Stewart et al., 1996).

The subjective meaning of QOL in dementia has also been qualitatively explored by direct observation or conversations with persons with dementia. The consistent thread that runs through these efforts is the assertion that persons with dementia do experience variations in QOL and that there can be meaning in their lives. More important, environments and interventions can impact their QOL. However, for the most part, this work has been phenomenological in nature and has not led to conceptual models (Gwyther, 1997; Kitwood & Bredin, 1992; Parse, 1996; Quayhagen & Quayhagen, 1996; Ronch, 1996).

From this qualitative work, Kitwood and Bredin (1992) found 12 indicators of well-being which they derived from many hours of detailed observations of patients in a variety of settings. They are: (1) the assertion of desire or will, (2) the ability to experience and express a range of positive and negative emotions, (3) initiation of social contact, (4) affectionate warmth, (5) social security, (6) self-respect, (7) acceptance of other dementia sufferers, (8) humor, (9) creativity and self-expression, (10) showing evident pleasure, (11) helpfulness, and (12) relaxation. They found that these domains were independent of the level of cognitive impairment so that "some who have long since reached a zero score on all cognitive tests still appear to be faring well as persons" (Kitwood & Bredin, 1992, p. 280). Further exploration by the authors of these 12 indicators suggested four global sentient states expressed by the indicators. These states are: (1) sense of personal worth, (2) sense of agency, (3) social confidence, and (4) hope.

Conceptual Models. In the larger field of health-related quality of life (both generic and disease-specific), there has been very little research that conceptualizes relationships among domains of QOL or describes its determinants and the intervening variables that may mediate these relationships. Two such generic models are worth noting: the model proposed by Lawton (1983) and Wilson and Cleary (1995). Lawton, (1983, p. 352) in his model, laid the conceptual foundation for defining QOL as being distinct from either objective or psychological domains. In one of the first pathway models of general QOL, Lawton described *perceived QOL* as a "set of evaluations that a person makes about each major domain of his or her life." In his conceptualization of the "good life," QOL was defined as distinct from behavioral competence, objective environment, and psychological well-being. The model of Wilson and Cleary proposes relationships between clinical and nonclinical variables to measures of health-related quality of life in the hope of facilitating effective clinical interventions to improve patient QOL. Further effort toward such a model that is dementia specific could help clarify some of the issues reviewed above.

Our own prior work in conceptualizing and measuring QOL in dementia began with the challenge to develop a disease-specific instrument that would assess QOL by directly querying the demented person, thus avoiding the known problems inherent in proxy assessments. This work has resulted in the development of the Dementia Quality of Life scale (D-QOL) (Brod, Stewart, Sands, & Walton, 1999). The underlying assumption in our prior work was that demented persons have experiences and interpretations of these experiences of which others may have little knowledge (Albert et al., 1996; Brod et al., 1999). "Objective and quantitative measurement of a priori identified QOL characteristics without sufficient prior attention to a full examination of the subjective and qualitative experiences of persons with dementia may lead us to measure aspects of quality of life that lack meaning for these persons" (Russel, 1996 (p.1401).

In our original framework, QOL was thought of as a multidimensional construct uniquely defined by the nature and experience of living with dementia. It was unclear at the outset if traditional domains of QOL were relevant for this population, or how they would interrelate. To address this issue, a series of expert panels were held with dementia patients, caregivers and care providers in which domains of QOL and factors which affected disease-specific QOL were explored. Thus, the intent was for the QOL domains identified to emerge from community dialogue (Post & Whitehouse, 1995). The expert panels confirmed that dementia affects all traditional domains of QOL, confirming our belief that the impact of dementia is multidimensional. This impact was disease specific, i.e., directly related to cognitive, behavioral and social changes accompanying disease progression. However, although the parent domains were similar, the behaviors and emotions associated with the domains were shaped by the presence of dementia and thus were substantially different in definition from other conceptualizations. For example, mobility did not focus on the physical ability to get around; rather it involved issues of confusion and disorientation which precluded going out alone. We found that self-concept needs to include the element of self-consciousness, and that negative affect should include embarrassment. Two new domains were also found to be important: domains we labeled "aesthetics" and "interaction capacity." Aesthetics is defined as the appreciation and pleasure obtained from sensory awareness on either a verbal or nonverbal level, such as viewing or creating art. Interaction Capacity is a disease-specific domain that includes difficulties in areas such as communication and reading.

This initial work has been presented elsewhere (Brod et al., 1999; Stewart et al., 1996) and is important to this discussion as it was the foundation for the refined conceptual framework of dementia-specific QOL presented below. In our original conceptual work, we did not make a distinction between determinants and QOL itself.

CONCEPTUAL MODEL OF QUALITY OF LIFE IN DEMENTIA

Figure 1.1 presents the refined conceptual model of dementia-specific QOL and its determinants. We are greatly indebted to the work of others, most notably Lawton (1991; 1983; 1994) and Wilson and Cleary (1995) from which this framework has evolved. The model in this initial presentation is intentionally simple and arrows are unidirectional solely to imply a chronology. We recognize that many of the associations between context, functioning, behavior, and QOL variables are most likely bidirectional and that variables within and between each of these domains do not exist in isolation of each other. For example, in context, interaction capacity may be impacted by comorbid illness, environment and/or individual characteristics. Engaging in discretionary activities may be affected by physical functioning and/or disabilities. Further research is needed to clarify these relationships. Variables listed within each category are presented as examples and are not meant to be exhaustive.

Context. Context refers to the individual characteristics and life circumstances that help shape the individual's subjective experience of QOL. They include: dementia signs and symptoms, comorbid illnesses, environment (physical and social), and nondisease-related individual characteristics. Dementia signs and symptoms are those reflecting the underlying physiological processes inherent in dementia. These include mental status, interaction capacity or degree of confusion, duration, and type of dementia. Comorbid illness includes the person's other physical conditions which may affect QOL. For example, a dementia patient who has arthritis may have related mobility problems which, distinct from the dementia, might also affect QOL. The physical and social environment of the person refers to external factors such as living arrangement (whom the person lives with and the nature of the relationship), degree of social support and the cultural influences which they experience. Nondisease-specific individual characteristics such as age,

DETERMINANTS

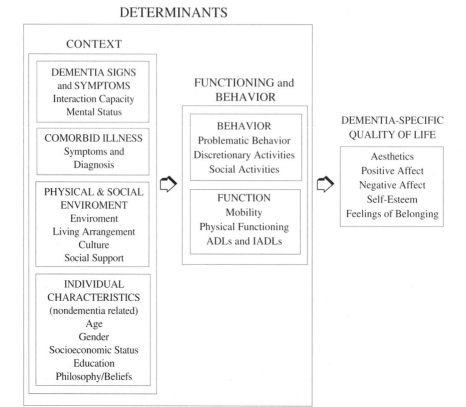

FIGURE 1.1   Conceptual Model of QOL in Dementia and its Determinants.

gender, socioeconomic status, philosophy and beliefs comprise the final contextual influences which help determine a person's QOL. Thus, the total context comprises both dementia-related and comorbid illness, environmental and individual characteristics.

Functioning and Behavior. In this model, objective functioning and behavior are considered as intermediate elements resulting from the context. Along with context, these are also determinants of quality of life. Thus, some domains traditionally considered as objective indicators of QOL are, in this model, determinants of QOL. Behaviors and functioning may impact QOL, but it is the individual's subjective experience and evaluation of his or her behavior and functioning that determines how one rates one's QOL. For example, a person may have a very active social life and yet feel lonely. This may help to explain why correlations between behaviors/functioning and subjective QOL, although sometimes significant, are only modest in strength (Nagatomo et al., 1997) and why objective measures of health, wealth, and relationships explain less than half the variance in perceived QOL for elders (Gwyther, 1997).

Functioning is defined as the extent of limitations or difficulties in basic activities such as bathing and toileting, walking, climbing stairs, instrumental activities such as telephoning and shopping, as well as areas such as mobility. As with behaviors, functioning in daily activities is observable and can be interpreted as either positive (absence of limitations) or negative.

Behaviors pertain to what people "do" as opposed to difficulties they may have with functioning. This domain includes the occurrence of the behavioral problems associated with dementia, such as wandering or shouting, social activities and discretionary activities such as participating in hobbies or exercise. Negative behaviors (wandering or shouting) can serve as an example of why such objective manifestations of the dementia are not considered part of QOL. First, the meaning of these behaviors in dementia is unclear. Some have even suggested that negative behaviors may be better conceived of as "problem-solving" behaviors wherein demented individuals try to redefine their sense of self (Russel, 1996). Albert (1997) echoes this idea in his statement (paraphrased) that behaviors included in this multivalent category, in the absence of other indicators of poor quality such as anxiety, should not in themselves be presumed as negative. An example of this provided by Albert is that excessive vocalization, which can be disturbing to caregivers and nursing home staff, may represent a demented person's attempt at self-stimulation in unsatisfying environments. Another example is repetitive questioning which may be an attempt at orientation or contact with a caregiver.

Dementia-Specific Quality of Life. Dementia-specific quality of life refers to individuals' subjective experience and evaluation of their life circumstances. Based on our previous qualitative work, literature reviews, and clinical experience, we define dementia-specific QOL as consisting of five domains: positive affect, negative affect, feelings of belonging, self-esteem, and sense of aesthetics. Positive affect includes the subjective experience of feeling happy, cheerful, content, and hopeful, as well as experiencing humor. Negative affect includes the subjective experience of feeling worried, frustrated, depressed, anxious, nervous, sad, lonely, afraid, irritable, embarrassed, and angry. Feelings of belonging includes feelings of being lovable, liked, and useful. Self-esteem includes feelings of accomplishment, confidence, satisfaction with oneself, and the perception of independent decision making. The aesthetics domain includes feelings of enjoyment from watching nature, the environment, from music, and from colors. Table 1.1 presents these domains.

Central to this model is the belief that although the objective dimensions of health are important in assessing the clinical course of illness, it is the person's subjective interpretation of the objective that truly defines QOL. We agree with Whitehouse and Rabins (1992) that although mental, social, and financial factors affect QOL, ultimately, it is up to each individual to evaluate and assess his or her own QOL, based on the degree of importance that he or she gives each component. We believe that inferring subjective QOL or well-being from external circumstances, or from

TABLE 1.1   Dementia-Specific Definition of Quality of Life

DOMAIN	DEFINITION
Aesthetics	enjoying/appreciating beauty, nature and surroundings (animals, music)
Positive Affect	experiencing humor (laughing, joking), feeling happy, cheerful, content, hopeful
Negative Affect	experiencing worry, frustration, depression, anxiety, sadness, loneliness, fear, irritability, nervousness, embarrassment, anger
Self-Esteem	feeling accomplished, confident or satisfied with self, able to make own decisions
Feelings of Belonging	feeling lovable and liked, useful

more objective domains such as functioning, does not fully take into account the values, needs, and adaptabilities of individuals to various life circumstances (Flanagan, 1982; Sanifort, Becker, & Diamond, 1996; Testa & Simonson, 1996). Although objective measures of health status are important, people may not always give their own health states sole or high priority in evaluating their own QOL (Lawton, 1991; O'Boyle, McGee, Hickey, O'Malley, & Joyce, 1992). This has been confirmed in reports of nonsignificant associations between clinical markers and the subjective experience of change in clinical trials (Dwosh, Giles, & Ford, 1983; Wilson & Cleary, 1995). A poignant example of this is provided by the experience of Christopher Reeves, who despite tragically becoming a quadriplegic, reports that his life is good and that he feels productive, loved, and hopeful about his future (Sloan, 1998).

Elucidating the way in which the determinants of QOL might be associated with one or more domains of QOL can help illustrate the distinction between determinants of QOL and QOL itself. For example, our research has shown that engaging in various discretionary activities is important to persons with dementia. Therefore, included in subjective QOL should be the feelings and emotions which are believed to accompany this behavior, such as feelings of accomplishment (self-esteem) or feeling useful (feelings of belonging). Another example might be social interactions. In this model, the frequency of social contacts is considered as an objective indicator. However, it is the subjective interpretation of feelings of loneliness (negative affect) or feelings of being liked (feelings of belonging) which constitutes QOL.

PRELIMINARY EMPIRICAL FINDINGS

In an iterative conceptual and statistical process, we developed the Dementia Quality of Life Scale (D-QOL), including items that reflect the subjective elements, i.e., the pure QOL elements. Ninety-five mild to moderately demented patients with MMSE (Mini-Mental State Exam) scores of 12 or greater were interviewed using the Dementia Quality of Life Instrument (see Brod, et al., 1997, for a full description of this work). The instrument has 29 items that comprise five subscales. Theory and prior research findings drove the assignment of items to hypothesized scales. We then conducted initial verification that items belonged to the assigned scales using statistical methods. We iteratively conducted principal components analyses on different subsets of items within the D-QOL to determine whether the structure of the components matched the conceptual framework specified above. For example, we combined into one component analysis the items that comprised the positive affect scale and the items from the aesthetics scale and assessed how many components emerged from the solution and which variables loaded highly on each component. Then we combined the items from the positive affect scales with the items from the self-esteem scales to determine the component structure of this new set of items. We continued this for all combinations of sets of items. This was necessary because the ratio of the number of subjects to the number of items was close to two. We consider this approach a first approximation to the statistical verification of the theoretical structure of the D-QOL. Consequently, we will not report component analysis results here other than to say that the component analyses revealed item groupings that closely matched the theoretical grouping of items discussed above. Thus, we consider these results using the D-QOL to be preliminary because of the many statistical limitations of analyzing many variables using a data set with a relatively small number of subjects.

Table 2 presents the five scales and representative items from the D-QOL. We computed internal-consistency reliability coefficients for each of the five scales. The reliabilities of the five scales are moderate to high, indicating that subjects' responses to items within a scale are consistent (range from .67 to .89). Correlations between the scales (range from .09 to .67) are shown in Table 3. The magnitude of the correlations indicates that the five scales represent QOL domains which are related, but do not overlap considerably.

CONCLUSIONS

Our model considers subjective QOL as the end product of many environmental, social, individual, health, behavioral and functional variables. Subjective QOL is not simply psychological well-being. Rather it is the subjective interpretation and evaluation of the individual's experience in each of the many important areas that contribute to well-being. For persons with dementia, we have presented five relevant domains: positive affect, negative affect, feelings of belonging, self-esteem, and aesthetics. We do not mean to imply that the determinants are not important to an individual's QOL, only that they cannot be used as proxy indicators of QOL until a high degree of empirical association between each determinant and QOL has been established. We also suggest that interventions at points along the pathway be evaluated in terms of their ability to affect QOL. As with Lawton's model (Lawton, 1983), it is not a given that improvement or deterioration in one sector of the pathway results in movement in other variables in the model, including QOL.

By defining QOL as subjective in nature, we imply that it can only reliably and validly be assessed directly from the person with dementia. The challenges presented by direct assessment of persons with dementia are significant, though not unsolvable. Our own work (Brod et al., 1999), as well as that of others (Albert, 1997;

TABLE 1.2   Quality of Life Scales and Representative Items From the D-QOL Instrument

Scale	# of Items	Internal Consistency Reliability	Sample D-QOL Items
Aesthetics	5	.77	1) Recently, how often have you enjoyed listening to music?
			2) Recently, how often have you enjoyed watching the clouds, sky, or a storm?
Positive Affect	6	.83	1) Recently, how often have you felt happy?
			2) Recently, how often have you found something that made you laugh?
Negative Affect	11	.89	1) Recently, how often have you felt frustrated?
			2) Recently, how often have you felt depressed?
Self-Esteem	4	.80	1) Recently, how often have you felt confident?
			2) Recently, how often have you felt satisfied with yourself?
Feelings of Belonging	3	.67	1) Recently, how often have you felt lovable?
			2) Recently, how often have you felt useful?

TABLE 1.3   Interscale Correlations

	Aesthetics	Positive Affect	Negative Affect	Self- Esteem	Feelings of Belonging
Aesthetics	1.0				
Positive Affect	.38	1.0			
Negative Affect	.09	.35	1.0		
Self- Esteem	.18	.67	.37	1.0	
Belonging	.29	.63	.33	.57	1.0

Lawton, 1996; Logsdon, 1996), provides promising methodologies to directly assess the QOL of persons with dementia. Both direct patient assessment, as well as observation of affective states, deserve considerable attention in future work. Direct assessment of mildly and moderately impaired individuals has been found to be reliable and valid (Brod et al., 1999; Logsdon, 1996). Observation of affective states, such as by the Apparent Affect Rating Scale (Lawton, van Haitsma, & Klapper, 1996), provides a methodology by which to understand the subjective experience, both negative and positive, in more severely demented persons who can no longer speak with words. Each of these methodologies is important in its own right and should be further explored.

Three of the domains of dementia-specific QOL in our model are very similar in nature to three of Kitwood and Bredin's four sentient states: self-esteem (ours) with sense of personal worth (theirs); feelings of belonging (ours) with social confidence (theirs); and positive affect (ours) with hope (theirs). It is encouraging to find that efforts from two very divergent perspectives and different countries (U.S. and England) have yielded similar findings.

Similar comparisons can also be made between many of the subjective experiences that the D-QOL measures and the dementia-specific relevant domains offered by Lawton (Lawton, 1997). These include, for example, meaningful time use (his) with sense of accomplishment (ours), and stimulation or aesthetic quality (his) with items in the aesthetics domain (ours), or family and friends (his) and feeling lovable and likable (ours). Further face validity is provided by the similarities of our domains of QOL and those variables identified as important in observations and case reports of dementia patients (Gwyther, 1997; Homma, 1995; Keane, 1994; Parse, 1996). Gwyther's work in particular (1997) reflects many of the subjective experiences we have also identified, such as feelings of anxiety and fear, lack of confidence and control, feeling valued and loved, and feeling useful and lonely.

Conceptualizing QOL in this way allows for appreciation of the belief that at least mildly and moderately demented persons have an awareness of their QOL, and a premise that at least some of this awareness may continue into the later stages of the disease. Further, although there is a progressive decline in some of the determinants of QOL, such as cognitive function and functional status, these inevitable declines may not inevitably translate into a decline in QOL in severe dementia (Albert, 1997; Callahan, 1992; Keane, 1994; Nagatomo et al., 1997). Just as good QOL has been reported at the end of life (Cohen & Mount, 1992; Lawton, Moss, & Glicksman, 1990), there can be good QOL even as the dementia progresses. As Callahan (1992, p. 143) eloquently argues in drawing a parallel between the state of dementia and that of a newborn baby, as long as an individual "still has the capacity to be comforted like a babe on its mother's breast and can still experience pleasure and nonverbal human contact," a quality of life continues to exist.

REFERENCES

Albert, S. (1997). Assessing health-related quality of life in chronic care populations. In J. Teresi, P. Lawton, D. Holmes, & M. Ory (Eds.), *Measurement in elderly chronic care populations* (pp. 210-227). New York: Springer Publishing Company.

Albert, S., Del Castillo-Castaneda, C., Sano, M., Jacobs, D., Marder, K., Bell, K., Bylsma, F., Lafleche, G., Brandt, J., Albert, M., & Stern, Y. (1996). Quality of life in patients with Alzheimer's disease as reported by patient proxies. *Journal of the American Geriatrics Society, 44,* 1342-1347.

Brod, M., Stewart, A., Sands, L., & Walton, P. (1999). Conceptualization and measurement of quality of life in dementia: The Dementia-QOL Instrument. *The Gerontologist, 39*(1), 25-36.

Callahan, S. (1992). Ethics and dementia: Current issues . . . Quality of life. *Alzheimer Disease and Associated Disorders, 6*(3), 138-144.

Cohen, S., & Mount, B. (1992). Quality of life in terminal illness: Defining and measuring subjective well-being in the dying. *Journal of Palliative Care, 8*(3), 40-45.

Cotrell, V., & Schulz, R. (1993). The perspective of the patient with Alzheimer's Disease: A neglected dimension of dementia research. *The Gerontologist, 33*(2), 205-211.

DeJong, R., Osterland, O., & Roy, G. (1989). Measurement of quality of life changes in patients with Alzheimer's Disease. *Clinical Therapeutics, 11*(4), 545-554.

Dwosh, I., Giles, A., & Ford, P. (1983). Plasmapheresis therapy in rheumatoid arthritis. *New England Journal of Medicine, 308,* 1124-1129.

Flanagan, J. (1982). Measurement of quality of life: Current state of the art. *Archives of Physical Medicine and Rehabilitation, 63,* 56-59.

Gwyther, L. (1997). The perspective of the person with Alzheimer Disease: Which outcomes matter in early to middle stages of dementia? *Alzheimer Disease and Associated Disorder, 11*(suppl. 6), 18-24.

Homma, A. (1995). Antidementia drugs: Are they effective in improving quality of life for elderly persons with dementia? *International Psychogeriatrics, 7*(3), 363-366.

Howard, K., & Rockwood, K. (1995). Quality of life in Alzheimer's Disease. *Dementia, 6,* 113-116.

Keane, W. (1994). The patient's perspective: The Alzheimer's Association. *Alzheimer Disease and Associated Disorders, 8* (suppl. 3), 151-155.

Kitwood, T., & Bredin, K. (1992). Towards a theory of dementia care: Personhood and well-being. *Aging and Society, 12,* 269-287.

Lawton, M., van Haitsma, K., & Klapper, J. (1996). Observed affect in nursing home residents with Alzheimer's Disease. *Journals of Gerontology: Psychological Sciences, 51B,* P3-14.

Lawton, M. P. (1991). A multidimensional view of quality of life in frail elders. *The concept and measurement of Quality of Life in the frail elderly* (pp. 3-23). San Diego: Academic Press, Inc.

Lawton, M. P., Moss, M., & Glicksman, A. (1990). The quality of the last year of life of older persons. *Milbank Quarterly, 68*(1), 1-28.

Lawton, P. (1983). Environment and other determinants of well-being in older people. *The Gerontologist, 23*(4), 349-357.

Lawton, P. (1994). Quality of life in Alzheimer Disease. *Alzheimer Disease and Associated Disorders, 8*(3), 138-150.

Lawton, P. (1997). Assessing quality of life in Alzheimer Disease research. *Alzheimer Disease and Related Disorders, 11* (suppl. 6), 91-99.

Logsdon, R. G. (1996, November). Assessment of quality of life, pleasant events and depression in Alzheimer's disease outpatients. In R. G. Logsdon (Chair), *Quality of life in Alzheimer's disease: Implications for research.* Symposium conducted at the 49th annual meeting of the Gerontological Society of America, Washington, DC.

Nagatomo, I., Kita, K., Takigawa, M., Nomaguchi, M., & Sameshima, K. (1997). A study of the quality of life in elderly people using psychological testing. *International Journal of Geriatric Psychiatry, 12*, 599-608.

O' Boyle, C., McGee, H., Hickey, A., O' Malley, K., & Joyce, C. (1992). Individual quality of life in patients undergoing hip replacement. *Lancet, 339*, 1088-91.

Parse, R. (1996). Quality of life for persons living with Alzheimer's Disease: The human becoming perspective. *Nursing Science Quarterly, 9*(3), 126-133.

Post, S., & Whitehouse, P. (1995). Fairhill guidelines on ethics of the care of people with Alzheimer's Disease: A clinical summary. *Journal of the American Geriatrics Society, 43*(1), 1423-1429.

Quayhagen, M., & Quayhagen, M. (1996). Discovering life quality in coping with dementia. *Western Journal of Nursing Research, 18*(2), 120-135.

Rabins, P., & Kasper, J. (1997). Measuring quality of life in dementia: Conceptual and practical issues. *Alzheimer Disease and Associated Disorders, 11*(suppl. 6), 100-104.

Ronch, J. (1996). Assessment of quality of life: Preservation of the self. *International Psychogeriatrics, 8*(2), 267-275.

Russel, C. (1996). Passion and heretics: Meaning in life and quality of life of persons with dementia. *Journal of the American Geriatric Society, 44*(11), 1400-1401.

Sanifort, F., Becker, M., & Diamond, R. (1996). Judgments of quality of life of individuals with severe mental disorders: Patient self-report versus provider perspectives. *American Journal of Psychiatry, 153*, 497-502.

Stewart, A., Sherbourne, C., & Brod, M. (1996). Measuring health-related quality of life in older and demented populations. In B. Spilker (Ed.),

Quality of life and pharmacoeconomics in clinical trials: Second Edition (pp. 819-829). Philadelphia: Lippincott-Raven.

Teri, L., & Logsdon, R. G. (1991). Identifying pleasant activities for Alzheimer's Disease patients: The pleasant events schedule-AD. *The Gerontologist, 31*((1)), 124-127.

Testa, M. A., & Simonson, D. G. (1996). Current concepts: Assessment of quality of life outcomes. *New England Journal of Medicine, 334*, 835-840.

Sloan, D. (Producer). (1998). *20/20* Interview with Christopher Reeves, conducted by Barbara Walters, New York: American Broadcasting Company.

Whitehouse, P., & Rabins, P. (1992). Quality of life and dementia. *Alzheimer Disease and Associated Disorders, 6*(3), 135-137.

Wilson, I., & Cleary, P. (1995). Linking clinical variables with health-related quality of life. *Journal of the American Medical Association, 273*(1), 59-65.

Acknowledgment. The chapter authors would like to thank the Alzheimer's Association, particularly Katie Maslow and Bill Fischer, for their continued support and encouragement of all of the authors' Alzheimer's disease research.

2

Quality of Life in Alzheimer's Disease: Patient and Caregiver Reports

Rebecca G. Logsdon, Laura E. Gibbons, Susan M. McCurry, and Linda Teri

lzheimer's Disease (AD) affects afflicted individuals' quality of life in profound ways. As cognitive and functional abilities are lost, individuals with dementia become unable to engage in many of the activities that once gave them a sense of purpose or pleasure (Logsdon & Teri, 1997; Teri & Logsdon, 1991). Behavior and social skills may also deteriorate, precipitating interpersonal conflict that causes the individual with AD to become socially isolated or avoided (Pearson, Teri, Reifler, & Raskind, 1989; Reisberg et al., 1987; Reisberg, Franssen, Sclan, Kluger, & Ferris, 1989; Teri, Borson, Kiyak, & Yamagishi, 1989; Teri, Larson, & Reifler, 1988). This, in turn, impacts the emotional state (Logsdon & Teri, 1997; Teri & Uomoto, 1991; Teri, Logsdon, Wagner, & Uomoto, 1994).

As new treatments to improve cognitive function, delay decline, and treat behavior problems have recently become available for AD, many investigators and clinicians have recognized that, in addition to specific symptom amelioration, it is important to evaluate the extent to which an intervention improves the quality of life (QOL) of the person being treated. Whitehouse and Rabins (1992) go so far as to describe quality of life as "not an isolated concept to be

included as one of many measurements of the benefits of our care, but rather
. . . it is the central goal of our professional activity, driving the organization
of both our clinical and our research efforts" (p. 136). Yet little has been done
to assess QOL of individuals with dementia.

To date, only one published study has empirically investigated QOL in AD.
This investigation by Albert and colleagues (1996) indicates that family and
institutional caregivers of AD patients in nursing homes show good agreement
on ratings of patient QOL, including positive and negative affect and frequency
and enjoyment of activities, but this investigation did not include patient
ratings of their own QOL.

The purpose of the current investigation was threefold. The first purpose
was to develop and provide psychometric data on a new scale that assesses
perceived QOL in AD patients. The scale was designed to tap the domains
identified as important to QOL, including interpersonal, environmental, functional, physical, and psychological status (Birren & Deutchman, 1991; Lawton,
1983, 1991, 1994).

The second purpose was to examine the ability of AD patients and caregivers to provide a reliable and valid report of these subjective states, and to
identify the point at which the patient's cognitive impairment would begin to
impact measurement reliability. A comparison of patient and caregiver reports
of patient QOL is also included to determine the extent to which caregivers and
patients agree or disagree in their assessments. It has been found that in
reporting depressive symptoms, patients consistently report fewer symptoms
in themselves than their caregivers report for them (Moye, Robiner, &
Mackenzie, 1993; Teri & Wagner, 1991) and that patients report their functioning on activities of daily living as higher than their caregivers report (Kiyak,
Teri, & Borson, 1994). It is important to evaluate differences in responses of
caregivers and patients in rating patient QOL to identify possible biases that
impact the accuracy of caregiver and patient reports. It was hypothesized that
both mildly and moderately cognitively impaired subjects would be able to
reliably report their own QOL, and that individuals with severely impaired
cognitive function would be unable to do so. In addition, it is important to
consider the primary caregiver's perception of the patient's QOL, because as
the disease progresses and the patient's communication skills become more
and more limited, the caregiver must report on how the patient is functioning
in a variety of areas.

The third purpose of this investigation was to evaluate the influence of
demographic factors (including patient and caregiver age, education, gender,
income, relationship, and living situation) on QOL in AD, and whether QOL
ratings could be explained by cognitive status, functional ability, mood, or
level of participation in pleasant events. It was hypothesized that higher
cognitive and functional status, fewer depressive symptoms, and higher levels
of participation in pleasant events would be related to better QOL.

METHOD

Subjects

Subjects were recruited from an ongoing patient registry of individuals with AD (Larson et al., 1990). This investigation included 77 AD patients who were community-dwelling, ambulatory, and had an actively involved caregiver who lived with them or spent every day with them. All subjects met National Institute of Neurological and Communicative Disease and Stroke and the Alzheimer's Disease and Related Disorders Association (NINCDS-ADRDA) criteria for "probable" or "possible" AD (McKhann et al., 1984), based on a comprehensive diagnostic evaluation (Larson et al., 1990).

Patients' mean age was 78.3 years (*SD* = 6.1), educational level was 12.7 years (*SD* = 3.4), and mean MMSE score was 17.1 (*SD* = 5.6). Fifty-three percent were male, 47% were female, 86% were Caucasian and 14% were African American. Caregivers' mean age was 69.8 years (*SD* = 13.8), and educational level was 13.7 years (*SD* = 2.7). Sixty-six percent of caregivers were female, 34% were male; 76% of caregivers were spouses, 10% were children, and 14% were other close relatives or friends who lived with and cared for the patient. Ninety-five percent of patients and caregivers lived together, 5% did not live together but saw each other every day.

Measures

The following measures were collected by an experienced interviewer (BA in psychology and 1 year experience interviewing older adults), who interviewed subjects in their homes.

Mini-Mental State Exam. The Mini-Mental State Exam (MMSE; Folstein, Folstein, & McHugh, 1975), one of the most widely used cognitive screening instruments, provides a total score, ranging from 0-30, with lower scores indicative of greater cognitive impairment.

Physical and Instrumental Self-Maintenance Scale. The Physical and Instrumental Self-Maintenance Scale (Lawton & Brody, 1969) is a 16-item caregiver-report measure that provides an assessment of basic activities of daily living (ADLs), such as bathing and dressing, and more complex instrumental activities (IADLs) such as shopping, transportation, and home management.

Hamilton Depression Rating Scale. The Hamilton Depression Rating Scale (HDRS; Hamilton, 1960; 1967) assesses the frequency and severity of various depression symptoms. It has been used with AD patients to identify individuals who may have major depressive disorder (Logsdon & Teri, 1995). In this investigation, the HDRS was administered to caregivers to assess symptoms of depression both in their patients and in themselves.

   Geriatric Depression Scale. The Geriatric Depression Scale (GDS; Yesavage et al., 1983) is a 30-item, self-report measure that is useful and reliable with older adults in residential care settings (Parmelee, Lawton, & Katz, 1989) and as a caregiver-report measure for AD patients (Logsdon & Teri, 1995). For this investigation, caregivers completed the questionnaire about their patients, and AD patients independently completed the GDS. Caregivers completed the measure as a questionnaire; patients were interviewed and asked to respond orally to the statements read to them, with their responses recorded by the interviewer.

   Pleasant Events Schedule-AD-Short Form. The Pleasant Events Schedule-AD-Short Form (PES-AD; Logsdon & Teri, 1997; Teri & Logsdon, 1991) asks caregivers to rate whether their patient now enjoys each of 20 activities, whether the patient enjoyed it in the past, and how frequently the patient engaged in each activity during the prior month. In a prior investigation, the PES-AD was demonstrated to have good internal consistency and to correlate with diagnosis and severity of depression in AD patients (Logsdon & Teri, 1997).

   Quality of Life-AD. The Quality of Life-AD (QOL-AD) was developed for this investigation. This measure obtains a rating of the patient's QOL from both the patient and the caregiver. Items for the QOL-AD were selected based on a review of relevant literature on QOL in older adults and on the assessment of QOL in other chronically ill populations. (For more information about relevant literature and domains of QOL, please refer to the Introduction to this special issue.) To optimize the measure's usefulness with mildly to moderately impaired AD patients, it uses simple and straightforward language and responses, with detailed instructions for the interviewer. During its development, the QOL-AD was reviewed by AD patients and caregivers, cognitively intact older adults, and experts in the field of geriatrics and gerontology, in order to maximize construct validity and to ensure that it addresses aspects of QOL that are particularly important to individuals with AD. Based on their feedback, an item on "energy level" was added and an item about "ability to perform tasks" was broken into two items: "ability to do chores around the house" and "ability to do things for fun." After administering the measure to 20 pilot subjects (patients and caregivers from the University of Washington Geriatric and Family Services Clinic), interviewer instructions were expanded and clarified based on recommendations of interviewers and caregivers. Response options were simplified to a 4-choice multiple choice format that is consistent across all questions, because this type of response was easier for patients to consistently follow than a Likert-type scale or more open-ended response. Patients were best able to complete the measure in interview format. Interviewers use a set of explicit instructions to avoid influencing the patient's responses; patients follow along on their own copy of the measure, and may respond verbally while the interviewer circles the response on the form, or may circle their own response. Caregivers were able to complete the measure as a questionnaire, with assistance from the interviewer if there was a question they didn't understand or if they were not sure how to respond. Caregivers in the pilot group required very little assistance.

In summary, the QOL-AD includes the patient's and caregiver's appraisal of the patient's physical condition, mood, interpersonal relationships, ability to participate in meaningful activities, financial situation, and an overall assessment of self as a whole and life quality as a whole. The measure has 13 items, rated on a 4-point scale, with "1" being poor and "4" being excellent. Total scores range from 13 to 52. Separate scores are calculated for patient and caregiver reports. These reports can also be combined into a single composite QOL score that incorporates both patient and caregiver ratings of the patient's QOL. Since the patient's QOL is the focus of the evaluation, a weighted composite QOL-AD score is calculated by multiplying the patient score by 2, adding the caregiver score, and dividing the sum by 3, to produce a composite score that weights the patient rating more heavily than the caregiver rating. The composite score consists of the same range of possible scores as the patient and caregiver report forms alone. (A copy of the measure, along with instructions for administration and a more detailed description of the instrument development process is available from the first author.)

RESULTS

Reliability of the QOL-AD

Table 2.1 shows the internal consistency of the QOL-AD. The correlation of each item with the total QOL-AD score, the correlation of each item with the single item on which subjects rated "life as a whole," and coefficient alpha are shown for both patient and caregiver report versions of the QOL-AD. Overall coefficient alpha levels for both patient and caregiver reports were well within the acceptable range (.88 and .87, respectively), indicating that the items did indeed measure a cohesive construct. In addition, correlations of each item with the single item where subjects rated "life as a whole" were good.

Table 2.2 shows the mean scores reported by patients and caregivers on each QOL-AD item, along with the Spearman correlation between patient and caregiver reports on each item and the Pearson correlation for the total measure. As can be seen, patients and caregivers achieved fairly good agreement on items related to mood, energy, physical health, and self, while agreement on items most affected by the patient's dementia, including memory and ability to do chores, was lower. This is consistent with prior findings that subjects with dementia rated their functional abilities higher than their caregivers rated them (Kiyak, Teri, & Borson, 1994; Magaziner, Simonsick, Kashner,

TABLE 2.1   Item–Total Correlation and Coefficient Alpha of the Quality of Life–AD Scale

Item	Patient Correlations (Total)	"Life as a Whole"	Caregiver Correlations (Total)	"Life as a Whole"
1. Physical health	.58	.53	.47	.29
2. Energy	.67	.39	.47	.38
3. Mood	.61	.52	.59	.40
4. Living situation	.65	.59	.45	.22
5. Memory	.42	.24	.34	.13
6. Family	.41	.29	.47	.27
7. Marriage	.58	.41	.63	.36
8. Friends	.46	.43	.60	.40
9. Self.	.60	.35	.58	.55
10. Ability to do chores	.56	.56	.49	.37
11. Ability to do things for fun	.54	.54	.53	.40
12. Money	.53	.43	.39	.44
13. Life as a whole	.67	—	.54	—
Coefficient Alpha	.88		.87	

TABLE 2.2   Mean Scores, Standard Deviations, and Correlations for Patient and Caregiver Reports on QOL-AD Items

Item	Patient Report	Caregiver Report	Correlation[a]
1. Physical health	2.84 (.78)	2.80 (.77)	.35**
2. Energy	2.70 (.71)	2.12 (.82)	.45***
3. Mood	2.82 (.77)	2.39 (.80)	.40***
4. Living situation	3.31 (.61)	3.19 (.61)	.21
5. Memory	2.26 (.71)	1.43 (.60)	.13
6. Family	3.39 (.61)	3.12 (.68)	.24*
7. Marriage	3.42 (.61)	3.16 (.70)	.21
8. Friends	3.00 (.67)	2.61 (.88)	.26*
9. Self	2.81 (.69)	2.63 (.63)	.31**
10. Ability to do chores	2.69 (.78)	2.05 (.73)	.04
11. Ability to do things for fun	3.06 (.68)	2.68 (.76)	.20
12. Money	2.66 (.74)	2.44 (.81)	.29**
13. Life as a whole	3.06 (.69)	2.73 (.58)	.22*
Total Score	38.03 (5.81)	33.35 (5.91)	.40***

[a]Spearman correlations are given for items; Pearson correlation is given for the total score. *$p < .05$. **$p < .01$. ***$p < .001$.

& Hebel, 1988). Agreement on the total score was adequate ($r = .40, p > .001$), particularly for a subjective scale with no behavioral anchors. It may be that the different methods of administration lowered the correlation between patient and caregiver reports.

Finally, test-retest reliability was evaluated on a subset of 30 patient-caregiver pairs, at a one week interval. Intra-class correlation coefficients were within the acceptable range (ICC = .76 for patients and .92 for caregivers).

Validity of the QOL-AD

Table 2.3 shows the correlation of QOL-AD scores with other constructs, including cognitive status, activities of daily living and instrumental activities of daily living, depression, and pleasant events. Patient QOL-AD scores were modestly correlated with MMSE scores ($r = .24, p < .05$), with higher scores on the MMSE related to higher QOL ratings. Interestingly, caregiver ratings on the QOL-AD were not correlated with patient MMSE scores. On the Physical and Instrumental-Self Maintenance Scales, the Activities of Daily Living score was significantly correlated with both the patient and caregiver ratings on the QOL-AD (r's = -.33 and -.32, respectively, $p < .01$), indicating that patients with the greatest impairment had lower QOL ratings. However, the Instrumental Activities of Daily Living score, which assesses less severe levels of functional impairment was not significantly correlated with the QOL-AD.

TABLE 2.3   Validity of the QOL-AD: Correlation With Related Measures

	Patient Report QOL-AD	Caregiver Report QOL-AD	Composite QOL-AD
Mini-Mental State Exam	0.24*	0.02	0.19
Activities of Daily Living[a]	-0.33**	-0.32**	-0.37***
Instrumental Activities of Daily Living[a]	-0.12	-0.08	-0.13
Hamilton Depression Rating Scale- Patient Depression	-0.43***	-0.25*	-0.43***
Geriatric Depression Scale (Patient report about self)	-0.56***	-0.14	-0.49***
Geriatric Depression Scale (Caregiver report about patient)	-0.40***	-0.57***	-0.53***
Pleasant Event Scale-AD	0.30**	0.41***	0.40***
Hamilton Depression Rating Scale- Caregiver Depression	0.00	-0.23*	-0.07

[a]Physical and Instrumental Self-Maintenance Scale.
*$p < .05$. **$p < .01$. ***$p < .001$

Depression correlated most highly with the QOL-AD. Patient report QOL-AD was significantly correlated with patient HDRS score ($r = -.43, p < .001$) and patient and caregiver reports on the GDS ($r = -.56$ and $-.40$, respectively, $p < .001$). Caregiver report QOL-AD was also correlated with patient HDRS ($r = -.25, p < .05$) and with caregiver-report GDS ($r = -.57, p < .001$). Both patient and caregiver reports on the QOL-AD were significantly correlated with caregiver reports of pleasant events ($r = .30, p < .01$ and $r = .41, p < .001$, respectively). Interestingly, caregiver depression (rated on the HDRS) was correlated with caregiver report QOL-AD ($r = -.23, p < .05$), but not with patient report QOL-AD scores.

For the composite QOL-AD score, a similar pattern of results was seen, with QOL most highly correlated with depression ($r = -.43$ to $-.53$) and pleasant events ($r = .40$), followed by ADL scores ($r = -.37$). The composite QOL-AD score was not significantly correlated with MMSE scores, IADLs, or caregiver depression.

Impact of Cognitive Impairment on Reliability and Validity of the QOL-AD

In order to evaluate the impact of patient cognitive status on ability to complete the QOL-AD, reliability and validity analyses were repeated with subjects divided into two groups according to their MMSE scores. Subjects with scores of less than 18 on the MMSE were placed in the "lower cognitive" group ($n = 41$), while those with scores of 18 or higher were placed in the "higher cognitive" group ($n = 36$). Table 2.4 shows the results of this analysis. For the

TABLE 2.4   Correlation of Patient Report QOL-AD With Related Measures

	Moderate Impairment MMSE < 18	Mild Impairment MMSE ≥ 18
Activities of Daily Living[a]	-0.30*	-0.07
Instrumental Activities of Daily Living[a]	-0.11	0.23
Hamilton Depression Rating Scale- Patient Depression	-0.51**	-0.22
Geriatric Depression Scale (Patient report about self)	-0.54***	-0.54***
Geriatric Depression Scale (Caregiver report about patient)	-0.44**	-0.21
Pleasant Event Scale-AD	0.44**	0.07
Hamilton Depression Rating Scale- Caregiver Depression	0.01	0.01
Caregiver QOL-AD	0.42**	0.31

[a] Physical and Instrumental Self-Maintenance Scale.
* $p < .05$. ** $p < .01$. *** $p < .001$.

"lower cognitive" (moderately impaired) group, the mean MMSE score was 13 (*SD* = 3; range 4-17), the mean patient report QOL-AD score was 36 (*SD* = 6; range 25-50), and coefficient alpha for the patient report QOL-AD was .90. For the "higher cognitive" (mildly impaired) group, the mean MMSE score was 22 (*SD* = 3; range 18-28), the patient QOL-AD was 40 (*SD* = 5; range 28-50), and coefficient alpha was .81. The correlation of patient QOL-AD with caregiver QOL-AD was .42 for the more impaired group, and .31 for the less impaired group. Thus, moderate levels of cognitive impairment did not have a negative impact on reliability or validity.

Characteristics of Quality of Life in Alzheimer's Disease

It was expected that QOL would be related to a variety of patient and caregiver characteristics. To determine which, if any, variables were related to QOL-AD scores, a series of correlations and regression analyses was conducted. To reduce the number of potential variables in the regression analysis, correlations were calculated for all demographic, cognitive, functional, and depression variables. Of the demographic variables, only patient educational level and caregiver educational level were significantly correlated with patient or caregiver reports on the QOL-AD. Correlations with other measures are shown in Table 2.3.

Stepwise linear regression analyses were conducted for the patient, caregiver, and composite ratings of QOL-AD, entering all theoretically relevant predictor variables (listed in Table 2.3), and two significantly correlated demographic variables (patient and caregiver education) as candidates for the models. Standardized regression coefficients for the models are shown in Table 2.5. The presence of depressive symptoms was the best predictor of QOL-AD scores. As hypothesized, individuals with fewer depressive symptoms reported

TABLE 2.5 Stepwise Multiple Regression to Identify Factors Associated With Quality of Life in AD

	Patient Report QOL-AD	Caregiver Report QOL-AD	Composite QOL-AD
Variables in the Equation	b[a]	b[a]	b[a]
Patient Education	0.320***	0.275**	0.356****
Geriatric Depression Scale (Patient report)	-0.566****	—	-0.360****
Geriatric Depression Scale (Caregiver report)	—	-0.548****	-0.326***
Activities of Daily Living	-0.260**	-0.201*	-0.281***
Adjusted R^2	0.485	0.429	0.567

[a]b = Standardized Regression Coefficient.
*p < .05. **p < .01. ***p < .001+.

higher QOL. More independent ADL functioning was also hypothesized to be related to higher QOL; this was confirmed. Educational level of the patient was the only demographic variable that was related to QOL, with more years of education related to higher QOL. Other variables hypothesized to relate to QOL, including IADL and MMSE scores, did not add significant predictive value to the model.

DISCUSSION

The proposed QOL-AD is a brief, easily administered assessment of QOL in AD. This investigation provides psychometric data for both a patient-interview version and a caregiver-questionnaire version of the measure, and it provides a method for calculating a composite score that combines both the patient and caregiver reports and is scaled in the same way as the individual reports. Each version of the measure appears to be reliable and valid. Further, patients appear able to provide a subjective assessment of their own QOL, and although patient and caregiver reports are related, they are not identical. It also appeared that caregiver depression may have influenced caregiver ratings of the patient's QOL, with depressed caregivers rating patient QOL lower than nondepressed caregivers. As QOL receives increasing attention in descriptive and treatment outcome research, the QOL-AD provides a useful tool for obtaining an assessment of the patient's QOL from both the patient and the caregiver.

The current investigation also provides data about factors related to QOL in AD. The factor most strongly associated with QOL-AD scores was depressive symptoms. Individuals with fewer depressive symptoms reported higher QOL. This is consistent with a recent investigation of social support, functional status, and QOL in nondemented older adults (Newsom & Schulz, 1996) which found that depression and life satisfaction ratings were highly correlated ($r = -.44$). More independent functioning in activities of daily living was also predictive of higher QOL in the present sample. Of the demographic variables examined, education was the only one that was related to QOL-AD scores, with more years of education related to higher QOL. Since education may be related to a number of other factors, including income, range of interests, and reading level, additional research is needed to clarify how educational achievement impacts QOL.

Although MMSE scores were modestly correlated with patient QOL-AD scores, cognitive status was not a significant predictor of QOL in the regression analysis. This is not to say that cognitive impairment does not affect QOL, but it does suggest that certain ADL losses are more significant to QOL than are purely cognitive changes, and that once the ADL scores were entered into the regression equation, MMSE did not add predictive value. The ability to perform more complex IADLs was not correlated with QOL. More investigation is needed to clarify the relationship between the ability to perform activities and QOL, and to determine whether the inability to independently perform IADLs (such as shopping, doing laundry, housework) is less disturbing to most individuals than is the inability to dress and bathe without assistance.

In the current investigation of QOL in community-residing AD patients, only 5 patients were unable to complete the QOL-AD interview. All 5 had MMSE scores of less than 10. In no case was a subject in the current sample with an MMSE score greater than 10 unable to complete the measure.

Finally, the frequency of pleasant events was related to QOL, with patients who engage in more pleasant events obtaining higher QOL-AD scores. Although the PES-AD score was not significant in the regression equation, once the impact of depression was explained, the correlation suggests that pleasant events may be important to QOL in AD.

In conclusion, the QOL-AD is a promising measure for investigations of QOL in AD. It is brief, readily accepted by individuals with AD and their caregivers, can be reliably used by individuals with MMSE scores between 10-28, and provides both the patient's and caregiver's assessments of QOL. Investigations currently underway will provide additional data regarding changes in QOL over time, and the relationship between QOL and behavioral disturbances. Future investigations will also address the impact of the quality of the patient-caregiver interpersonal relationship on QOL, and evaluate changes in QOL with both pharmacological and behavioral treatments. The increasing recognition of QOL as an important outcome variable in research with individuals with AD, and the development of measures such as the QOL-AD, marks an important milestone in AD research, which will encourage and allow a more global and clinically relevant assessment of individuals with AD.

REFERENCES

Albert, S. M., Del Castillo-Castaneda, C., Sano, M., Jacobs, D. M., Marder, K., Bell, K., Bylsma, F., Lafleche, G., Brandt, J., Albert, M., & Stern, Y. (1996). Quality of life in patients with Alzheimer's disease as reported by patient proxies. *Journal of the American Geriatrics Society, 44*, 1342-1347.

Birren, J. E., & Deutchman, D. E. (1991). Concepts and content of quality of life in the later years: An overview. In J. E. Birren, J. E. Lubben, J.C. Rowe, & D. E. Deutchman (Eds.), *The concept and measurement of quality of life in the frail elderly* (pp. 344-360). New York: Academic Press, Inc.

Folstein, M. F., Folstein, S. E., & McHugh, P. R. (1975). Mini-Mental State Exam: A practical method for grading the cognitive state of patients for the clinician. *Journal of Psychiatric Research, 12*, 221-231.

Hamilton, M. (1960). A rating scale for depression. *Journal of Neurology, Neurosurgery, and Psychiatry, 23*, 56-62.

Hamilton M. (1967). Development of a rating scale for primary depressive illness. *British Journal of Social and Clinical Psychology, 6*, 278-296.

Kiyak, H. A., Teri, L., & Borson, S. (1994). Physical and functional health assessment in normal aging and in Alzheimer's disease: Self-reports vs. family reports. *The Gerontologist, 34,* 324-330.

Larson, E. B., Kukull, W. A., Teri, L., McCormick, W. C., Pfanschmidt, M., van Belle, G., & Sumi, M. (1990). University of Washington Alzheimer's Disease Patient Registry (ADPR): 1987-1988. *Aging: Clinical and Experimental Research, 2,* 404-408.

Lawton, M. P. (1983). The dimensions of well-being. *Experimental Aging Research, 9*(2), 65-72.

Lawton, M. P. (1991). A multidimensional view of quality of life in frail elders. In J. E. Birren, J. E. Lubben, J. C. Rowe, & D. E. Deutchman (Eds.), *The concept and measurement of quality of life in the frail elderly* (pp. 4-27). New York: Academic Press, Inc.

Lawton, M. P. (1994). Quality of life in Alzheimer disease. *Alzheimer Disease and Associated Disorders, 8,* 138-150.

Lawton, M. P., & Brody, E. (1969). Assessment of older people: Self-maintaining and instrumental activities of daily living. *The Gerontologist, 9,* 179-185.

Logsdon, R. G., & Teri, L. (1995). Depression in Alzheimer's disease patients: Caregivers as surrogate reporters. *Journal of the American Geriatrics Society, 43,* 150-155.

Logsdon, R. G., & Teri, L. (1997). The Pleasant Events Schedule-AD: Psychometric properties of long and short forms and an investigation of its association to depression and cognition in Alzheimer's disease patients. *The Gerontologist, 37*(1), 40-45.

Magaziner, M., Simonsick, E. M., Kashner, T. M., & Hebel, J. R. (1988). Patient-proxy response comparability on measures of patient health and functional status. *Journal of Clinical Epidemiology, 41,* 1065-1074.

McKhann, B., Drachman, D., Folstein, M. F., Katzman, R., Price, D., & Stadlan, E. M. (1984). Clinical diagnosis of Alzheimer's disease: Report of the NINCDS-ADRDA work group under the auspices of Department of Health & Human Services Task Force on Alzheimer's disease. *Neurology, 34,* 939-944.

Moye, J., Robiner, W. N., & Mackenzie, T. B. (1993). Depression in Alzheimer patients: Discrepancies between patient and caregiver reports. *Alzheimer Disease and Associated Disorders, 7,* 187-201.

Newsom, J. T., & Schulz, R. (1996). Social support as a mediator in the relation between functional status and quality of life in older adults. *Psychology and Aging, 11,* 34-44.

Parmelee, P. A., Lawton, M. P., & Katz, I. R. (1989). Psychometric properties of the Geriatric Depression Scale among the institutionalized aged. *Psychological Assessment, 1,* 331-338.

Pearson, J. L., Teri, L., Reifler, B. V., & Raskind, M. A. (1989). Functional status and cognitive impairment in Alzheimer's patients with and without depression. *Journal of the American Geriatrics Society, 37*, 1117-1121.

Reisberg, B., Borenstein, J., Salob, S. P., Ferris, S. H., Franssen, E., & Georgotas, A. (1987). Behavioral symptoms in Alzheimer's disease: Phenomenology and treatment. *Journal of Clinical Psychiatry, 48* (supplement), 9-15.

Reisberg, B., Franssen, E. Sclan, S. G., Kluger, A. & Ferris, S. H. (1989). Stage specific incidence of potentially remediable behavioral symptoms in aging and Alzheimer's disease: A study of 120 patients using the BE-HAVE-AD. *Bulletin of Clinical Neuroscience, 54*, 95-112.

Teri, L., Borson, S., Kiyak, H. A., & Yamagishi, M. (1989). Behavioral disturbance, cognitive dysfunction, and functional skill: Prevalence and relationship in Alzheimer's disease. *Journal of the American Geriatrics Society, 37*, 109-116.

Teri, L., Larson, E. B., & Reifler, B. V. (1988). Behavioral disturbance in dementia of the Alzheimer's type. *Journal of the American Geriatrics Society, 36*, 1-6.

Teri, L., & Logsdon, R. G. (1991). Identifying pleasant activities for Alzheimer's disease patients: The Pleasant Events Schedule-AD. *The Gerontologist, 31*, 124-127.

Teri, L., Logsdon, R. G., Wagner, A., & Uomoto, J. (1994). The caregiver role in behavioral treatment of depression in dementia patients. In E. Light, B. Lebowitz, & G. Niederehe (Eds.), *Stress effects on family caregivers of Alzheimer's patients* (185-204), NY: Springer Publishing Co.

Teri, L., & Uomoto, J. (1991). Reducing excess disability in dementia patients: Training caregivers to manage patient depression. *Clinical Gerontologist, 10*, 49-63.

Teri, L., & Wagner, A. (1991). Assessment of depression in patients with Alzheimer's Disease: Concordance between informants. *Psychology and Aging, 6*, 280-285.

Whitehouse, P. J., & Rabins, P. V. (1992). Quality of life and dementia. *Alzheimer Disease and Associated Disorders, 6*, 135-137.

Yesavage, J. A., Brink, T. L., Rose, T. L., Lum, O., Huang, V., Adey, M., & Leirer, V. O. (1983). Development and validation of a geriatric depression screening scale: A preliminary report. *Journal of Psychiatric Research, 17*, 37-49

Acknowledgment. The investigation presented in this chapter was supported by grants from the Alzheimer's Association (FSA-95-009) and the National Institute on Aging (AG-10845-04, AG-13757). Portions were presented at the Annual Meetings of the Gerontology Society of America, Washington, DC, November 20, 1996, and Cincinnati, OH, November 18, 1997. The chapter authors are indebted to colleagues Soo

Borson, MD, M. Powell Lawton, PhD, Murray Raskind, MD, Peter Vitaliano, PhD, Myron Weiner, MD, and Peter Whitehouse, MD, PhD, and the patients and caregivers of the Geriatric and Family Services Clinic, who contributed their efforts and expertise to the development and testing of the QOL-AD. They also gratefully acknowledge the contributions of Amy Moore, MS, who served as project manager, and Kari Mae Hickman, BA, and Julie Sorenson Starks, MD, who interviewed subjects and assisted with data entry.

3

The Quality of Life Assessment Schedule (QOLAS)—A New Method for Assessing Quality of Life (QOL) in Dementia

Caroline E. Selai, Michael R. Trimble,
Martin N. Rossor, and Richard J. Harvey

Q uality of Life (QOL) data are now an established outcome measure in the assessment of therapeutic interventions (Bowling, 1995; Brooks, 1995). Since all pharmacological and other treatments have implications for quality of life, the prospect of drug treatment for Alzheimer's disease (AD) raises questions about the most appropriate methods to measure the QOL of this patient group (Burns, 1995; Kelly, Harvey, & Cayton, 1997). By far the most common and best known of the dementias is Alzheimer's disease which is characterized by progressive global deterioration of intellect and personality (Lezak, 1995). Although Alzheimer's is predominantly a disease of old age, some patients have symptoms as early as their fourth decade (Rossor, 1993). The assessment of QOL in dementia raises a number of complex methodological issues (Rabins & Kasper, 1997; Whitehouse et al., 1997) and research in this patient group is just beginning. Since QOL assessment requires a highly complex procedure of introspection and evaluation, involving several components of cognition including implicit and explicit memory (Barofsky, 1996), it follows that, at a certain stage of cognitive decline, there will come a point where QOL self-assessment will no longer be possible. It has been suggested, therefore, that both patient self-report and proxy ratings of QOL are important in dementia (Lawton, 1994; Stewart, Sherbourne, & Brod, 1996). Patients' ability to evaluate and communicate aspects of their well-being will be determined by a number of clinical features such as the decline of cognitive skills, insight, denial, anosognosia, and a range of neuropsychiatric symptoms. One question, therefore, is to establish at what stage of the disease self-report is no longer possible (Fletcher, Dickinson, & Philip, 1992).

QOL: Measurement Issues

There is a fundamental tension in the measurement of QOL. Since what is deemed important for QOL is acknowledged to be subjective and idiosyncratic, differences being influenced by a variety of personal and cultural factors, an appraisal of QOL should strive to capture the individual's subjectively appraised phenomenological experience. On the other hand, the hallmark of scientific measurement is reliable, "objective," empirical data collection. QOL researchers have addressed measurement at various stages of this 'subjective/objective' continuum and there now exist over 1,000 instruments that have been developed taking a variety of approaches to measurement (Hedrick, Taeuber, & Erickson, 1996). The two aspects of the qualitative-quantitative continuum have different strengths. It has been suggested that qualitative methods are more valid while quantitative methods are more reliable (Mays & Pope, 1996).

The QOL literature advocates a robust and rigorous program of instrument development and testing, and most QOL measures are developed within the psychometric tradition (Juniper, Gayatt, & Jaeschke, 1996; McDowell & Newell, 1987). Some researchers have argued, however, that since quality of life is a uniquely personal perception, most standardized measurements of QOL in the medical literature seem to aim at the wrong target (Gill, 1995). It is argued that quality of life can be suitably measured only by determining the opinions of patients and by supplementing (or replacing) the instruments developed by "experts" (Gill & Feinstein, 1994). Scales developed within the psychometric tradition often omit items important to the beliefs and values of individual patients (Gill, 1995) and the psychometric aim of internal reliability is in conflict with the goals of achieving comprehensiveness and content validity (Brazier & Deverill, 1999). In response to this, a number of "individualized," patient-driven techniques have been developed whereby the patient can nominate items of importance to him/herself (Fraser; 1993; Geddes et al., 1990; Guyatt et al., 1987a, 1987b; O'Boyle et al., 1993; Ruta et al., 1994; Tugwell et al., 1990).

There are strong arguments in favor of a number of approaches to QOL measurement and, since there is no gold standard, this debate is likely to continue. In practice, the choice of QOL assessment technique depends on the goal of the study and the type of data required which, in turn, will depend upon the use to which the data will be put. Uses include the simple description of QOL, screening in the clinical context, population surveys of perceived health problems, medical audit and cost-utility analyses (Fitzpatrick et al., 1992). Assessment of QOL in dementia is in its infancy and it is likely that, as with other patient groups, a number of approaches will be developed, each appropriate for a different purpose.

QOL in Dementia: Recent Work

Research in this area has only recently begun and the definition of QOL in dementia and a number of other conceptual, practical, and ethical issues remain the subject of some debate (Rabins & Kasper, 1997; Rockwood & Wilcock, 1996; Whitehouse et al., 1997). Several scales, focussing on proxy reports, observational methods, and patient self-reports are in the early stages of development (Selai & Trimble, 1999a; Whitehouse et al., 1998). Some of the new scales are reported in this volume.

A number of scales purporting to measure QOL have been used in clinical trials of antidementia drugs but these measures have been criticized for a number of reasons. The QOL scales used in these trials have either not been fully validated for use in dementia (Howard & Rockwood, 1995) and/or have assessed only some aspects of activities of daily living, or affect, rather than comprehensively assessing QOL (Salek, Walter, & Bayer, 1998). To date, no QOL instrument used in clinical trials of antidementia drugs appears to be satisfactory (Walker, Salek, & Bayer, 1998).

The Development of the Quality of Life Assessment Schedule (QOLAS) for Use in Dementia

Since so little data have been published on patient self-report, the Quality of Life Assessment Schedule (QOLAS) was developed and refined as a technique that is subject-driven, i.e., personally tailored to each individual patient. This approach yields both qualitative and quantitative data. The QOLAS was derived from the psychological theories and methods of the Personal Construct Theory and the Repertory Grid Technique (RGT) (Fransella & Bannister, 1977). The RGT was initially developed as a generic tool to assess the QOL of patients with neurological disorders, particularly epilepsy (Kendrick & Trimble, 1994). The full Repertory Grid Technique was lengthy and cumbersome and it was deemed desirable to streamline the method. The brief version has been used in a study of patients going on to adjunctive, antiepileptic drugs (Selai & Trimble, 1998a), a study to assess QOL pre- and postdefinitive surgical treatment for intractable epilepsy (Selai, Trimble, Rosser, & Harvey, in press) and Gilles de la Tourette Syndrome (Elstner, Selai, Trimble, & Robertson, submitted). Preliminary results have shown the revised method to be reliable, valid and more sensitive to post-treatment changes than some other QOL measures.

QOLAS as Used in Dementia

After piloting the QOLAS in dementia, modifications were made and the technique used in this investigation is as follows:

1. Introduction and rapport-building
2. Respondents are invited to recount what is important for their QOL and ways in which their current health condition is affecting their QOL. Key constructs are extracted from this narrative. Prompting is sometimes required.
3. In total, 10 "constructs" are elicited, two for each of the following five domains of QOL: physical, psychological, social, daily activities, and cognitive functioning.
4. The patient is asked to rate how much of a problem each of these is *now* on a 0-5 scale where 0 = no problem; 1 = very slight problem; 2 = mild problem; 3 = moderate problem; 4 = big problem and 5 = it could not be worse.
5. At follow-up interview, the respondents' individual constructs are read out to them and they are invited to re-rate each on the 0-5 scale for how much of a problem there is with each "now."

Scoring

The scores for the two constructs per domain are summed to give a domain score out of 10. The total for each of the five domains is summed to give an overall QOLAS score out of 50.

Example

Domain	Construct	Construct Score	Domain Score	Total Score
Physical:	Head-aches	3		
	Tiredness	2	5	
Psychological:	Anxious	4		
	Feel sad	4	8	
Social/family:	Don't go out dancing anymore	4		
	Children no longer visit us	5	9	
Daily activities:	Difficulties watching television	4		
	Gardening	3	7	
Cognitive:	Memory	5		
	Finding the right word	3	8	
Total:				37

Current Study Aims

The present study had three aims: (i) to assess until what stage of the disease patient self-report is possible; (ii) to test the psychometric properties of the QOLAS for the assessment of QOL of patients with dementia, and (iii) to compare the patients' ratings of their own QOL with the ratings given by the main carers.

METHODS

Subjects

A total of 37 patient-carer dyads were recruited. The cognitive status of 13 patients precluded interviews and for these only carer proxy data were obtainable. Two patients were subsequently found not to have a regular carer and they were excluded from the study. In this chapter we report the results for two subgroups of patients: (i) the QOL of the 22 patients with mild-to-moderate dementia who could be interviewed and for whom a primary carer was identified and interviewed; (ii) the QOL of the 13 patients who could not be interviewed themselves but for whom a carer proxy-rating was obtained. The interviews took place either at The National Hospital, Queen Square, London, or at home. Most of the patients had presenile dementia of the Alzheimer's type (DSM-IV criterion of onset before age 65 years) and in this preliminary study the patients were not further subgrouped according to aetiology. Standard socio-demographic data were collected from carer. The patients who were able to be interviewed completed: (i) the Quality of Life Assessment Schedule (QOLAS); (ii) the Mini-Mental State Examination (MMSE); (iii) the EuroQol EQ-5D and (iv) a selection of the Dartmouth COOP charts. The carer rated the QOL of the patient using (i) the QOLAS; (ii) the Interview to Determine Deterioration in Daily Functioning in Dementia (IDDD); (iii) the Neuropsychiatric Inventory (NPI); and (iv) the EuroQol EQ-5D. These instruments are briefly described below.

QOL Assessment: Patient on Self

(1) Modified QOLAS (described above).

(2) Mini-Mental State Examination (MMSE) (Folstein, Folstein, & McHugh, 1975). This is probably the most widely used brief screening instrument for dementia (Lezak, 1995). The test consists of two parts: verbal and performance. The scores range from 0-30 with a lower score indicating greater cognitive impairment.

(3) EQ-5D (Brooks, 1996; EuroQol Group, 1990). This generic instrument, which measures health-related quality of life, has 5 domains: mobility,

self-care, usual activities, pain/discomfort and anxiety/depression. Respondents also rate their own health today on a visual analogue scale (VAS) from 100 (best imaginable health state) to 0 (worst imaginable health state). The data can be presented descriptively as a health profile and a single index utility score can be calculated. The EQ-5D is designed for self-completion but in the current study it was interviewer assisted, i.e., copy given to patient but wording also read out to patient.

(4) Dartmouth COOP Charts (Nelson et al., 1987). These generic self-rated health status questions were developed for the assessment of patients' functional health in routine clinical practice. Each chart consists of a question referring to the past month, with 5 response choices, each illustrated with a drawing. The scoring for each questions is from 1 = no difficulty to 5 = cannot do, with higher scores representing worse QOL. A subset of 5 questions was chosen which assessed the domains: (i) overall health, (ii) daily activities, (iii) physical fitness, (iv) social activities, and (v) feelings.

Proxy QOL Assessment:
Carer Describing Patient

(1) QOLAS (as above). Carers were asked to nominate the QOL items they perceived to be of most importance for the patient's QOL. Carers were reminded that this part of the interview concerned their perception of the patient's QOL and that there would be an opportunity later in the interview for carers to discuss their *own* QOL.

(2) Interview to Determine Deterioration in Daily Functioning in Dementia (IDDD) (Teunisse et al., 1991). This scale has 33 items concerning changes in patient's daily functioning. The questions refer to self-care and daily activities. A higher score indicates poorer abilities.

(3) The Neuropsychiatric Inventory (NPI) (Cummings et al., 1994). This scale, which assesses neuropsychiatric problems, has 12 domains. If a positive response is elicited from an initial screening question, further questions about each item are asked and total score based on frequency and severity can be calculated for each of the 12 items.

(4) EQ-5D (carer on patient). The EQ-5D was interviewer administered and the question plus response options were read out replacing, e.g., "Do you have any problems in walking about?" with "Does you wife/husband (etc.) have any problems in walking about?".

Staging of Dementia

The staging of dementia was calculated using cutoffs on the MMSE as follows: scores 0 to 10 = severe; 11 to 20 = moderate; 21 to 30 = mild (Mega, Cummings, Fiorello, & Gornbein, 1996).

Data Analysis

Psychometric testing of the QOLAS. We assessed the validity and reliability of the QOLAS on the subset of patient-carer dyads where the patient could complete the full interview. We assessed the criterion validity by examining the correlations between the QOLAS and other measures assessing similar aspects of well-being (Streiner & Norman, 1995). Construct validity was assessed in two ways: first, we tested the hypothesis that the patients with greater deterioration in skills of daily activities, as measured by the IDDD, would have a worse QOL than patients with less deterioration in these skills. We arbitrarily chose a cutoff of 50 on the IDDD and compared the two groups (n = 11 patients per group) using independent t-tests. Second, we tested the hypothesis that the QOLAS total score (patient self-rating) would correlate with the MMSE.

We assessed internal reliability by looking at the correlation of each item/domain with the total score and coefficient alpha. Although a repeat interview 1 week later had been planned to assess test-retest reliability, in practice a follow-up after this short interval was felt to have been too intrusive and burdensome since most of the interviews were conducted in the patients' homes after considerable negotiation with carers to find a convenient time.

Patient / Proxy Comparison. To compare patient and proxy reports, we looked at the correlations between the patients' and the carers' scores for each QOLAS domain. Since the QOLAS is an individual, respondent-tailored technique, one would not expect, a priori, as much agreement between any two raters as with fixed questionnaires with identical wording. We therefore also looked at the head-to-head comparison of the EQ-5D, patient rating self and carer rating patient.

Predictors of QOL. We investigated the contribution of the various predictor variables assessed (neuropsychiatric symptoms, dementia severity, patient and carer gender etc.) in determining QOL, i.e., the total QOLAS score as rated by the patient and by the carer using an all-subsets regression technique.

RESULTS

The patient could be interviewed in 22 of the patient-carer dyads. These patients all had MMSE scores within the range 11-30 and thus were in the mild-to-moderate stages of dementia (Mega et al., 1996). The mean age of these patients was 65 years, $SD = 8$ (range 48-80). Twelve patients were male and 10 were female. Eighteen of the carers were spouses and all carers were living with the patient at the time of interview. The mean age of the carers was 61 years, $SD = 13$ (range 30-77). Eight of the carers were male and 14 were female. The mean time of onset of dementia prior to interview was 5 years, $SD = 3$ years.

Thirteen patients could not complete the QOL interview. All of these individuals had MMSE scores of less than 10. In these cases carers were interviewed to provide proxy QOL data. The mean age of these patients was 65 years ($SD = 4$; range 58-70 years). Nine of these patients were male and 4 were female. The mean age of the carers was 63 years ($SD = 6$ years; range 52-71 years). Four of the carers were male and 9 were female. The mean onset prior to interview was 6 years ($SD = 4$ years; range 1-15 years).

Psychometric Testing - Patients With Mild-to-Moderate Dementia

Qualitative data: QOLAS Semi-Structured Interview. One main advantage of the QOLAS interview is that each respondent can identify the items of importance to his own QOL, thus maximizing the validity of the method. The items most frequently mentioned by the patients and by the carers are summarized in Appendix 3.1; full details of the constructs elicited can be obtained from the authors. The QOLAS subscale scores for both the patients' and the carers' ratings are shown in Figure 3.1. For each domain, the carers rated the patients as having a worse QOL than did the patients themselves.

Validity. The QOLAS was shown to be valid in this patient group (Selai et al., in press). The QOLAS total score as rated by the patient correlated with measures of affect, social life, and activities, whereas the carers' rating of the QOL of the patient correlated with more objective measures of mobility, activities of daily living, and neuropsychiatric symptoms. Construct validity was assessed, first, by testing the hypothesis that the patients with greater deterioration in skills of daily activities, as measured by the IDDD, would have a worse QOL than patients with less deterioration in these skills. The mean scores were significantly different, $t = 2.85$, $p = 0.01$ (Selai et al., in press). While the patient self-rated QOLAS total score for the whole group ($n = 22$) did not correlate with the MMSE score, in patients with mild dementia only ($n = 12$), the patient self-rated QOLAS total did correlate with the MMSE score, $r = 0.6$, $p = .05$.

Reliability. The QOLAS was found to have good internal consistency. Each domain correlated highly with the total QOLAS score. The coefficient alpha, for patient rating self and carer rating patient was in each case 0.78, and this result is well within the acceptable range (Selai et al., in press).

Head-to-Head Comparison: Patient Self-Rating and Carer Rating Patient on the EQ-5D

We directly compared the results of the patient self-rated EQ-5D with the EQ-5D rated by the main carer to look at the level of agreement. The three levels per domain (no problem, some problems, and extreme problems) yield ordinal

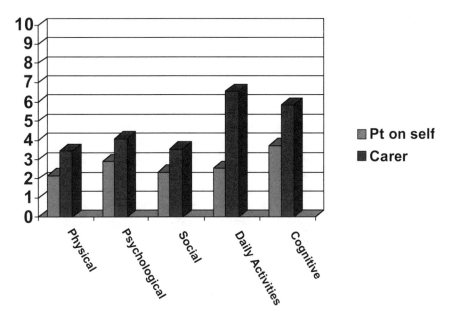

FIGURE 3.1 Histogram comparing QOLAS subscale scores: patient rating own QOL and carer rating QOL of the patient.

scale data, and agreement in each domain was assessed using Cohen's kappa statistic with the strength of agreement for each value of K rated using the convention from "poor" to "very good" as per the current literature (Altman, 1991; Landis & Koch, 1977). The results for each EQ-5D domain for the mild-to-moderate group (n = 22) were as follows: Mobility = fair; Self-care = good; Usual activities = poor; Pain/discomfort = good; Anxiety/depression = moderate (Selai et al., in press). The results for the "usual activities" domain were poor and qualitative data revealed that both patient and carer asked "what is usual..?" In cases where the patient had been retired early on medical grounds, sometimes months or years previously, it was not clear whether work was a "usual activity." This finding would suggest that a less ambiguous question would be more appropriate for patients with dementia.

Regression Analysis

For *patient self-rated* QOL, the optimal model had 11 parameters: patient age; patient gender; MMSE; IDDD; COOP overall; COOP daily activities; COOP fitness; COOP social; COOP feelings; profile of mood states; GHQ. For *carer-rated* patient QOL a model with six parameters was optimal: patient gender, age at onset, IDDD, NPI, Co-op daily activities and Co-op feelings (Selai et al., in press).

Comparison of Proxy QOL Ratings of the Patients With Mild-to-Moderate Dementia and Patients With Severe Dementia

The results of the two groups, the patients who could be interviewed (n = 22) and those who could not be interviewed (n = 13) were compared using either t-tests or the nonparametric Mann Whitney U. The results of the *QOLAS* (carer rating patient) are shown in Table 3.1. For comparison, the proxy results for the patients who could not complete the interview (n = 13) are shown alongside the patients (n = 22) who could complete the interview. The missing data in the "Daily activities" domain are mainly the result of this question being judged irrelevant because the patient could perform few activities, if any.

The mean *IDDD* score for the patients who could not be interviewed (n = 13) was 88.23 (*SD* = 17.49; range 49-99). The mean IDDD score for the patients who could be interviewed (n = 22) was 53.32 (*SD* = 12.37; range = 40.86). The scores for the two groups were significantly different, t = 6.91, p = 0.000.

The results of the *NPI* are shown in Table 3.2. There were significant differences between the two groups on the subscales of agitation and eating and on the NPI global score.

The results of the *EQ-5D* descriptive, carer-rating patient, are shown in Table 3.3. As might be predicted, compared to those patients with mild-to-moderate dementia, more patients with severe dementia had problems (and more severe problems) on every subscale of the EQ-5D.

Most respondents had problems giving an overall score for the EQ-5D Visual Analogue Scale (VAS). The most frequently mentioned problem with giving an overall rating was that the respondent wanted to give one score for physical well-being (health or fitness), and a separate score for what they called "mental" functioning. In the group where the patients had mild-to-moderate dementia (n = 22), a total of 6 respondents gave a VAS rating. In the group where the patients had severe dementia, a total of 5 respondents gave a VAS rating. Since the comment about wanting to give two scores was so frequently expressed, respondents were given the opportunity to score the two

TABLE 3.1   Mean QOLAS Scores for the Patients Who Could (*n* = 22) and Could Not (*n* = 13) Be Interviewed. All Carer Rating Patient

QOLAS Domain	*n* = 13 Mean	*n*=22 Mean	Parametric statistics *t*-tests *t-value*	2-tailed sig.	Nonparametric Mann-Whitney U *U*	2-tailed sig.
Physical	5.92	3.45	2.12	0.041*	87.0	0.05*
Psychol.	6.55	4.09	2.20	0.035*	69.0	0.048*
Social	7.77	3.55	4.58	0.000***	36.0	0.0001***
Daily acs.	2.50(*n* = 8)	6.55(*n* = 13)	4.35	0.000***	38.5	0.0001***
Cognitive	8.54	5.86	4.01	0.000***	47.0	0.0007***

* $p = 0.05$; ** $p = 0.01$;*** $p = 0.001$.

TABLE 3.2   Mean N.P.I. Scores for Patients Who Could ($n = 22$) and Who Could Not ($n = 13$) Be Interviewed

NPI scale	Interviewed ($n = 22$)		Not intervwd.($n = 13$)		t-value	2-tailed
	Mean	SD	Mean	SD		Signif.
Euphoria	0.36	1.29	0.15	0.38	-0.57	0.574
Disinhibition	1.56	2.52	0.54	1.33	-1.27	0.213
Hallucinations	0.73	2.60	0.92	1.89	0.24	0.815
Delusions	0.95	2.80	1.23	2.62	0.29	0.775
Anxiety	2.18	2.50	2.23	2.86	0.05	0.958
Depression	1.41	2.81	2.46	2.50	1.11	0.273
Irritability	1.86	2.83	2.54	2.93	0.67	0.506
Night behav.	1.50	2.84	3.38	4.57	1.51	0.141
Agitation	1.32	1.84	3.62	2.99	2.83	0.008**
Eating	1.00	2.39	4.31	4.13	3.01	0.005**
Motor	2.36	3.51	4.62	4.03	1.74	0.092
Apathy	3.68	4.34	5.38	5.69	1.00	0.325
Global	18.86	14.61	31.38	16.94	2.31	0.027*

* $p = 0.05$; ** $p = 0.01$.

TABLE 3.3   Results of the EQ-5D (Carer Rated) for Patients Who Could ($n = 22$) and Who Could Not ($n = 13$) Be Interviewed. The Figures Are Percentages

Domain	Missing		No problems		Some problems		Extreme problems	
	$n = 13$	$n = 22$	$n = 13$	$n = 22$	$n = 13$	$n = 22$	$n = 13$	$n = 22$
Mobility	—	—	39	68	39	32	22	0
Self-care	—	—	15	73	08	23	77	4
Usual acs.	—	—	0	32	15	50	85	18
Pain/disc.	23	—	54	73	15	27	08	0
Anx/depr.	8	—	39	68	39	32	14	0

components of well-being separately. The results are presented in Table 3.4. The mean VAS-total score was much higher (indicating better health) for the mild-to-moderate group than for the severely affected group. Then 'VAS-physical' was, somewhat surprisingly, higher for the group of patients with 'severe' dementia than for the group with mild-to-moderate dementia but the 'VAS-mental' score was, predictably, lower for the more severely affected group. Because of the very small sample sizes in each group, no statistical tests were performed on these data.

Finally, in Table 3.5 we compare the results of the EQ-5D descriptive profile for 4 groups: (i) a group of patients being assessed for their suitability for definitive surgical treatment for intractable epilepsy, (ii) a large UK population survey (Kind, Dolan, Guder, & Williams, 1998), (iii) the carers' rating of the patients with mild-to-moderate dementia, and (iv) the carers' rating of the patients with severe dementia.

DISCUSSION

We present the results of a study to assess the feasibility of using an individualized assessment technique, the QOLAS, to rate the QOL of patients with dementia as rated by both the patients themselves and the patients' main carers. Although some health services researchers are sceptical about the feasibility of asking patients with dementia to rate their own well-being (Bond, 1999), in this study, the patients with mild-to-moderate dementia understood the interview and were able to answer questions about their QOL, providing both qualitative and quantitative data.

In the current study, the QOLAS was administered alongside a number of other measures of well-being to assess its psychometric properties. Since it is

TABLE 3.4   EQ-5D Visual Analogue Scale (VAS) Scores (All Carer Rated)

	Mild-to-moderate dementia (*n*=6)			Severe dementia (*n*=5)		
	M	*SD*	Range	*M*	*SD*	Range
VAS Total	70.58	18.13	35–95	27.00	22.25	0–50
VAS Physical	76.67	15.06	50–90	82.50	15.00	70–100
VAS Mental	27.50	13.32	10–50	2.50	5.00	0–10

Note. Most respondents had difficulty giving an overall VAS score.Since almost all of the respondents expressed the wish to give a separate score for physical and mental health, these separate scores were noted.

TABLE 3.5   EQ-5D Descriptive—Percentage Reporting "No Problems" for Four Groups of Respondents

EQ domain	Surgery study (*n*=125)	UK survey (*n*=3395)	Dementia study Carer rating pt. Mild-to-mod. (*n*=22)	Dementia study Carer rating pt. Severe (*n*=13)
Mobility	88	82	68	39
Self-care	93	96	73	15
Usual activities	78	84	32	0
Pain/discomfort	82	67	73	54
Anxiety/depress	65	79	68	39

a subjective, respondent-driven approach, the method has optimum face (or content) validity. This study demonstrated that the QOLAS had good criterion validity and concurrent validity. Reliability was good, as assessed by internal consistency and the coefficient alpha. In this study we were not able to address test-retest reliability or sensitivity to change.

The QOLAS is one of a growing number of patient-tailored approaches, which take account of the individual's perspective, in a way that cannot be addressed by the fixed, standardized questionnaire. The need for such an approach has been strongly argued for in the QOL literature (Bowling, 1995; Gill, 1995).

The finding of poor agreement for the EQ-5D domain "usual activities" highlights the problem. The patients and their carers found this question ambiguous and asked "What is a 'usual' activity . . . ?" An individualized approach would have allowed the respondent to identify an activity, the performance of which mattered greatly to their QOL. Individualized approaches do not compete with the fixed questionnaire. Rather, they take a different approach to QOL measurement which yields complementary data. We compared the two groups, those who could be interviewed and were in the mild-to-moderate stages of dementia and those who could not be interviewed and who were in the severe stage of dementia. The results show significant differences between the two groups, i.e., those with mild-to-moderate dementia (n = 22) and those with severe dementia (n = 13) on all subscales of the QOLAS. Qualitative data collected at the time of interview revealed an ambiguity in the question concerning daily activities since, for most of these patients, this question was no longer applicable. Because most of the patients with severe dementia no longer engaged in any purposeful, goal-directed activities, a question about problems with daily activities elicited either the response that the patient was having extreme problems or, conversely, the response that (since the patient was no longer aware) he/she was having no problems with daily activities, or that the question was "not relevant."

On the Neuropsychiatric Inventory (NPI) differences between the two groups were observed on the agitation, eating, and the global NPI subscales. The EQ-5D descriptive data showed marked differences between the groups. The 'Usual activities' question was sometimes difficult to score when this question was no longer applicable and/or when the patient had no insight. In the group with severe dementia, 23% of carers could not give a rating for pain/discomfort and 8% could not rate the anxiety/depression question. The most frequent comment made by carers was that the patient sometimes made a gesture or a facial grimace or otherwise behaved such that the carer thought that the patient might be in pain or be anxious but that it was impossible to be sure. Published studies suggest that there will be less agreement for nonobservable things, e.g., pain and psychological problems compared to concrete, observable items such as "ability to walk" (Magaziner, 1997; Zimmerman & Magaziner, 1994).

In Table 3.5 we compare the results of the EQ-5D descriptive profile for 4 groups: (i) our patients being assessed for their suitability for definitive surgical treatment for intractable epilepsy, (ii) the UK population survey (Kind et al., 1998), (iii) the carers' rating of the patients with mild-to-moderate dementia, and (iv) the carers' rating of the patients with severe dementia. Because of the differences in sample sizes and the fact that two of the groups were proxy rated, no statistical analyses have been performed. It is nevertheless of interest to informally compare the groups in Table 3.5. It was previously reported (Selai, Elstner, & Trimble, 1999b) that the percentage of patients in our epilepsy surgery study reporting "no problems" on each EQ-5D domain was similar to that in the UK survey and this was surprising, given that they had chronic, intractable epilepsy (these patients were being interviewed while undergoing in-patient video-telemetry). Table 3.5 shows that the dementia (carer-rating-patient) results were quite different. Overall, both the mild-to-moderate and the severe dementia groups had smaller percentages reporting "no problems" (carer-rated) on any question than respondents in either the surgery study or the UK survey. It is of note that a larger percentage of the group of patients with mild-to-moderate dementia and a larger percentage of the surgery group had "no problems" with pain/discomfort than did the UK survey population. On the other hand, the dementia carers reported being unsure whether the patient was experiencing any pain in cases where the patient could no longer speak.

The other interesting comparison is between the patients with mild-to-moderate dementia and the epilepsy surgery group on the anxiety/depression domain. A slightly larger percentage (68%) of patients with mild-to-moderate dementia was rated by their carers as having no problems with anxiety/depression, compared to the surgery patients (65%). This might be explained by the fact that, as documented in the literature, carers underreport affective states because they have difficulties in knowing about "inner," subjective states of well-being. It also suggests that spending time on the telemetry unit, having tests which might lead to major brain surgery, is just slightly more anxiety inducing than being in the mild-to-moderate stages of dementia (the latter being proxy-rated).

CONCLUSION

We present some preliminary data which show that the modified Quality of Life Assessment Schedule (QOLAS) is a feasible technique to assess QOL in patients with dementia. Our sample was relatively small and we acknowledge the need to replicate the study with a larger sample size. Nevertheless, preliminary psychometric testing showed the method to be reliable and valid. Patients with mild-to-moderate dementia clearly can rate their QOL but the discrepancy between patient and carer proxy views needs further debate, since the question as to whose views are important raises many technical and ethical issues. Attention has only relatively recently turned to the assessment of QOL in dementia. As with the assessment of QOL in other patient groups, the most suitable QOL measure for use in dementia will depend upon the use to which the data will be put and it is likely that a variety of assessment methods will be useful for different purposes. The QOLAS, an individualised technique, is a promising method and we suggest it is likely to have a role to play in the assessment of QOL in dementia.

REFERENCES

Altman, D. G. (1991). *Practical statistics for medical research.* Chapman and Hall.

Barofsky, I. (1996). Cognitive aspects of quality of life assessment. In B. Spilker (Ed.), *Quality of life and pharmacoeconomics in clinical trials.* Philadelphia, New York: Lippincott-Raven Publishers.

Bond, J. (1999). Assessing quality of life for people with dementia. *Progress in Neurology and Psychiatry, 3*(2), 29-34.

Brazier, J., & Deverill, M. (1999). A checklist for judging preference-based measures of health related quality of life: *Learning from psychometrics. Health Economics, 8,* 41-51.

Brooks, R. G. (1995). Health status measurement: *A perspective on change.* Macmillan Press Ltd.

Brooks, R. G. (1996). EuroQol: The current state of play. *Health Policy, 37,* 53-72.

Bowling, A. (1995). Measuring disease: A *review of disease-specific quality of life measurement scales.* Open University Press.

Burns, A. (1995). Alzheimer's disease: Pharmacological developments to the year 2000. *Human Psychopharmacology, 10*(Suppl. 4), S247-S251.

Cummings, J. L., Mega, M., Gray, K., Rosenberg-Thompson, S., Carusi, D. A., & Gornbein, J. (1994). The Neuropsychiatric Inventory: Comprehensive assessment of psychopathology in dementia. *Neurology, 44,* 2308-2314.

Elstner, K., Selai, C. E., Trimble, M. R., & Robertson, M. M. (submitted). *Quality of Life in Gilles de la Tourette Syndrome.*

EuroQol Group. (1990). EuroQol: A new facility for the measurement of health related quality of life. *Health Policy, 16,* 199-208.

Fitzpatrick, R., Fletcher, A., Gore, S., Jones, D., Spiegelhalter, D., & Cox, D. (1992). Quality of life measures in health care, I: Applications and issues in assessment. *British Medical Journal, 305,* 1074-1077.

Fletcher, A. E., Dickinson, E. J., & Philp, I. (1992). Review: Audit measures: Quality of life instruments for everyday use with elderly patients. *Age and Ageing, 21,* 142-150.

Folstein, M. F., Folstein, S. E., & McHugh, P. R. (1975). Mini Mental State: A practical method for grading the cognitive state of patients for the clinician. *Journal of Psychiatric Research, 12,* 189-198.

Fransella, F., & Bannister, D. (1977). *A manual for repertory grid technique.* New York: Academic Press. Harcourt Brace Jovanovich Publishers.

Fraser, S. C. A., Ramirez, A. J., Ebbs, S. R., Fallowfield, L. J., Dobbs, H. J., et al. (1993). A daily diary card for quality of life measurement in advanced breast cancer trials. *British Journal of Cancer, 67,* 341-346.

Geddes, D. M., Dones, L., Hill, E., Law, K., Harper, P. G., et al. (1990). Quality of life during chemotherapy for small cell lung cancer: Assessment and use of a daily diary card in a randomized trial. European *Journal of Cancer, 26*(4), 484-492.

Gill, T. M. (1995). Quality of Life Assessment: Values and pitfalls. *Journal of the Royal Society of Medicine, 88,* 680-682.

Gill, T. M., & Feinstein, A. R. (1994). A critical appraisal of the quality of quality of life measurements. *Journal of the American Medical Association, 272,* 619-26.

Goldberg, D. P., & Williams, P. (1988). *A user's guide to the general health questionnaire.* Windsor: NFER-Nelson.

Guyatt, G. H., Berman, L. B., Townsend, M., Pugsley, S. O., & Chambers, L. W. (1987a). A measure of quality of life for clinical trials in chronic lung disease. *Thorax, 42,* 773-778.

Guyatt, G. H., Townsend, M., Pugsley, S. O., Keller, J. L., Short, H. D., et al. (1987b). Bronchodilators in chronic air-flow limitation. *American Review of Respiratory Disorders, 135,* 1069-1074.

Hedrick, S. C., Taeuber, R. C. & Erickson, P. (1996). On learning and understanding quality of life. In B. Spilker (Ed.), *Quality of life and pharmacoeconomics in clinical trials.* Philadelphia, New York: Lippincott-Raven Publishers.

Howard, & Rockwood. (1995). Quality of life in Alzheimer's disease: A review. *Dementia, 6,* 113-116.

Juniper, E. F., Guyatt, G. H., & Jaeschke, R. (1996). How to develop and validate a new health-related quality of life instrument. In B. Spilker (Ed.), *Quality of life and pharmacoeconomics in clinical trials* (2nd ed.). Lippincott-Raven .

Kelly, C. A., Harvey, R. J., & Cayton, H. (1997). Drug treatments for Alzheimer's disease. *British Medical Journal, 314,* 693-694.

Kendrick, A. M., & Trimble, M. R. (1994). Repertory Grid in the assessment of Quality of Life in patients with epilepsy: The Quality of Life Assessment Schedule. In M. R. Trimble & W. E. Dodson (Eds.), *Epilepsy and the quality of life.* Raven Press.

Kind, P., Dolan P., Gudex, C., & Williams, A. (1998). Variations in population health status: Results from a United Kingdom national questionnaire survey. *British Medical Journal, 316,* 736-741.

Landis, R. J., & Koch, G. G. (1977). The measurement of observer agreement for categorical data. *Biometrics, 33,* 159-174.

Lawton, M. P (1994). Quality of life in Alzheimer disease. *Alzheimer's Disease and Associated Disorders, 8*(Suppl. 3), 138-150.

Lezak, M. D. (1995). Neuropsychological assessment (3rd ed.). New York: Oxford University Press.

Magaziner, J. (1997). Use of proxies to measure health and functional outcomes in effectiveness research in persons with Alzheimer's disease and related disorders. *Alzheimer Disease and Associated Disorders, 11*(Suppl. 6), 168-174.

Mays, N., & Pope, C. (1996). Rigour and qualitative research. In N. Mays & C. Pope (Eds.), *Qualitative research in health care.* BMJ Publishing Group.

McDowell, I., & Newell, C. (1987). Measuring health: A *guide to rating scales and questionnaires.* New York: Oxford University Press.

McNair, D. M., Lorr, M., & Droppleman, L. F. (1992). *EdITS manual for the profile of mood states.* San Diego: EdITS/Educational and Industrial Testing Service.

Mega, M. S., Cummings, J. L., Fiorello, T., & Gornbein, J. (1996). The spectrum of behavioural changes in Alzheimer's disease. *Neurology, 46,* 130-135.

Nelson E., Wasson, J., Kirk, J., Keller, A., Clark, D., et al. (1987). Assessment of function in routine clinical practice: Description of the COOP chart method and preliminary findings. *Journal of Chronic Disease, 40*(Suppl. 1), 55S-63S.

O'Boyle, C. A., McGee, H. M., Hickey, A., Joyce, C. R. B., Browne, J., O'Malley, K., & Hiltbrunner, B. (1993). *The Schedule for the Evaluation of Individual Quality of Life (SEIQoL). Administration manual.* Department of Psychology, Royal College of Surgeons in Ireland.

Rabins, P. V., & Kasper, J. D. (1997). Measuring quality of life in dementia: Conceptual and practical issues. *Alzheimer Disease and Associated Disorders, 11*(Suppl. 6), 100-104.

Rockwood, K., & Wilcock, G. K. (1996). Quality of life. In S. Gauthier (Ed.), *Clinical diagnosis and management of Alzheimer's disease.* Butterworth-Heinemann.

Rossor, M. (1993). Alzheimer's disease. *British Medical Journal, 307,* 779-782.

Ruta, D. A., Garratt, A. M., Leng, M., Russell, I. T., & MacDonald, L. M. (1994). A new approach to the measurement of quality of life: The patient-generated index (PGI). *Medical Care, 32*(11), 1109-1126.

Salek, S. S., Walker, M. D., & Bayer, A. J. (1998). A review of quality of life in Alzheimer's disease. Part 2: Issues in assessing drug effects. *Pharmacoeconomics, 14*(6), 613-627.

Selai, C. E., & Trimble, M. R. (1998). Adjunctive therapy in epilepsy with the new antiepileptic drugs: Is it of any value? *Seizure, 7,* 417-418.

Selai, C. E., & Trimble, M. R. (1999a). Assessing quality of life in dementia. *Aging and Mental Health, 3*(2), 101-111.

Selai, C. E., Elstner, K., & Trimble, M. R. (1999b). *Quality of life pre and post epilepsy surgery.* Epilepsy Research.

Selai, C. E, Trimble, M. R., Rossor, M., & Harvey, R. (in press). Assessing Quality of life (QOL) in dementia: The feasibility and validity of the Quality of Life Assessment Schedule (QOLAS). *Journal of Neuropsychological Rehabilitation.*

Stewart, A. L., Sherbourne, C. D., Brod, M. (1996). Measuring health-related quality of life in older and demented populations. In B. Spilker (Ed.), *Quality of life and pharmacoeconomics in clinical trials.* Philadelphia, New York: Lippincott-Raven.

Streiner, D. L., & Norman, G. R. (1995). *Health status measurement* (2nd ed.). New York: Oxford University Press.

Teunisse et al. (1991). Interview to determine deterioration in daily functioning in dementia (IDDD). *Archives of Neurology, 48,* 274-277.

Tugwell, P., Bombardier, C., Buchanan, W. W., Goldsmith, C., Grace, E., Bennett, K. J., Williams, J., Egger, M., Alarcon, G. S., Guttadauria, M., Yarboro, C., Polisson, R. P., Szydlo, L., Luggen, M. E., Billingsley, L. M., Ward, J. R., Marks, C. (1990). Methotrexate in rheumatoid arthritis: Impact on quality of life assessed by traditional standard item and individualized patient preference health status questionnaires. *Archives of Internal Medicine, 150,* 59-82.

Walker, M. D., Salek, S. S., & Bayer, A. J. (1998). A review of quality of life in Alzheimer's disease. Part I: Issues in assessing disease impact. *Pharmacoeconomics, 14*(5), 499-530.

Ware, J. E., & Sherbourne, C. D. (1992). The MOS 36-item short form health survey (SF-36): I. Conceptual framework and item selection. Medical Care, *30,* 473-83.

Whitehouse, P. J., Orgogozo, J.-M., Becker, R. E., Gauthier, S., Pontecorvo, M., Erzigkeit, H., Rogers, S., Mohs, R. C., Bodick, N., Bruno, G., & Dal-Bianco, P. (1997). Quality of life assessment in dementia drug development. Position paper from the International Working Group on Harmonization of Dementia Drug Guidelines. *Alzheimer Disease and Associated Disorders, 11*(Suppl. 3), 56-60.

Whitehouse, P. J., Winblad, B., Shostak, D., Bhattacharjya, A., Brod, M., Brodaty, H., Dor, A., Feldman, H., Forette, F., Gauthier, S. Hay, J. W., Hill, S., Mastey, V. Neumann, P. J., O'Brien, B. J. Pugner, K. Sano, M., Sawada, T., Stone, R., & Wimo, A. (1998). 1st International Pharmacoeconomic Conference on Alzheimer's Disease: Report and Summary. *Alzheimer Disease and Associated Disorders , 12,* 266-280.

Zimmerman, S. I., & Magaziner, J. (1994). Methodological issues in measuring the functional status of cognitively impaired nursing home residents: The use of proxies and performance-based measures. *Alzheimer Disease and Associated Disorders, 8*(Suppl. 1), S281-S290.

APPENDIX 3.1   QOLAS: Describing the QOL of the Patient. The Three Constructs Most Frequently Elicited per Domain by the Patients and by the Carers. Whole Group (*n* = 22).

QOLAS Domain Patients Self-Report		Carer on Patient
Physical:	No problems/healthy	Physical health is good
	Head-aches	Tiredness
	Various symptoms, e.g., back/chest pain	Various e.g., excema, deafness
Psychological:	No problems/happy	Seems mainly happy
	Depressed/down	Anxious
	Feel vulnerable/unsafe	Up-and-down/agitated
Social/family:	Going out	Relationship with family
	Seeing friends/leisure activities	Going out
	Seeing family	Friends backing off
Daily activities:	Gardening	Cooking/housework
	Going for a walk	Going for a walk
	Doing things round home	
Cognitive:	Memory/forgetting	Memory
	Concentration, e.g., TV	Concentration
	Thinking and speaking (finding the right words)	Repeatedly asks the same question

Part II

Proxy Reports
of
Quality of Life

4

Concepts and Methods in the Development of the ADRQL: An Instrument for Assessing Health-Related Quality of Life in Persons With Alzheimer's Disease

*Peter V. Rabins, Judith D. Kasper, Leah Kleinman,
Betty S. Black, and Donald L. Patrick*

Health-related quality of life is recognized as an essential component in the overall evaluation of health, and is used increasingly to reflect patients' perspectives in studies of medical treatment effectiveness and outcomes (Ware, 1995). There are proponents of both generic and disease-specific measures (Wiklund & Karlberg,1991), and both have important uses (Guyatt, Feeny, & Patrick, 1993). Health-related quality of life measures, whether generic or not, have a shared objective: to provide information about the effects of treatment beyond the traditional focus on mortality and clinical indicators. Determining whether people are "better off" as a result of medical intervention has become increasingly salient as clinicians and patients face choices among alternative treatments or therapies, and payers and policy makers try to determine which alternatives are most cost-effective.

Research definitions of quality of life are usually quite broad, e.g., "those aspects of life and human function considered essential for living fully" (Mor, 1987), and build upon an extensive social science literature concerning quality of life and associated concepts such as well-being and life satisfaction (Andrews & Withey, 1976; Andrews & Inglehart, 1979; Diener, 1984; Lawton, 1984). Health-related quality of life (HRQOL) focuses more narrowly on the "value assigned to the duration of survival as modified by impairments, functional states, perceptions, and social opportunities influenced by disease, injury, treatment, or policy" (Patrick & Erickson, 1993). HRQOL is intended to concentrate attention on those areas of life directly influenced by health; although, as noted elsewhere, "when a patient is ill or diseased, almost all aspects of life can become health-related" (Guyatt et al., 1993).

Although health-related quality of life measures have been developed for many specific diseases, e.g., asthma (Juniper, Guyatt, Ferrie, & Griffith, 1993) and HIV (Wu et al., 1991), only recently has HRQOL begun to receive attention for Alzheimer disease (AD) and other dementias. One reason may be the expectation that assessment of HRQOL must be obtained through self-report which is not feasible for many AD patients. As Lawton, one of several researchers arguing for the need to consider quality of life for patients with Alzheimer's observes, "most cognitively impaired patients do not introspect, or at least do not report reliably on interior phenomena" (Lawton, 1994). Many patients with dementia either are unaware of their impairments and disabilities or are unable to communicate them, having lost the capacity to verbalize and the ability to remember information necessary to assess their own status. The fact that many individuals with dementia reside in nursing homes also may have discouraged application of HRQOL methodologies, since measures would need to be applicable to institutional settings as well as community-living environments. This is a crucial issue since the influence of environment on functioning and opportunities for social interaction, often reflected in HRQOL instruments, may differ considerably across these settings.

In spite of these obstacles, several arguments support the development of a measure of quality of life in individuals with dementia. First and foremost is the observation that many individuals with dementia improve with therapeutic intervention (Rabins, 1994). Treatments can have desirable and undesirable outcomes. Since these are observed by family members and clinicians, they should be accessible to measurement. In this regard, measures of quality of life are similar to other phenomena such as physical function, cognitive function, activities of daily living and behavior disorder, all of which are commonly used as outcome measures. Second, while the view is sometimes expressed that the life of a person with dementia is by definition of negligible quality, this is inconsistent with both clinical experience and other research. Onset of serious, disabling disease or terminal illness does not eliminate variation in quality of life or well-being among those afflicted (Tsevat et al., 1998), although the metric on which these are measured is often different from what would be applicable to a broad segment of the population. Positive quality of life has been identified in many groups of patients with severe illness, including those with end-stage renal disease (Churchill, Wallace, Ludwin, Beecroft, & Taylor, 1991), terminal cancer (Mor, 1987), and HIV-infection (Hays & Shapiro, 1992). Health-related quality of life also has been measured successfully in persons with severe mental illness (Lehman, 1988). People with dementia, like others with a serious debilitating disease, still have quality in their lives, even though it may be difficult for persons *not* in this state to see it. An underlying assumption of our work on HRQOL in AD is that all human life has quality and that it can be quantitated.

A necessary first step in developing an instrument to evaluate health-related quality of life is to determine the basic areas or domains that are to be assessed. For populations who cannot communicate for themselves, which include young children and individuals with disease-related impairments in communication, there are two alternative approaches, (1) to define the domains *a priori* or, (2) to use proxy respondents to identify domains of importance. As described below, we took the second approach, using caregivers and AD experts to shape the content of the instrument (a process described in more detail below) rather than adopting existing classifications from other instruments already in use. This method yielded some domains that are equivalent to those in other HRQOL instruments and some domains that appear distinct in concept, definition, or both.

This paper describes the development of the ADRQL, a health-related quality-of-life instrument for use in patients with Alzheimer's disease. The conceptual framework for the instrument and its relationship to other established instruments measuring HRQOL are described, as are the unique challenges of assessing HRQOL in persons with dementia. Other stages of the instrument development process are described as well. The ADRQL was specifically designed to contain concepts and domains most important to caregivers and providers of care for people with AD and to detect change in health-related quality of life in response to treatment interventions. As such, it is disorder-specific and incorporates the unique characteristics of the daily life of persons with dementia.

The potential uses for this instrument include evaluations of behavioral interventions, environmental settings, and drug treatments in AD patients. Instruments intended for evaluations of medical effectiveness of treatment interventions must demonstrate several key measurement properties including a strong conceptual foundation, content validity, and responsiveness to change (Guyatt et al., 1993).

CONCEPTUAL DEVELOPMENT OF THE ADRQL

The ADRQL was developed to produce a multidimensional disease-specific HRQOL instrument for use with people with AD. The conceptual process was guided by two objectives:

— to develop an instrument that would be consistent, both conceptually and methodologically, with previous approaches used in measuring health-related quality of life

— to develop an instrument that would detect change and yield a quantitative assessment of health-related quality of life, making it suitable for clinical trials and medical effectiveness studies.

Table 1 provides a comparison of the content of the ADRQL with that of other HRQOL instruments, both generic and disease-specific. This comparison provides a basis for evaluating the ADRQL in the broader context of HRQOL instrumentation. Two of the instruments selected for comparison, the Short-Form 36 (SF-36)(Ware & Sherbourne, 1992) and the Quality of Well-Being scale (QWB) (Kaplan & Bush, 1982; McDowell & Newell, 1996), are global or general instruments that are intended for use in assessing individuals and populations regardless of health levels or type of disease. As defined by Ware (1993), generic measures assess health concepts that "represent basic human values that are relevant to everyone's functional status and well-being" and are not "age, disease, or treatment specific." Also included is Patrick and Erickson's (1993) general framework of core concepts and domains of health-related quality of life. Although not an instrument, this comprehensive listing serves as a useful guide for assessing any HRQOL instrument. The two disease-specific comparisons are the Arthritis Impact Measurement Scales 2 (AIMS2) (Meenan, Mason, Anderson, Guccione, & Kazis, 1992) and Lawton's formulation of quality of life issues in AD (Lawton, 1994). The AIMS2 is designed for use in a particular age group, elderly people suffering from arthritis. Similarly, Lawton frames the domains of importance in measuring HRQOL in Alzheimer's disease and identifies methods that could be used for assessment (Lawton, 1994).

All health-related quality of life instruments share a common goal, to quantify individual subjective feelings about day-to-day living experiences as they are affected by health and illness. Operationally, these experiences are conceptualized as major domains in which the effects of health and illness on individuals are expressed. HRQOL instruments are characterized by multiple domains as well, since it is generally acknowledged that the effects of illness or treatment can vary across domains. The process of developing and defining domains for a particular instrument nonetheless leads to considerable differences across instruments. These include varying numbers and types of domains, as well as differences in definition even when measuring a similar concept.

Similarities and differences in content and structure among existing HRQOL instruments are apparent in Table 4.1. The ADRQL, which is the focus of these comparisons, consists of 5 domains: Social Interaction, Awareness of Self, Feelings and Mood, Enjoyment of Activities, and Response to Surroundings. The SF-36, by contrast, assesses 8 areas (physical functioning, social functioning, general health, bodily pain, mental health, vitality, role—physical, role—

TABLE 4.1   Comparison of Health-Related Quality of Life Domains in the ADRQL With Other Generic and Disease Specific Measures

Alzheimer Disease Related Quality of Life (ADRQL)	Generic			Disease-Specific	
	Short Form 36 (SF-36)[1] *incl Bodily pain*	Quality of Well-Being Scale (QWB)[2]	Core Concepts of Quality of Life (Patrick & Eriskson)[3]	Arthritis Impact Measurement Scale 2 (AIMS2)[4]	Quality of Life in Alzheimer Disease (Lawton)[5]
Social Interaction	Social funtioning	Social activity	Social contact	Social activities Suppprt from family and friends	Socially appropriate behavior
Awareness of Self	Role-Limitations due to physical problems	Social activity	Limitations in usual role	Work	
	Role-Limitations due to emotional problems				
Feelings and Mood	General mental health		Affective functioning	Mood Level of tension	Psychological well-being Presence of positive/ negative affect states
Enjoyment of Activities		Symptom/ problem list	Social integration		Engagement in positive activities
Response to Surroundings					

[1]From Table 4.1, Information about SF-36 Health Status Scales and the Interpretation of Low and High Scores (Lehman, 1988).
[2]From Table 4.1, The QWB Scale, Showing the Combinations of Mobility, Physical Activity and Social Activity Items and Associated Social Preference Weights (Kaplan & Bush, 1982).
[3]From Table 4.1, Core Concepts and Domains of Health-related Quality of Life (Patrick & Erickson, 1993).
[4]From Table 4.1, AIMS2 Scale Scores in Rheumatoid Arthritis and Osteoarthritis Subject Groups (Ware, 1993).
[5]Quality of Life in Alzheimer's Disease (Lawton, 1994).

emotional; not all are shown in Table 4.1); the QWB assesses 3 areas (mobility, physical activity, social activity); and the AIMS2 consists of 12 areas (among these are arthritis pain, work, mood, hand and finger function, self-care; not all are shown in Table 4.1). A major difference between these instruments and the 2 instruments developed for Alzheimer's disease, is the inclusion of domains reflecting physical activity (discussed in more detail below). All five domains of the ADRQL fall within the concepts of social and psychological functioning as described by Patrick and Erickson (1993). Only domains related to these concepts are included for the other instruments shown in Table 4.1, since the main objective is comparison of these instruments with the ADRQL.

Four areas of social functioning are identified by Patrick and Erickson (1993), 2 of which appear in the ADRQL as well as in the other four instruments shown in Table 4.1. These are interaction with others (talking to or seeing family and friends) and role performance (in work or school, as a spouse or child). Interaction or involvement with other people is characterized in the ADRQL as Social Interaction. Lawton's framework, which is concerned with Alzheimer's disease specifically, evaluates "socially appropriate behavior" (1993), while the AIMS2 includes domains on "social activities" and "support from family and friends." The SF-36 assesses "social functioning," and the QWB includes contact with family and friends under social activity.

Role performance is included in both generic instruments. The SF-36 distinguishes between role limitations due to physical impairments and those due to emotional problems, while the QWB assesses presence/ absence of limitations in work, school, housework (again under the social activity dimension). In the AIMS2, the only role-related domain is work. Ability to perform one's role in a work or family setting is inevitably affected by the progression and severity of Alzheimer disease. Lawton, for example, does not suggest any assessment in role-related activities as a component of quality of life in Alzheimer (1994). The ADRQL domain that most closely approximates role functioning is Awareness of Self. Unlike the domains that focus on limitations in role performance, how-ever, this domain of the ADRQL is intended to reflect whether a "contin-ued connection" to these roles is observed in the subject's behavior.

In addition to social functioning, the other domain consistently represented across HRQOL instruments is an appraisal of perceived emotional well-being or distress. Patrick and Erickson identify two areas of psychological function, affective and cognitive (1993). The first includes "distress and well-being," while the second reflects attributes such as alertness and problems in reason-ing. The instruments in Table 4.1 focus on domains that reflect affective functioning; none includes cognitive functioning as a domain. Clearly, changes in cognitive functioning are an important outcome in treatment interventions for AD. There is little precedent for including it in an HRQOL instrument, however, perhaps because, as Patrick and Erickson note, the relationship of cognitive functioning to psychological well-being or social functioning is not well understood (1993). The affective component of psychological function is captured in the ADRQL under Feelings and Mood, and is most similar to the two disease-specific instruments which assess "psychological well-being" and "presence of positive/negative affect states" (Lawton, 1994) and "mood" and "level of tension" (Meenan, Mason, Anderson, Guccione & Kazis 1992). The SF-36 deals with psychological functioning by characterizing general mental health in four areas—anxiety, depression, loss of behavioral/emotional control, and psychological well-being. The QWB focuses on the functional end result of disease expressed in mobility and social/physical activity limitations, and does not provide a means of evaluating psychological well-being or mental health.

The last two domains of the ADRQL, Enjoyment of Activity and Response to Surroundings, have few counterparts in the other instruments. They are salient for persons with dementia in the eyes of caregivers and providers, however. Lawton notes that most contemporary QOL assessment methodologies focus on limitations and disabilities, paying little attention to positive behaviors (Lawton, 1994). Given the severe impairments in social behavior and activity that result from Alzheimer's disease, he argues the need for understanding "which behaviors can survive dementia." The Enjoyment of Activity domain in the ADRQL is intended to evaluate this type of behavior in AD and is similar to "enjoyment of positive activities" suggested by Lawton (1994). Patrick and Erickson's (1993) "social integration" concept which is directed at participation in community life and the social ties that result, has some common ground with Enjoyment of Activity as well. The level and types of participation in activities among persons with dementia, however, will necessarily be quite different from what would be viewed as appropriate in individuals without cognitive impairment. Social integration, leisure behavior and activities or, in Lawton's terminology, "lifestyles outside the work domain," (Lawton, 1994) are not reflected in either of the generic measures (QWB and SF-36). These focus instead on role performance and ability to engage in more instrumental task-oriented activities (e.g., activities of daily living, household tasks, work).

Response to Surroundings has no counterpart in the other instruments shown in Table 4.1. Just as "arm function" is unique to the AIMS2, Response to Surroundings is unique to the ADRQL. This domain is intended to address both positive and negative interactions with one's physical environment. The design and configuration of physical environments (both community and nursing homes) is seen as potentially important in AD treatment (Cohen & Weisman, 1991) and is a field in which considerable advances may occur in the near future. In the general population, this dimension has not been considered relevant to health-related quality of life, perhaps because the physical environment has not been viewed as having an impact on health-related quality of life except indirectly through enhancing or limiting physical functioning.

While the ADRQL draws on concepts that have been included in many other efforts to assess health-related quality of life, the specific items or indicators for each domain will differ from what would be used in a general population. A generic instrument, such as the SF-36, includes indicators of social interaction that reflect the impact of physical or emotional health on normal social activities. However, use of these indicators in an AD population would result in a "floor" effect, whereby virtually all individuals would be grouped at the worst scores. Since the items within each domain must discriminate among individuals, an instrument designed for use in persons with AD must reflect the range of scores (and functioning) possible among these individuals, rather than the much higher levels of functioning that would be expected in nonaffected individuals. Items that discriminate within an AD population, on the other hand, will not be suitable for discriminating among individuals without dementing diseases, since virtually all of these individuals will be capable of performing at the highest level.

One major difference between the ADRQL and many other instruments assessing quality of life is the absence of a domain reflecting physical functioning. Cognitive functioning, as already noted, is rarely included in HRQOL instruments, even though Patrick and Erickson list it as a domain of psychological functioning (1993). Both physical functioning and cognitive functioning are important components of the full battery of assessments that are needed to evaluate treatment interventions for Alzheimer disease. Cognitive functioning is critical, of course, because it is impaired in all individuals affected with the disease. For both cognitive and physical functioning, however, several well-established scales exist. The ADL (Katz, Ford, Moskowitz, Jackson, & Jaffe, 1963) and IADL (Lawton & Brody, 1969) are extensively used to evaluate the impact on functional performance of physical limitations in basic and complex areas of task functioning. There also are valid and reliable measures of cognitive functioning that have been used extensively in studies of the Alzheimer population (Folstein, Folstein, & McHugh, 1975; Rosen, Mohs & Davis, 1984). There are additional reasons, however, for not incorporating these domains in an HRQOL instrument for persons with AD.

First, declines in cognitive function are a necessary component in diagnosing Alzheimer disease. Furthermore, progressive and ultimately overwhelming physical deterioration accompanies dementing illness such as AD. Because cognitive and physical decline are closely aligned with disease progression or severity, inclusion of these domains in an HRQOL instrument runs the risk of building into the measurement process a strong correlation between a decline in functioning and a decline in quality of life. How change in physical and cognitive functioning resonate in other aspects of life is far from clear. Excluding physical functioning and cognitive functioning as domains in the

ADRQL allows hypotheses to be tested concerning the relationship of changes in quality of life to changes in physical and cognitive functioning.

Another reason for excluding cognitive and physical functioning is the strong likelihood that these would dominate the assessment of health-related quality of life in Alzheimer patients, and render the instrument less sensitive to changes in other domains. Mor (1987), for example, in using the Spitzer Quality of Life Index, noted that its central organizing principle was physical functioning and that "if the index serves only as a physiological marker, it is probably not sufficiently sensitive for use as an outcome variable in studies evaluating the effect of a medical or health care system intervention on patients' lives." Ideally, HRQOL measures, which are inherently subjective, should be sensitive to changes that may not be reflected in measures of physical or cognitive functioning. Small improvements in cognitive functioning, for example, may have little or no impact on quality of life domains, while interventions that do not measurably affect cognitive functioning may show improvement in quality of life. It is critical to evaluate the impact of treatment interventions in the areas of cognition, physical function, *and* HRQOL and to do so with measures that do not assume that a change in one evokes a change, or a change of equal magnitude, in another.

Lawton has proposed conceptualizing quality of life across 4 sectors—psychological well-being, perceived quality of life, behavioral competence (social, physical, cognitive), and objective environment (1994). The ADRQL has domains and indicators that have a common ground with three of the four qualities (psychological well-being, perceived quality of life, and the social component of behavioral competence). With the addition of instruments that evaluate physical and cognitive functioning, and measures of the external environment (e.g., quality of care), an evaluation of Lawton's broad concept of quality of life could be achieved. Such a battery could also form the basis for evaluating the impact of AD treatments in both functioning and health-related quality of life.

INSTRUMENT DEVELOPMENT

Given the inability of those with the disease to make such assessments, caregivers and health care professionals were viewed as best suited to identify health-related quality of life issues in Alzheimer disease. Caregivers, most often close family, are well informed concerning the day-to-day activities and behavior of people with Alzheimer disease, although their views may be influenced by their own experience. Health care professionals offer a clinical perspective and, based on experiences with many patients, are in a position to identify behaviors that appear common to persons with AD. Both groups were used in the iterative process of identifying domains of HRQOL in AD and in developing and selecting items.

Initially, the authors developed an item pool based on objectives for the instrument, knowledge of other health-related quality of life measures, and clinical and research experience with Alzheimer's disease. Next, a local expert panel of health care professionals was convened. It consisted of nurses working in long-term care and outpatient dementia assessment centers, physicians working in outpatient and inpatient psychiatric and long-term-care facilities that specialize in treating persons with dementia, an activity therapist, a social worker and a representative of the local Alzheimer Association. After being presented with the objectives of the instrument, these individuals were asked to develop a list of potential items, and then to review the items developed previously by the authors. Finally, the group was asked to develop a list of major life domains.

After including the panel's recommendations, the draft instrument contained 9 domains of 4 or more items in each. This list of items and domains was mailed to 12 experts with national reputations in research or treatment of AD. Among them were individuals with clinical (psychology, psychiatry, nursing) expertise, research experience, or both. The national expert panel was asked to review the draft instrument and to identify items for inclusion or deletion among both items and domains. Once responses were obtained from this external panel (11 out of 12 responded), a revised instrument was constructed that reflected the modifications contributed by the local and national expert panels. Decisions concerning modifications were based on consistency with the initial conceptual framework, inclusion of items and domains that had not been considered, and the elimination of redundancy.

The instrument was then presented to a focus group of 12 family caregivers of persons with Alzheimer's disease. Among them were spouse and adult child caregivers, men and women, and African American and White individuals. Participants were asked to consider what behaviors or observable indicators they would use to evaluate a good or poor quality of life for someone with AD. Subsequent to this discussion, they were asked to examine the draft instrument, to comment on existing items and domains and to add or change any items they felt were missing or inadequately represented. Modifications suggested in the caregiver focus group were incorporated into another draft of the instrument and reviewed a final time by the local expert panel. Useful modifications were made at each stage of this process, but at no point was there serious disagreement about the key domains for assessing HRQOL in AD.

The final stage in the development process involved efforts to verify the placement of items within domains and the ability of caregivers to comprehend content. For the first, 5 researchers in gerontology and health services research were given the titles of the domains and asked to sort the pool of items into them. For 80% of the items, at least 4 participants sorted them into the expected domain. Two items out of 48 were sorted incorrectly by all participants; these had been placed in the Feelings and Mood domain but were sorted into Social

Interaction because the presence of other people was mentioned in the items. All missorted items were reviewed by the investigators. Minor modifications were made including placing one item in a different domain and slightly rewording others.

The final step was an additional effort to ensure that the items and definitions used in the instrument would be clearly understood by caregivers. Three cognitive interviews were conducted with current caregivers who were chosen to reflect diverse demographic backgrounds (one White male spouse, one Black female spouse, one Black adult child caregiver). Cognitive interviews provide a means of identifying words or phrases that are confusing or difficult to understand, and are used to explore the thought processes respondents use in deciding on answers to questions (Fowler, 1992; Willis, Royston, & Bercini, 1989). No changes were made to content based on these interviews, but instructions were shortened and simplified, and wording complexity was reduced.

Table 4.2 reflects the final conceptual domains of the ADRQL and their definitions. Representative items, both positive and negative, are also shown. It is important to note that items rely primarily on observable behaviors and actions such as physical gestures, speech and facial expression, although some, e.g.,"shows sense of humor," call for a more subjective assessment.

Concomitant with the focus group and mail survey, a review of the literature was undertaken with particular attention to instruments addressing (1) aspects of well-being or health-related quality of life in Alzheimer's disease, and (2) assessment of patient characteristics or attributes through observable behavior. Table 4.3 compares 4 instruments described in the literature that address health-related quality of life in Alzheimer's disease. The instruments included were developed to measure well-being or distress in persons with AD. All use a proxy respondent to evaluate the subject's status. Caregivers are used in the Progressive Deterioration Scale (PDS) (DeJong, Osterlund, & Roy, 1989), the Pleasant Events Scale (PES-AD) (Logsdon & Teri, 1997), and the ADRQL, while observer/raters, either clinicians or other trained observers, are used in the Discomfort Scale for Persons with Dementia of the Alzheimer Type (DS-DAT) (Hurley, Volicer, Hanrahan, House, & Volicer, 1992) and the Affect Rating Scale (Lawton, Van Haitsma, & Klapper, 1996). The PDS and the PES-AD have content that reflects activities characteristic of community residence (helping around the house, ability to safely travel distances alone). The DS-DAT and the Affect Rating Scale, on the other hand, focus on manifestations of a person's emotional and physical state (e.g., noisy breathing, contentment) and were developed using nursing home patients in later stages of the disease.

The ADRQL shares both content and methods with these other instruments. Proxy respondents will be used in administering the ADRQL. Like the PDS and PES-AD, interaction with others and participation in activities or tasks are assessed in the ADRQL (Social Interaction, Awareness of Self, and Enjoyment

**TABLE 4.2   Conceptual Domains of the ADRQL, Definitions and
Representative Items**

Domains	Definitions	Examples of Items
Social Interaction	Relates to family members, friends, neighbors, or professional caregivers in some observable way through physical gestures, talking, or facial expression	Smile or laughs when around other people Becomes upset or angry when approached by other people
Awareness of Self	Awareness of a person's own special personal identity and of his/her major relationships in the family, in friendships, or in work or community	Shows interest in event, places or habits from person's past No longer responds to own name
Enjoyment of Activities	Participation and enjoyment in daily life, for example in leisure and recreational activities or hobbies	Enjoys solitary activities such as listening to music or watching T.V. Dozes off or does nothing most of the time
Feelings and Mood	Signs that can be seen or heard by others of how a person often feels. These may be spoken statements, expressions, or physical gestures	Shows sense of humor Throws, hits, kicks, or bangs objects
Response to Surroundings	How a person responds to their living environment and other places in some observable way through physical gestures, talking, facial expression	Experiences enjoyment from or is calmed by possessions or belongings Makes repeated efforts to leave places

of Activities Domains). The dimension Feelings and Mood includes items like those in the DS-DAT and Affect Rating Scale that are designed to be "signs that can be seen or heard by others of how a person often feels" (Table 4.2).

The ADRQL differs in several important respects. It has been conceptualized as an evaluation of HRQOL in AD, whereas the instruments above focus on single components of experience (affect, pleasant activities). The ADRQL was developed through a process that elicited the instrument's content from caregivers and providers, rather than relying on existing classifications of quality of life to generate concepts and items. Unlike the instruments above, the ADRQL will incorporate views of caregivers concerning the contribution of various indicators to HRQOL, which has both advantages and disadvantages described more fully below. Finally, the ADRQL has been designed specifically to evaluate change in HRQOL. Longitudinal analyses will be undertaken to test "responsiveness" of the instrument to change.

TABLE 4.3   Comparison of the ADRQL With Other Instruments for Assessment of Well-Being in AD Patients

Instrument	Domains of Items	Respondent
ADRQL	Social interaction Awareness of self Enjoyment of activities Feelings and mood Response to surrounding	Caregivers

Progressive Deterioration Scale (PDS) (DeJong et al., 1989)	(Content areas)
	Extent to which patient can leave
	  immediate neighborhood
	Ability to safe travel distance alone
	Confusion in familiar settings
	Use of familiar household implements
	Participation/enjoyment of leisure/
	  cultural activities
	Extent to which patient does household chores
	Involvement in family finances, budgeting, etc.
	Interest in doing household tasks
	Travel on public transportation
	Self-care and routine tasks
	Social function/behavior in social settings
		Caregivers

Pleasant Events Schedule - AD (PES - AD) (Logsdon & Teri, 1997)	2 domain, passive-active, social-nonsocial, 20 items, examples: Listening to music Laughing Helping around the house Recalling and discussing past events	Caregivers or patient/ caregiver teams
Discomfort Scale for Persons with Dementia of the Alzheimer's Type (DS - DAT, Hurley et al., 1992)	Noisy breathing Negative vocalization Content facial expression Sad facial expression Frightened facial expression Frown Relaxed body language Tense body language Fidgeting	Observer/ Rater
Affect Rating Scale (Lawton et al., 1996)	Pleasure Interest Contentment Anger Anxiety/Fear Sadness	Observer/ Rater

APPROACH TO MEASUREMENT IN THE ADRQL

The ADRQL was developed using a methodology that incorporates into the instrument preferences among individual indicators of quality of life. The Underlying this approach is the recognition that preferences for various health states vary among individuals and that this variation can be identified, quantified and used to produce individual scores which lend themselves to statistical analysis. The items and domains of the ADRQL have been developed with the view that not every item or domain is equal in what it brings to quality of life. By developing weights for items, these differences can be incorporated into the measurement of HRQOL. A weighted scale of this type has several advantages. Within each domain, there may be some items that are more commonly performed or observed than others. These would always carry greater influence in overall HRQOL were not their importance (preference weight) also considered. Weighting a scale also increases its sensitivity to differences among individuals because it provides a continuous measure rather than a series of discrete yes/no responses. Finally, using a preference-based weighting approach provides opportunities for both single and subscale HRQOL scores for each person.

Once a weighted approach is selected, it is necessary to determine which groups should make judgments about the relative importance of each item to overall HRQOL (i.e., provide the weights). For the ADRQL, family caregivers with major caregiving responsibilities for persons with Alzheimer's disease were selected. Sixty-one caregivers were interviewed and asked to rank, on a scale from 1 to 10, the importance of each item to good/poor health-related quality of life in persons with Alzheimer's disease (psychometric analyses of the weights resulting from this process are in progress). Information was also obtained about caregivers (race, socioeconomic status, relationship to subject, current health status, caregiver burden, depression) and the person they care for. Final item selection and weighting of the instrument is based on psychometric analyses. The procedures being used followed parallel those used in developing such well-known instruments as the Sickness Impact Profile (Bergner et al., 1976).

USE OF CAREGIVERS TO ASSESS HRQOL IN PERSONS WITH AD

The ADRQL uses caregivers as proxy respondents for persons with AD. As Table 4.3 indicates, use of proxies for patient assessment in AD is common (DeJong et al., 1989; Lawton et al., 1996; Logsdon & Teri, 1995). Caregivers, health care providers and trained observers are all routinely employed as proxy respondents. In quality of life and health status assessment, however, use of proxy respondents is less common. The SF-36, for example, is structured for self-assessment. Studies of proxy assessment of health status, usually indicators of physical functioning, have yielded mixed results (Epstein, Hall, Tognetti, Son, & Conant, 1989;

Rothman, Hedrick, Bulcroft, Hickman, & Rubenstein, 1991; Spranger & Aaronson, 1992). For the most part provider ratings of general health perceptions and changes in health status are only moderately correlated with those of patients (Berlowitz, Du, Kazis, & Lewis, 1995). Some studies of patients' ratings and relatives' ratings of the patient also yield conflicting results. In several studies, greater disability was reported by proxies rather than subjects (Epstein et al., 1989; Magaziner, 1992). Concordance between patient and proxy is greatest, however, when the areas being rated are concrete and observable (Sprangers & Aaronson, 1992).

One major challenge to the validity of caregiver evaluations is the extent to which their assessment may be colored by the effects of the subjects' illness on their own quality of life. Many studies have demonstrated high rates of emotional distress in persons caring for individuals with dementia (Rabins, Mace, & Lucas, 1982; Schultz, Alison, O'Brien, Bookwala, & Fleissner, 1995). Caregiver ratings of "burden" have been found to correlate poorly if at all, however, with measures of disease severity in the person cared for (Fitting, Rabins, Lucas, & Eastham, 1986; George & Gwyther, 1986). Another recent study indicates caregivers are able to act as surrogate reporters of depression in persons with AD (Logsdon & Teri, 1995). The structure of the ADRQL should reduce the influence of caregiver characteristics on responses, since caregivers are not asked to assess how well an individual is functioning in various areas but rather about the occurrence of observable behaviors during a recent period. The relationship of caregiver characteristics to preferences among quality of life indicators is an important issue. Our working hypothesis is that there is no relationship between the two.

 An underlying assumption of our choice to develop a rating that can include all persons with AD is that each person with AD has a "personhood," no matter how severe the illness. An extensive discussion of this issue is beyond the scope of this paper (see Post, 1995 and Moody, 1992, for helpful discussions) but we believe our use of a proxy who has some knowledge of the ill person and the choice to measure quality of life in ill persons with AD is the best methodologic solution to the question of how to assure that personhood is appreciated throughout the illness.

CONCLUSIONS

This article describes the concepts and methods underlying development of the ADRQL, an instrument for assessing health-related quality of life in persons with Alzheimer disease. It was developed for use in evaluating the impact that treatment interventions in AD have on health-related quality of life or, in lay terms, whether the intervention makes the patient better off in ways that matter to patients and their families. This paper reports on the conceptual development of the instrument and its place in the broader context of health-related quality of life assessment.

REFERENCES

Andrews, F. M., & Inglehart, R. F. (1979). The structure of subjective well-being in nine western societies. *Social Indicators Research, 6,*73-90.

Andrews, F. M., & Withey, S. B. (1976). *Social indicators of well-being: Americans' perceptions of life quality.* New York: Plenum.

Bergner, M., Bobbit, R. A., Kressel, S., Pollard, Gilson, & Morris (1976). The sickness impact profile: Conceptual formulation and methodology for the development of a health status measure. *International Jornal of Health Services, 6,*393-415.

Berlowitz, D. R., Du, W., Kazis, L., & Lewis, S. (1995). Health-related quality of life in nursing home residents: Differences in patient and provider perceptions. *Journal of the American Geriatric Society, 43,* 799-802.

Churchill, D. N, Wallace, J. E., Ludwin, D., & Taylor (1991). A comparison of evaluative indices of quality of life and cognitive function in hemodialysis patients. *Controlled Clinical Trials,12,*159S-167S.

Cohen, U., & Weisman, G. D. (1991). *Holding on to home.* Baltimore: The Johns Hopkins University Press.

DeJong, R., Osterlund, D. W., & Roy, G. W. (1989). Measurement of quality of life changes in patients with Alzheimer's Disease. *Clinical Therapeutics,11,*545-554.

Diener, E. (1984). Subjective well-being. *Psychological Bulletin, 95(3),* 542-575.

Epstein, A. M., Hall, J. A., Tognetti, J., Son, & Conamt (1989). Using proxies to evaluate quality of life. Can they provide valid information about patients' health status and satisfaction with medical care? *Medical Care, 27,*S91-S98.

Fitting, M., Rabins, P., Lucas, M. J., & Eastham, J. (1986). Caregivers for dementia patients: A comparison of husbands and wives. *The Gerontologist, 26,*248-252.

Folstein, M. F., Folstein, S.E., & McHugh, P. R. (1975). The Mini-Mental State Exam: A practical method for grading the cognitive state of patients for the clinician. *Journal of Psychiatric Research,12,* 89-198.

Fowler, F. J. (1992). How unclear terms affect survey data. *Public Opinion Quarterly, 1975, 56,* 218-231.

George, L. K., & Gwyther, L. P. (1986). Caregiver well-being: A multidimensional examination of family caregivers of demented adults. *The Gerontologist, 26,* 253-259.

Guyatt, G. H., Feeny, D. H., & Patrick, D. L. (1993). Measuring health-related quality of life. *Annals of Internal Medicine, 118,* 622-629.

Hays, R. D., & Shapiro, M. F. (1992). An overview of generic health-related quality of life measures for HIV research. *Quality of Life Research, 1,* 91-97.

Hurley, A. C., Volicer, B. J., Hanrahan, P. A., House, & Volicer, L. (1992). Assessment of discomfort in advanced Alzheimer patients. *Research in Nursing & Health, 15*, 369-377.

Juniper, E. F., Guyatt, G. H., Ferrie, P. J., & Griffith (1993). Measuring quality of life in asthma. *American Review of Respiratory Disease,147*, S832-S838.

Kaplan, R. M., & Bush, J. W.(1982). Health-related quality of life measurement for evaluation research and policy analysis. *Health Psychology, 1,* 61-80.

Katz, S., Ford, A. B., Moskowitz, R. B., Jackson, B. A., & Jaffe, M. W. (1963). Studies of illness in the aged: The index of ADL, a standardized measure of biological and psychosocial function. *Journal of the American Medical Association, 185,* 914-919.

Lawton, M. P. (1984). The varieties of wellbeing. In C. Z. Malateota & C. E. Izard (Eds.), *Emotion in adult development* (p. 67). Beverly Hills, CA: Sage.

Lawton, M.P. (1994). Quality of life in Alzheimer disease. *Alzheimer Disease and Associated Disorders, 8(3)*, 138-150.

Lawton, M. P., & Brody, E. (1996), Assessment of older people: Self-maintaining and instrumental activities of daily living. *The Gerontologist, 9,* 179-186.

Lawton, M. P., Van Haitsmam, K., & Klapper, J. (1996). Observed affect in nursing home residents with Alzheimer's Disease. *Journal of Gerontology:Psychological Sciences, 51BS,* 3-14.

Lehman, A. F. (1988). A quality of life interview for the chronically mentally ill. *Evaluation and Program Planning,11*, 51-62.

Logsdon, R., & Teri, L. (1995). Depression in Alzheimer's disease patients: Caregivers as surrogate reporters. *Journal of the American Geriatric Society, 43,* 150-155.

Logsdon, R. G., & Teri, L. (1997). The pleasant events schedule-AD: Psychometric properties and relationships to depression and cognition in Alzheimer's disease patients. *The Gerontologist, 37,* 40-45.

Magaziner, J. (1992). The use of proxy respondents in health surveys of the aged. In R. B. Wallace & R. F. Wolfson (Eds.), *The epidemiologic study of the elderly.* New York: Oxford University Press, 120-129.

McDowell, I., & Newell, C. (1996). *Measuring health: A guide to rating scales and questionnaires* (2nd ed.). New York: Oxford University Press.

Meenan, R. F., Mason, J. H., Anderson, J. J., Guccione, A. A., & Kazis, L. E. (1992) The content and properties of a revised and expanded arthritis impact measurement scales health status questionnaire. *Arthritis and Rheumatism, 35,* 1-10.

Moody H. R. (1993). *Ethics in an aging society* (2nd ed.). Baltimore: Johns Hopkins University Press.

Mor, V. (1987). Cancer patients' quality of life over the disease course: Lessons for the real world. *Journal of Chronic Disease, 40(6)*, 535-544.

Patrick, D. L., & Erickson, P. (1993). Concepts of health-related quality of life. In D.L. Patrick & P. Erickson, *Health status and health policy* (pp. 76-112). Oxford University Press.

Post, S. G. (1995). *The moral challenge of Alzheimer disease*. Baltimore: The Johns Hopkins University Press.

Rabins, P. V. (1994). Noncognitive symptoms in Alzheimer disease. In R. D.Terry, R. Katzmen, K. L. Bick (Eds.), *Alzheimer disease* (419-429). New York: Raven Press Ltd.

Rabins, P. R., Mace, N. L., & Lucas, M. J. (1982). The impact of dementia on the family. *Journal of the American Medical Association, 248*, 333-335.

Rosen, W., Mohs, R., & Davis, K. (1984). A new rating scale for Alzheimer's disease. *American Journal of Psychiatry,141*, 1356-1364.

Rothman, M. L., Hedrick, S. C., Bulcroft, K. A., Hickam, D. H., & Rubenstein, L.Z. (1991). The validity of proxy-generated scores as measures of patient health status. *Medical Care, 29*, 115-124.

Rubenstein, L. Z., Schairer, C., Wieland, G. D., & Kane, R. (1984). Systematic biases in functional status assessment of elderly adults: Effects of different data sources. *Journal of Gerontology, 39*, 686-691.

Schultz, R., O'Brien, A., Bookwala, J., & Fleissner, K. (1995). Psychiatric and physical morbidity effects of dementia caregiving: Prevalence, correlates and causes. *The Gerontologist, 35*, 771-791.

Sprangers, M. A. G., & Aaronson, N. K. (1992).The role of health care providers and significant others in evaluating the quality of life of patients with chronic disease: A review. *Journal of Clinical Epidemiology,45*, 43-760.

Tsevat J., Dawson, N. V., Wu A. W., Lynn, J., Soukup, J. R., Cook, E. F., Vidaillet, H., & Phillips, R. S. (1998). Health values of hospitalized patients 80 years or older. *Journal of the American Medical Association, 279*, 71-375.

Ware, J. E., & Sherbourne, C. D. (1992). The MOS 36-item short-form health survey (SF-36): I. Conceptual framework and item selection. *Medical Care, 30*, 473-483.

Ware, J. E. (1993). *SF-36 Health survey manual and interpretation guide*. Boston, MA: Nimrod Press.

Ware, J. E. (1995). The status of health assessment 1994. *Annual Review of Public Health, 16*, 327-354.

Wiklund, I., & Karlberg, J. (1991). Evaluation of quality of life in clinical trials: Selecting quality-of-life measures. *Controlled Clinical Trials,12*, 204S-216S.

Willis, G. B., Royston, P., & Bercini, D. (1989). *Problems with survey questions revealed by cognitively-based interviews* (pp. 345-360). Proceedings of the 5th Annual Research Conference, U.S. Bureau of the Census.

Wu, A. W., Rubin, H. A., Mathews, W. C., Ware, J. E., Brysk, L. T., Hardy, W. D., Bozzette, S. A., Spector, S. A., & Richman, D. D. (1991). A health status questionnaire using 30 items from the Medical Outcomes Study. *Medical Care, 29*, 786-798.

5

Proxy-Reported Quality of Life in Alzheimer's Patients: Comparison of Clinical and Population-Based Samples

Steven M. Albert, Caridad Castillo-Castanada, Diane M. Jacobs, Mary Sano, Karen Bell, Carol Merchant, Scott Small, and Yaakov Stern

Quality of life (QOL) measures for Alzheimer's disease (AD) assess the impact of dementia on domains considered important to a patient's well-being. Some candidate domains include independence in the activities of daily living, positive affect, interaction with friends and family, and physical discomfort (Sano, Albert, Trachtenberg, & Schittini, 1999). Yet because of memory decline and loss of verbal skills, AD patients often cannot describe the impact of the disease and may not perceive subjective states as we perceive them (Albert, 1997). Moreover, with severe cognitive impairment it is not clear how these domains should be interpreted. For example, if a patient no longer recognizes family, how should one interpret a rating of frequency or satisfaction regarding time spent with family?

These difficulties have in some cases forced investigators to devise alternative indicators of QOL in AD, especially in the case of proxy-reported measures, since these measures are most often employed when patients can no longer speak or reliably report on subjective states. Here we report our experience with one such proxy-based rating system, extending our initial findings in a clinic-based sample with research from a population-based survey of people with AD. Use of a common QOL measure in two very different AD samples — one highly educated and clinic based; the other largely minority, low-income, and drawn from a population survey—offers a revealing contrast and some insight on measurement of QOL in AD.

DEVELOPMENT OF A PROXY-BASED QOL MEASURE: EXPERIENCE IN A CLINIC-BASED SAMPLE

In prior research, we have described a simple proxy-based measure useful for the assessment of quality of life in patients with Alzheimer's disease (Albert et al., 1996; Albert, 1997). The measure involves a combination of two domains: the frequency with which patients participated in caregiver-guided activities over the prior two weeks, and the frequency with which patients demonstrated visible positive and negative affect over the same reporting period.

For the first activity measure, we adapted Teri & Logsdon's "Pleasant Events Schedule-AD" (Teri & Logsdon, 1991; Logsdon & Teri, 1997), identifying 15 caregiver-cued or guided activities that patients could perform frequently ($\geq$ 3x/wk), infrequently (<3x/wk), or not at all. Of the 15 activities, five refer to activities that take place outside the home (going outdoors, taking a ride in a car, going with the caregiver to a public place), and 10 to indoor activities of varying complexity. Relatively complex activities include exercising, reading, and making handicrafts, while simpler tasks include watching television and visiting with family.

For the second, we adapted Lawton's Affect Rating scale (Lawton, 1994, 1997; Lawton, Van Haitsma, & Klapper, 1996), in which six well-identified affects (*positive*: happy, content, interested; *negative*: angry, anxious, depressed) are again rated according to frequency, ranging from never to more than 3x/day. This measure was originally designed for use in behavioral observation studies, in which raters score patients for the presence and duration of such affects. We have shown that the measure performs well in caregiver reports that elicit the frequency of such affects over a 2-week period.

The use of two such disparate measures was guided by our desire to capture both a relatively objective indicator of behavioral engagement (participation in activity) and an indicator of subjective states (affective expression), each of which could be considered a measure of QOL in patients unable to report on their quality of life. The choice of the activity measure should be viewed in light of the decision of Brod and colleagues (this issue) to exclude activity as a measure of health-related quality of life in AD. They consider activity a component of patient functional status and hence disease status, rather than an element of QOL. We take a different approach for two reasons. First, we have found that patients with similar levels of functional deficit are quite variable in reported activity (Albert et al.,1996); thus, functional status and participation in these activities cannot be considered equivalent. Second, health-related QOL, as the name implies, cannot be completely distinct from indicators of disease. Patients with similar levels of functional deficit may still *use* functional ability differently, depending on environmental opportunity, caregiver initiative, and other features of patient health status. We would thus argue that participation in activity by AD patients is an important indicator of health-related QOL.

In our initial experience with this measure, test-retest reliability was adequate, and institutional and family caregivers did not differ in reports of patient activity or affect (Albert et al., 1996). We also assessed the construct validity of the measure, as demonstrated by appropriately high correlations between proxy-reported QOL and measures of patients' functional and cognitive abilities. In cross-sectional analyses, frequency of activity declined with increasing severity of dementia, as indicated by lower modified Mini-Mental Status scores (MMSE). Similarly, one affect, "interest," was reported to be less frequent among more severely demented patients. Other affect-MMSE correlations, however, did not achieve significance in these cross-sectional analyses. We noted as well a possible curvilinear relationship between expressed negative affect and dementia severity, with levels of negative affect highest in patients with severe dementia and lower in patients with early and terminal disease.

A major effort in the development of the measure was to combine the activity and affect measures to form a reasonable composite QOL indicator (Albert et al., 1996). Our strategy was to identify a group that frequently participated in activity and also frequently experienced positive affect, or, alternatively, frequently participated in activity and infrequently experienced negative affect. We kept the two affect indicators separate because of a consistent body of research showing that positive and negative affects represent separate components of experience rather than ends of a single continuum. The cross-classification of these indicators would then define a group with the most favorable profile on both the activity and affect measures.

To construct such a measure, we first divided the sample at the median of the reported activity distribution; in the absence of normative data this seemed the safest course. We then defined two desirable affect states. Subjects were considered to have "high positive affect" if they were reported to experience all three of the positive affects at least 3x/day (the maximum score). They were considered to have "low negative affect" if they experienced all three of the negative affects no more than once a day. We did not require the absence of all three negative affects because some expression of negative affect can be considered a reasonable indicator of QOL and may be a normal aspect of daily engagement in activity.

Our reasoning in establishing these definitions deserves comment. We did not assume that participation in activity (going outside, exercising, working on a craft, reading or being read to) necessarily implies active engagement in such activity. For example, a caregiver may read to a patient and yet not be able to determine if the patient comprehends what she has heard. She may also take the patient outside or to an event outside the home but not be sure the patient is aware of changes in the environment. We would still score this behavior as a measure of engagement because participation in such activity, relative to no reported activity, is likely to imply greater variety of stimuli, greater chance for movement, and more likelihood of social interaction. Similarly, a high frequency of positive affect or low frequency of negative affect minimally implies that patients are less often distressed and are at least comfortable, compared to patients with less favorable affect profiles.

This conjoint definition of high QOL was very revealing in our initial clinic sample. By this indicator about a quarter of the sample could be said to have high QOL, some two-thirds of elders residing in the community and less than 10% of patients residing in nursing homes. Community patients with high QOL were significantly less impaired in function and cognition than patients not meeting criteria for high QOL. Patients in nursing homes with high QOL were significantly less likely to be taking antipsychotic medicines than those with low QOL. As expected, high QOL was strongly related to dementia severity. In patients with mild dementia (Clinical Dementia Rating scale [CDR, Hughes, Berg, & Danziger, 1982] score of 1), 56% met criteria for high QOL on both the high positive affect and low negative affect conditions. By contrast, among those with moderate or greater dementia severity (CDR $\geq$ 2), only 15% met criteria for high QOL on the basis of positive affect and 11% on the basis of low negative affect (Albert et al., 1996).

Given these findings, we wished to examine, first, whether the proxy-based activity and affect measures "traveled well" to nonclinical samples. Would reports of activity and affect be similarly correlated? Would proxy-reported QOL using the same measures be similarly related to patient cognitive and functional status? Second, given comparable dementia severity in patients, could we expect a similar prevalence of patients to meet criteria for high QOL? At the same time, our clinic sample has now grown, so that we have at least one affect and activity rating on 145 patients. In this report, then, we also update our prior clinic investigation.

PERFORMANCE OF THE PROXY-REPORTED QOL MEASURE IN A MINORITY, POPULATION-BASED SAMPLE

We had an opportunity to investigate these issues in patients with AD recruited in a population-based sample, the Washington Heights-Inwood Columbia Aging Project (WHICAP). In 1992, 2,128 Medicare beneficiaries from this primarily low-income, minority community in northern Manhattan, New York City, were enrolled into WHICAP. In addition, 209 elders from an AD disease registry (ascertained from Columbia-Presbyterian Medical Center discharge lists, local senior housing, and area social service agencies) were added to the sample and have been similarly followed. In 1994-95, the first follow-up survey of the cohort was completed, which included an informant interview for patients meeting criteria for AD. The informant interview was conducted with the person provid-ing the majority of care to the patient and included both family members and home health aides or nursing assistants (nonfamily represented 44% of the sample). The same affect and activity measures were employed, and we defined high QOL according to the published criteria described above.

These patients all met NINDS-ADRDA criteria for AD, and all met criteria for cognitive impairment using a standardized neuropsychological paradigm (Stern et al., 1992). Based on the results of our follow-up data, we excluded some patients who met criteria for AD at only one visit, or who were discovered to have alternative etiologies for their dementia, or who had clear evidence of basal ganglia disease. We were left with a sample of 296 AD patients for whom proxy reports were obtained (70% of all AD patients followed in WHICAP). We compared these patients to patients without proxy interviews and determined that the two groups did not significantly differ in patient sociodemographic characteristics or features of disease. Proxies provided reports of activity in 222 patients and reports of affect in 196 patients (reflecting the later introduction of the affect measure in the first follow-up). Interviews with Spanish-speaking proxies were conducted in Spanish by bilingual research assistants, and a Spanish version of the QOL form was developed and pretested before field use.

The population-based sample and clinic sample were quite different. While 10% of the clinic sample consisted of minority elders, over 90% of the population-based sample was Hispanic (56%) or African American (35%). Moreover, while the mean education in the clinic sample was 13.2 years ($\pm$ 3.6), the mean education in the community group was 6.0 ($\pm$ 4.2). The mean age of subjects in the community sample was 83.5 ($\pm$ 7.2), some 7.5 years higher than that of elders in the clinic sample, in which the mean age at assessment was 76.0 ($\pm$ 8.7). Nonfamily served as proxies for the QOL reports in 34% of the clinic sample, while nonfamily served as proxies in 44% of the community sample. In the clinic sample, patients with nonfamily proxies were largely in skilled care settings (30.1%). In the community, by contrast, proxy reporters were likely to be home health aides, and only 18.5% of the community AD patients were in nursing homes.

These differences are notable, reflecting the different populations from which each sample was drawn and different recruitment strategies; thus, we do not present statistical tests for differences between the two samples. Comparison of the two samples, even when stratified by dementia severity, is therefore confounded by differences in age, racial-ethnic identity (insofar as these may influence proxy reporting or access to care), education, and potential differences in the prevalence and severity of other comorbid medical conditions (also likely to be higher in the urban minority sample). Because of these differences, our main interest must be in the performance of the QOL measures *within* each sample, i.e., whether the measures are similarly correlated with each other and with indicators of impairment. However, it is also worth examining broad differences in reported QOL between clinic and community AD samples.

RELATIONSHIP BETWEEN PROXY-REPORTED
AFFECT AND ACTIVITY IN THE TWO SAMPLES

To assess performance of the QOL measure, we began by examining correlations between the affect and activity measures within each sample. We wished to determine if these correlations were comparable. This strategy allows us to determine if proxies in the two samples differ in the way they report on patient QOL. Table 5.1 presents such correlations for the two samples ($n = 145$ in the clinic sample, $n=196$ in the community sample, because not all patients completed both measures).

Significant correlations between reported positive affect and frequency of activity were found in both samples, with correlations of roughly the same magnitude (0.35 among clinic patients and 0.30 in community patients; $p < .001$ in each case). Activity and negative affect were less highly correlated, and correlations were lower in the community sample (-0.16 among clinic patients and -0.01 in community patients). Finally, correlations between positive and negative affect were low in both samples but much lower in the community sample (-0.20, clinic; -0.02, community).

We also correlated the QOL indicators with measures of dementia severity. Cognitive status was indexed by performance on the modified Mini-Mental Status Exam (clinic sample) and Selective Reminding Test (community sample) (Bushke & Fuld, 1974). Functional status was indexed by scores on the dependency scale (Stern et al., 1994). Finally, scores on the Clinical Dementia Rating (CDR) scale were used as a composite indicator of dementia severity encompassing both cognitive and functional deficits. Pearson correlations within each sample are shown in Table 5.2.

The pattern of correlations suggests that the proxy-report measure travels reasonably well over the samples, though, again, affect ratings in the community sample were less highly correlated with measures of disease severity than in the clinic sample. For example, the correlation between positive affect ratings and dependency scores was -0.24 in the clinic sample and only 0.03 in

TABLE 5.1   Correlations Between Proxy-Reported Affect and Activity in Clinic and Population-Based AD Samples

	Clinic Sample ($n = 145$)		Population-Based Sample ($n = 196$)	
	Activity Sum	Positive Affect	Activity Sum	Positive Affect
Positive Affect	.35***		.30***	
Negative Affect	-.16	-.20	-.01	-.02

***$p < .001$, Pearson correlations.

the community sample. On the other hand, reported activity was highly correlated with all measures of dementia severity in both samples. Also, correlations between affect ratings and CDR stage were comparable in both samples (positive affect: -0.22 clinic, -0.19 community; negative affect: 0.27 clinic, 0.13 community).

COMPARISON OF QOL AMONG AD PATIENTS ACROSS THE TWO SAMPLES

Table 5.3 summarizes results for the two samples using the proxy-reported QOL indicators. The samples are stratified according to severity of dementia (mild, moderate, and severe, as indicated by Clinical Dementia Rating scale scores). The table shows that proxies in the community sample report poorer QOL for AD subjects than proxies in the clinic sample within any given stage of dementia severity. The mean frequency of activities in the clinic sample was 15.1 vs. 11.8 in the community for mildly demented elders, 11.7 vs. 8.8 for moderately demented elders, and 6.4 vs. 5.3 for severely demented elders. The same pattern obtains when one simply counts the number of activities elders performed, ignoring frequency, though the gap is narrowed (4.8 vs. 3.9 for mild dementia, 3.4 vs. 2.9 for moderate dementia, 1.9 vs. 1.6 for severe dementia).

Proxies to clinic patients also reported superior positive affect in AD patients: 50% vs. 12% in mildly demented elders, 33% vs. 6% in moderately demented elders, and 21% vs. 5% in severely demented elders. These differences were less pronounced in the case of proxy-reported negative affect: 50% vs. 40% in mildly demented elders, and 27% vs. 20% in moderately demented elders. Among severely demented elders, however,

TABLE 5.2 Correlations Between QOL Indicators and Measures of Dementia Severity Across Two Samples

	Clinic Sample (*n* = 145)			Community Sample (*n* = 196)		
	Cognitive Function	Functional Status	CDR	Cognitive Function	Functional Status	CDR
Activity	.44***	-.64***	-.60***	.33***	-.45***	-.53***
Affect						
Positive	.09	-.24	-.22	.09	.03	-.19
Negative	-.17	.21	.27	-.01	.16	.13

***p < .001.

Cognitive function: modified Mini-Mental Status (clinic);
  Selective Reminding Test (community).
Functional status: Dependency scale score.
CDR, Clinical Dementia Rating scale score.

TABLE 5.3   Comparison of Clinic and Population-Based Minority Samples, by AD Severity

	Clinic Sample	Population-Based, Minority Sample
Mild Dementia		
Activities, frequency	14.5	11.8
Activities, (#)	4.8	3.9
High positive affect (%)	50	12
Low negative affect (%)	50	40
Hi activity, high positive affect (%)	42	9
Hi activity, low negative affect (%)	50	28
Moderate Dementia		
Activities, frequency	11.7	8.8
Activities, (#)	3.4	2.9
High positive affect (%)	33	6
Low negative affect (%)	27	20
Hi activity, high positive affect (%)	22	3
Hi activity, low negative affect (%)	16	3
Severe Dementia		
Activities, frequency	6.4	5.3
Activities, (#)	1.9	1.6
High positive affect (%)	21	5
Low negative affect (%)	17	47
Hi activity, high positive affect (%)	8	0
Hi activity, low negative affect (%)	6	5

Dementia severity: mild (CDR 1), moderate (CDR 2), severe (CDR 3+).
Activity sum: frequency of 15 caregiver-guided activities, range 0-30 (0, none;
1, < 3x/wk; 2, ≥ 3x/wk); activity number: count of number of activities performed.
High positive affect: ≥ 3x/day of all three positive affects (happy, content, interested).
Low negative affect: ≤ 1x/day of all three negative affects (angry, anxious, depressed).
Composite high QOL: above median on activity frequency and favorable affect profile.
Clinic sample, $n = 26$, mild; $n = 70$, moderate; $n = 48$, severe.
Community sample, $n = 133$, mild; $n = 37$, moderate; $n = 45$, severe.

there was a large difference in the proportion with low negative affect: 17% of clinic patients compared to 47% in community elders. This difference may indicate a bias in reporting among home health attendant proxies, who provided ratings for more than half the severely demented elders in the community. These home health attendants were more likely to report low negative affect than family proxies.

Finally, the composite QOL indicator showed an expected gradient across dementia severity in both groups, though the proportion of elders meeting criteria for high QOL was again lower in the community sample. The difference was most pronounced using the positive affect criterion for the QOL composite: for mildly demented patients, 42% of clinic vs. 9% of community patients met this criterion; for moderately demented patients, 22% vs. 3%; and for severely demented patients, 8% vs. 0%. These differences were somewhat smaller using the negative affect criterion for the QOL composite: 50% vs. 28% for mild dementias, 16% vs. 3% for moderate dementias, and 6% vs. 5% for severe dementias.

A final concern is potential differences in QOL ratings obtained from family and nonfamily proxies. We have already drawn attention to the greater likelihood of home attendants in the community sample to report low negative affect among severely demented elders. However, we did not find evidence of bias in the other QOL indicators. In both samples, the proportion meeting criteria for QOL was higher for elders with family proxies across strata defined by dementia severity. This held for both the positive- and negative-affect criterion used to define high QOL.

DISCUSSION

This inquiry shows the value—and limitations—of a simple proxy-based QOL indicator in patients with AD. We sought to determine if proxies from two disparate samples of AD patients (one clinic-based, relatively affluent, and mostly White; the other population-based, low-income, and mostly minority) reported on patient affect and activity in similar ways. The consistently high correlation in both samples between patient activity and indicators of dementia severity is very reassuring and suggests that proxy reports of patient activity offer a reliable and valid indicator of patient QOL. For example, counts and frequency of reported patient activity across levels of dementia severity were remarkably similar.

The affect measure, and in particular, reports of patient negative affect, were less consistent across the two samples. Proxy reports of high positive affect were consistently higher in the clinic sample than in the population-based sample (mild dementia: 50% vs. 12%; moderate dementia: 33% vs. 6%; severe dementia: 21% vs. 5%). Reports of negative affect, however, were less consistent across the two samples. We conclude that the affect measure, because it is less clearly linked to observed behaviors, may be a less reliable indicator of patient QOL when reported by caregiver proxies. Lawton and colleagues (this issue) also suggest that reliability in affect reports may require fairly extensive training of nurse's aides and research assistants.

These results should be interpreted within the limitations of our study design. First, the inherent differences between the samples suggest caution in the interpretation of the low correlations between the QOL measures and indicators of disease severity. The population-based sample is likely to be more heterogeneous with regard to dementia diagnosis (since these patients, unlike the clinic sample, were not ascertained in physician offices seeking treatment for memory disorders). Also, proxies in this sample were more likely to be home health attendants and were therefore more likely to have occasional or intermittent contact with patients. An important consideration for future research is to determine if family and paraprofessional caregivers differ in their ratings of activity and affect in people with AD.

A second consideration is the nature of our validation effort. These correlations should not be viewed as an example of a true multitrait-multimethod validation effort. That effort requires a similar source for ratings for different constructs, and different sources for ratings for similar constructs (Campbell & Fiske, 1959). Our measurement approach sought only to examine proxy ratings relative to standard indicators of disease severity. High correlations between proxy reports of patient QOL and such indicators of dementia severity—across two very different samples—would offer reassuring evidence that these proxy reports are reliable indicators of patient experience.

These considerations should be kept in mind when examining differences in the proportion of elders meeting criteria for high QOL in the two samples. Across categories of dementia severity, both samples show a reasonable gradient of decline in proxy reports of patient QOL. Yet the samples clearly differ in the proportion meeting such criteria within any level of dementia severity. As we have seen, in the clinic sample 42% of the mildly demented, 22% of the moderately demented, and 8% of the severely demented met criteria for high QOL using the positive affect criterion. The corresponding proportions in the community were 9%, 3%, and 0%. At this point it is hard to know how much of this difference should be attributed to true differences in environment that might affect patient QOL.

The activity measure should be sensitive to true differences in environmental opportunity. A number of the activities assessed (taking a drive in a car, reading, going to a movie or public event, performing a craft or hobby) may be linked to income or may be more difficult in an urban environment (Albert, Marks, Barrett, & Gurland, 1997). The higher reports of activity by proxies in the clinic sample, whatever the severity of dementia, may reflect such differences in opportunity.

Lastly, it should be stressed that our QOL measures depend on proxies. Proxy reports may introduce error. For example, Seltzer and Buswell (1994) found poor convergence between caregiver reports of psychiatric symptoms and formal evaluations conducted by physicians. Physician evaluations were more highly related to severity of disease. Zimmerman and Magaziner (1994) and Teresi and Holmes (1997) suggest that such discrepancies are typical of proxy measures. On the other hand, with AD patients in home environments it is hard to see how proxy reports can be avoided. The goal, as we and others have suggested (Rabins and colleagues, this issue), is to develop proxy measures that keep such error to a minimum, without requiring extensive training. Our results suggest that the activity report meets this requirement.

REFERENCES

Albert, S. M. (1997). Assessing quality of life in chronic care populations. *Journal of Mental Health and Aging, 3*(1), 101-118.

Albert, S. M., Castillo-Castenada, C., Sano, M., Jacobs, D. M., Marder, K., Bell, K., Bylsma, F., Lafleche, G., Brant, J., Albert, M., & Stern, Y. (1996). Quality of life in patients with Alzheimer's disease as reported by patient proxies. *Journal of the American Geriatrics Society, 44*, 1342-1347.

Albert, S. M., Marks, J., Barrett, V., & Gurland, B. (1997). Home health care and quality of life of patients with Alzheimer's disease. *American Journal of Preventive Medicine, 13(6)*, 63-68.

Brod, M., Stewart, A. L., & Sands, L. (1999). Conceptualization of quality of life in dementia. *Journal of Mental Health and Aging, 5*(1), 7-19.

Bushke, H., & Fuld, P. A. (1974). Evaluating storage, retention, and retrieval in disordered memory and learning. *Neurology, 24*, 1019-1025.

Campbell, D. T., & Fiske, D. W. (1959). Convergent and discriminant validation by the multitrait-multimethod matrix. *Psychological Bulletin , 56*, 85-105.

Hughes, C. P., Berg, L., & Danziger W. L. (1982). A new clinical scale for the staging of dementia. *British Journal of Psychology, 140*, 556-572.

Lawton, M. P. (1994). Quality of life in Alzheimer's disease. *Alzheimer Disease and Associated Disorders, 8*(3), 138-150.

Lawton, M. P. (1997). Assessing quality of life in Alzheimer disease research. *Alzheimer Disease and Associated Disorders, 11(suppl. 6)*, 91-99.

Lawton, M. P., Van Haitsma, K., & Klapper, J. (1996). Observed affect in nursing home residents with Alzheimer's disease. *Journal of Gerontology: Psychological Sciences, 51B*, P3-14.

Lawton, M. P., van Haitsma, K., Perkinson, M., & Ruckdeschel, K. (1999). Observed affect and quality of life in dementia: Further affirmations and problems. *Journal of Mental Health and Aging, 5*(1), 21-32.

Logsdon, R. G., & Teri, L. (1997). The Pleasant Events Schedule-AD: Psychometric properties of long and short forms and an investigation of its association to depression and cognition in Alzheimer's disease patients. *The Gerontologist, 37*(1), 40-45.

Rabins, P. V., Kasper J. D., Kleinman, L., Black, B. S., & Patrick, D. L. (1999). Concepts and methods in the development of the ADRQOL. *Journal of Mental Health and Aging, 5*(1), 33-48.

Sano, M., Albert, S. M., Trachtenberg, R., & Schittini, M. (1999). Developing utilities for stages of Alzheimer's disease using the Clinical Dementia Rating. *Journal of Mental Health and Aging, 5*(1).

Seltzer, B., & Buswell, A. (1994). Psychiatric symptoms in Alzheimer's disease: Mental status examination versus caregiver report. *The Gerontologist, 34,*103-109.

Stern, Y., Andrews, H., Pittman, J., Sano, M., Tatemichi, T., Lantigua, R., & Mayeux, R. (1992). Diagnosis of dementia in a heterogeneous population. *Archives of Neurology 49,* 453-460.

Stern, Y., Albert, S. M., Sano, M., Richards, M., Miller, L., Folstein, M., Albert, M., Bylsma, F., & Lafleche, G. (1994). Assessing patient dependency in Alzheimer's disease. *Journal of Gerontology: Medical Science 49,* M216-222.

Teresi, J., & Holmes, D. (1997). Reporting source bias in estimating prevalence of cognitive impairment. *Journal of Clinical Epidemiology 50,* 175-184.

Teri, L., & Logsdon, R. G. (1991). Identifying pleasant activities for Alzheimer's disease patients: The Pleasant Events Schedule-AD. *The Gerontologist, 31*(1), 124-127.

Zimmerman, S. I., & Magaziner, J. (1994). Methodological issues in measuring the functional status of cognitively impaired nursing home residents: The use of proxies and performance-based measures. *Alzheimer Disease and Associated Disorders 8(suppl 1),* S281-290.

Acknowledgments. The research presented in this chapter was supported by NIH grants AG07370, AG07232, and RR00645; an Alzheimer's Association grant (93-026); and the Charles S. Robertson Memorial Gift for Alzheimer's Disease Research from the Banbury Fund.

6

Developing Utilities: Quantifying Quality of Life for Stages of Alzheimer's Disease as Measured by the Clinical Dementia Rating

Mary Sano, Steven M. Albert,
Rochelle Tractenberg, and Mario Schittini

Although "Quality of Life" (QOL) is a complex and multifaceted concept, it is recognized as a critical component to assessing the impact of disease and the effect of interventions. This volume has reviewed many approaches to quantifying QOL and described several instruments to assess this concept. In the context of clinical trials and the assessment of interventions these instruments could be used to assess QOL as a distinct and separate entity. An alternative approach is to determine the QOL attributed to the primary outcome measure of a clinical trial.

Recent trends in pharmacologic intervention in Alzheimer's disease (AD) have been to design trials to determine if an agent can delay the progression of the disease. A commonly used outcome measure is the Clinical Dementia Rating (CDR) (Schafer, Sano, Mackell, Ernesto, & Morris, 1996). This scale provides a global rating of dementia severity, ranging from mild (CDR=1) to severe (CDR =3), by evaluating six domains of functioning. We have demonstrated that the total CDR assigned by trained professionals is very reliable, although the rating of the individual domains is less so (Morris et al., 1997). In this study we attempted to develop utilities for mild and severe dementia using Time Trade-Off (TTO) and Visual Analog Scale (VAS).

Utilities are ratings of preferences for a particular state of health. Perfect health receives the highest rating of 1, with poorer health states associated with lower ratings. This concept assumes that lower ratings (less preferred states) are associated with poorer quality of life (QOL). A low utility assigned to a health state indicates that the health state is less desirable than other states and that it is ranked lower than a state of optimal health. That is, the utility rating expresses the rater's perception of the degree to which the health state is worse than optimal health (Patrick & Erickson 1993). To this degree the utility rating for a particular state of health can be considered an indicator of health-related QOL. In theory utilities can be established for any type of outcome, allowing the comparison of QOL across different types of efficacy measures.

Historically, utilities have been assigned based on judgments made by expert clinicians. These were often collected through unstructured or nonstandardized techniques (open-ended interviews). It is recognized that this may not be the most appropriate representation of preference (Weeks, 1997), and more recent studies have used patient- and population-based samples for generating utility data through the use of standardized ratings such as the visual analog scale (VAS) and time trade-off (TTO). Given the complexity of AD it would seem valuable to have knowledgeable experts use these standardized techniques to generate utilities for its stages.

We conducted two studies using an identical protocol to generate utilities for stages of dementia. One study used clinical and research experts currently working in Alzheimer's disease and the other used a group of university students with little experience of the disease.

We examined two commonly used techniques for the assignment of utilities: VAS and TTO. VASs were used to generate a global rating and ratings for components of QOL. In the TTO, one is asked how many years of life one would give up in return for perfect health. In this developmental work ratings were generated for individuals with mild and severe dementia which covers the range of patients typically enrolled in clinical trials for AD. It was assumed that if these extreme stages could be quantified, future work could examine intermediate and early stages.

These techniques involve different cognitive and emotional demands. The TTO requires an estimate of "life given up" which may be more aversive than a visual quantification of one's health state. Many raters do not wish to give up *any* of their remaining life span to be restored to perfect health. For this reason, TTO ratings are often higher than visual analogue ratings for the same health state, with smaller variance (Frybeck et al. 1993; Nease, Tsai, Hynes, & Littenberg 1996). However, there should be proportionality between the two techniques at both ends of the disease spectrum. Also convergence of ratings across the two types of raters would indicate a common understanding of the impact of dementia on QOL.

METHODS

Study 1

Expert Raters. All attendees at the winter business meeting of the Alzheimer's Disease Cooperative Study were invited to participate. Participants included physicians, nurses and other clinical and research staff. Forty-one individuals participated.

Study 2

Student Raters. Thirteen students from the Columbia University School of Public Health participated in this study.

All raters answered a series of demographic and professional background questions and were asked if they had ever personally cared for a demented person.

Videotapes. Raters were shown two videotapes, each consisting of an interview with a patient and informant. The semi-structured interview for the CDR assesses capacity in memory, orientation, judgment and problem solving, home and hobbies, community affairs, and personal care. The first tape was of a patient who had been rated a CDR of 1, or mild dementia; the second was of a patient rated a CDR of 3, or severe dementia. All raters saw both videotapes and rated each using the VAS and TTO technique described below.

Questionnaire. A two-part questionnaire was used. Part 1 (administered only to the expert raters,) was completed prior to viewing the videotapes (described above) and the elicitation of utilities, and consisted of a series of questions about the longest length of life desired under four conditions of physical and cognitive impairment. These questions required a forced choice response and are described in Table 6.1 and were not used for the determination of utilities.

Part 2 consisted of two types of rating scales which were administered to both groups of raters, in conjunction with viewing videotapes of the semistructured CDR interview. A VAS was used to rate global QOL and four previously defined components (Albert & Sano, 1997). The global QOL rating was assigned using a VAS consisting of a vertical broken line with 100 at the top, 0 at the bottom and decile anchors. Raters were asked: "Based on what you have seen on the videotape, please rate the overall quality of life of this person. Let 100 represent the best quality of life and 0 the worst. Please mark with an X the quality of life of this person."

Next, four components of QOL were rated: (1) Happiness, (2) Physical Comfort, (3) Independence and (4) Relations with friends and family. The instructions were: "Rate the extent to which this condition has affected the following components of quality of life. Draw a line to indicate the effect." The lines were drawn so as to intersect a 6.5" horizontal line which was labeled "Totally destroyed" on the left end and "Spared, no effect" on the right.

TABLE 6.1   Summary of Part 1 of the Utility Questionnaire

Indicate the longest length of time you would want to live, given the following conditions:

Physical Impairment	Cognitive Impairment

Mild

You are conscious and able to make decisions but **unable to engage in physically demanding activity** (i.e., walking a few blocks, carrying groceries).

You are conscious but **unable to exercise judgment reliably,** so that you are unable to travel to new places on your own. **Memory** problems make it difficult to understand complex directions or complicated plots. **Language problems** make it hard for you to carry on conversations.

Moderate

You are conscious and able to make decisions but unable to **bathe or dresson** your own. You require help from family or health aides.

You are conscious but difficulties with memory and concentration **require that you receive help in household activities,** i.e., using the telephone, handling money, preparing a meal.

Severe

You are conscious and able to make decisions but are **limited to bed and chair at home.** You require constant help from family or health aides.

You are conscious but difficulties with memory and concentration **require that you receive help bathing and dressing.** You require help from family or home health aides for personal care.

Devastating

You are conscious and able to make decisions but are limited to bed and chair at a **nursing home or skilled care facility.** You require constant help from family or health aides.

You are conscious but problems with memory and concentration make you **unable to follow what is going on around you,** where you are or who is caring for you. You require nursing home care or its equivalent.

Forced choice response categories: 1) would not want to live;
2) 1-6 months;
3) 7- 12 months;
4) >12 months.

TTO was also used to rate the CDR stages depicted on the videotapes. A hypothetical situation was described that offered a treatment option that would return a patient to full health but would shorten life. Participants were asked if they would recommend participation in the treatment. Those who answered "yes" were asked two forced choice questions with different amounts of "life given up" to determine if responses met minimum logical criteria (see Figure 6.1). They were then asked an open question about how much of a 10-year life span they would give up to regain predementia state. Since TTO requires comprehension of a complex conditional statement, the analysis also examined the response to the open question to determine if it was consistent with the forced choice responses.

Data Analysis. Demographic and descriptive variables of the raters were summarized. The frequency of each response category was tallied for the "length-of-life" questions. Ratings for the global and component VASs were converted to decimal values. TTO values for those who would not recommend treatment were set to zero. To provide a response in the same direction as the VAS, TTO (which was recorded as the number of years given up assuming a 10-year life expectancy) was converted to percent of time desired as follows: (10-TTO)/10. Spearman correlations were performed to assess the association between demographic/descriptive variables and QOL ratings and between the two rating methods (the TTO and the global VAS).

RESULTS

1) The Raters

The expert raters were primarily male (76%), physicians (66%) with a mean age of 46.0 (±7.9) and 11.1 (±5.6) years experience working in dementia. Forty-six percent had personally cared for a person with dementia.

The mean age of the student raters was 25 years (*SD*) with a range of 22-65 years. One MD, one RN and 11 students in a master program in Public Health participated. Only one (4%) had ever personally cared for a demented person.

2) The Questionnaire: Part 1

The results of Part 1 of the questionnaire, which was administered to the expert raters, are summarized in Table 6.2. Responses to the "longest length-of-life desired" items were in the maximum category (>12 months) for the majority of the mild (61%) and moderate (75%) cognitive impairment conditions. The percent responding in the maximum category was reduced for severe (46%) and devastating (10%) cognitive impairment. Overall the trend follows an expected pattern of greater length of life desired with less impairment. The exception to this observation occurs in mild cognitive impairment, with fewer individuals rating the maximum category (>12 months) than in moderate cognitive impairment.

Responses to the "longest length-of-life desired" items for physical impairment followed a more uniform pattern. The maximum response was less frequently endorsed under conditions of increasing impairment. Table 6.2

Scenario

Assume that you know the family of this man with dementia. He can expect to live 10 years in this condition. Suppose a new experimental treatment (e.g., brain implant) could restore him to his pre-dementia state but would shorten his life. Cost is not an issue because a pharmaceutical company will pay for the procedure and has received approval from FDA for safety.

Would you recommend that the family volunteer for the treatment?

Yes   No

If Yes, Proceed

The treatment will reduce the man's life span, that is, he will live **less** than 10 years.

		Question 1 If the man lived only 2 years in his predementia state after the treatment (that is, gave up 8 years), would it be worth having the treatment?	
		Requirement for consistent response to Question 3	
Question 2 If the man lived only 8 years in his pre-dementia state (that is, gave up two years), would it be worth having the treatment?		Yes	No
	Yes	$> =8$ years[1]	between 2 and 8 years[1]
	No	illogical response [2]	less than 2 years[1]
		Question 3 If you were in a position to make this decision, how many of the 10 years would it be worth **giving up** to have someone restored to his/her pre-dementia state?	

FIGURE 6.1   Time Trade-Off Elicitation of Utilities.

[1] Range of responses to question 3 demonstrating consistency with questions 1 and 2.
[2] Illogical response to questions 1 and 2. Question 3 cannot be assessed in this condition.

illustrates several trends. First, raters tended to indicate longer life desired for less impaired states. Second, even mild cognitive impairment tended to generate shorter life desired than severe physical impairment. Twenty-seven percent indicated they would want to live 6 months or less given mild cognitive impairment while 2%, 20%, and 19% gave this response to mild, moderate, and severe physical impairment, respectively. Finally, it appears that the negative impact on length-of-life-desired accelerates with each level of cognitive impairment but is equivalent with each level of physical impairment.

TABLE 6.2   Expert Raters' Responses to the Questions About "Longest Life Desired" Given Increasing Levels of Physical and Cognitive Impairment. Numbers Refer to Percent Responding to Each Category

	Response Categories for Longest Length of Life Desired			
	Would not want to live	1-6 month	7-12 months	> 12 months
Physical Impairment				
Mild	0	2	0	98
Moderate	0	10	12	78
Severe	7	12	17	63
Devastating	17	29	10	44
Cognitive Impairment				
Mild	7	20	12	61
Moderate	5	10	10	75
Severe	22	20	10	46
Devastating	54	27	7	10

Study 1: VAS and TTO in Expert Raters

Table 6.3 describes the responses of the expert raters to the global and component VASs for the CDR 1 and CDR 3 patients. These ratings followed an expected pattern of lower VAS rating in more severe disease, as described in Table 6.3. The pattern of response to VAS for the components of QOL was comparable in both the mild and severe case, with independence receiving the lowest rating and physical comfort receiving the highest rating, followed by happiness and relationships with family and friends.

To the initial question of the TTO 15 (37%) of the expert raters said they would not recommend a treatment that shortened life for the CDR 1 patients. In contrast, all recommended the treatment for the CDR 3. All those who completed the forced-choice questions provided internally consistent answers. However, 24% gave a response to the open question which was inconsistent with the forced-choice questions. Time trade-off responses indicated willingness to give up one-third of remaining life to return to the predementia state from mild dementia and two-thirds of life from severe dementia.

To assess the sensitivity of raters to dementia severity, paired t-tests were carried out on VAS (global and component) and TTO ratings, comparing each rater's CDR 1 and CDR 3 ratings. In every case the ratings were significantly higher for mild dementia than for severe dementia ($p < .001$) (see Table 6.3).

The TTO rating and global VAS correlated significantly for both the CDR 1 ($rho=.498; p < .001$) and CDR 3 ($rho=.401; p = .01$) indicating considerable association between the rating methods.

TABLE 6.3   Mean (SD) Visual Analog Scale (VAS) and Time-Trade-Off (TTO) as Rated by Expert Raters. Global and Component Quality of Life Ratings are Expressed as Proportion Preserved. TTO is Presented as Proportion of Time Desired

	CDR 1	CDR 3
VAS: Global	.75 (.14)	.26 (.18)
Physical comfort	.96 (.73)	.55 (.26)
Happiness	.78 (.11)	.48 (.23)
Relationships	.71 (.15)	.28 (.18)
Independence	.63 (.19)	.14 (.13)
TTO: Time desired	.67 (.32)	.31 (.27)

We examined the association between ratings (VAS and TTO) and expert rater characteristics (demographic and descriptive). The number of years working in dementia was negatively correlated with global VAS for CDR 1 ($rs = -.377$; $p = .015$). There was no other significant association between these ratings and age, gender, years working in dementia, areas of specialty (neurology vs. other), professional degree (MD vs. other) and report of personally caring for someone with dementia.

Study 2: VAS and TTO in Student Raters

Table 6.4 summarizes the VAS and TTO ratings of the student raters. The mean global VAS rating for mild dementia was .65 ($\pm$.17) and for severe dementia was .30 ($\pm$.13). In general mild dementia was rated lower by the student raters than by the expert raters on all VAS ratings. However, the pattern of responses of the components of QOL was quite comparable, with independence the most affected component and physical comfort the least affected. This trend is less obvious for severe dementia. Of note, student raters viewed "happiness" as highly impaired in the mildly demented patient, perhaps reflecting awareness of the patient's insight and distress about self-reported memory loss. Also, for severe dementia, physical comfort is rated lower and happiness is rated higher by the student raters compared to expert raters.

All of the student raters recommended treatment for mild dementia. Eleven of 13 completed the TTO for severe dementia. All those who completed the forced choice questions provided internally consistent answers. One responder to the severe dementia gave a response to the open-ended TTO that was not consistent with the forced choice responses. For mild dementia, the mean TTO rating was .58 ($\pm$.23). For severe dementia, the mean TTO rating was .29 ($\pm$.22). As in Study 1 the TTO rating and global VAS correlated significantly for both the CDR 1 ($rho=.49; p<.01$) and CDR 3 ($rho=.45; p< 0.01$).

DISCUSSION

This report describes the development of utilities for mild and severe stages of AD as defined by the CDR, using both expert and student raters. In general, the findings follow the predicted pattern of poorer ratings for poorer health states. The pattern is seen in the "desired length of life" ratings for both physical and cognitive conditions, although the experts appear to rate the cognitive conditions lower than the physical ones. The VAS ratings of QOL demonstrate a large difference between CDR 1 and 3, with the same pattern of order among the component QOL ratings. The TTO procedure yielded consistent responses for most raters, indicating that they were able to understand and follow the task. As with the VAS ratings, there was a significant difference between years given up for mild and severe dementia.

Together these studies demonstrate consistency in judgments regarding impact of dementia on QOL across a range of ages and levels of expertise. The two samples, one relatively naive to dementia care, the other professionally engaged in care and research, provided similar ratings on two standard modalities for eliciting such ratings. Utilities for a mild dementia (CDR 1) ranged from .65-.75 for VAS ratings and .58 -.67 for TTO ratings. Utilities for severe dementia ranged from .30-.33 for VAS and .29-.31 for TTO.

The correlations between TTO and VAS ratings were significant for both mild and severe disease demonstrating that the elicited utilities are robust and sensitive across the spectrum of dementia. Examination of the components of QOL suggests that independence is perceived the most impaired while physical comfort and happiness are least impaired. The consistency of this pattern supports the idea that the utility is based on a well-defined construct of dementia that can be universally perceived across dementia severities and levels of experience with the disease.

TABLE 6.4   Mean (SD) Visual Analog Scale (VAS) and Time-Trade-Off (TTO) as Rated by Student Raters. Global and Component Quality of Life Ratings are Expressed as Proportion Preserved. TTO is Presented as Proportion of Time Desired

	CDR 1	CDR 3
VAS: Global	.65 (.17)	.30 (.13)
Physical Comfort	.74 (.16)	.55 (.22)
Happiness	.57 (.19)	.46 (.14)
Relationships	.54 (.20)	.23 (.18)
Independence	.42 (.24)	.12 (.12)
TTO: Time desired	.58 (.23)	.29 (.21)

Across all VAS ratings students judged dementia somewhat worse than the experts. It may be that exposure and familiarity with a disease reduces aversiveness. This trend is seen in other diseases. Higher utility weights for dialysis programs were observed among dialysis patients than among the general public (Sackett & Torrance, 1978). Because of their exposure to patients, the experts may be aware of greater tolerance of disease states in those with disease, perhaps allowing them some latitude in their own perception of illness.

Ultimately utilities are developed to help evaluate treatment outcomes by providing a common metric for comparison. The present study may permit the comparison of treatments which preserve or prolong mild dementia and/or delay the time to severe dementia. However, we do not know the utility or value of other outcome measures such as cognitive test scores, functional measures or clinical impression of change. Future work needs to be done to demonstrate the universality of utility weights from different perspectives such as that of the patient or caregiver. In addition the development of utilities for specific cognitive and functional outcomes is also needed. Such studies would allow for decision analyses to determine the costs and benefits of different treatment approaches.

These raters represented experts from Alzheimer's Disease Centers across the U.S. and students at a major U.S. university. The demographic and descriptive features of the expert raters suggest we have captured different professionals with a range of experience. These factors did not systematically affect utility ratings and one might expect that these ratings would parallel those of other dementia experts. It must be acknowledged that these student and expert raters place a high value on cognitive ability. They are highly sensitive to cognitive disability and, conversely, relatively insensitive to physical disability. However, it is important to note that even these diverse groups may not represent a full range of exposure to other health-related aspects of aging. Medical experts exposed to physical disability of the elderly rather than cognitive disability may attribute different value to these conditions. It is equally important to recognize that neither of these groups may represent patient or family caregiver perspectives, which may differ from lay or clinician judgments. We leave this determination as a goal for future research.

The convergence of professional and lay raters as well as the commonality of the pattern of VAS component ratings offers some confidence that a broad consensus governs perceptions of the impact of dementia on QOL. In this study the utility weight of mild dementia was comparable to that of other chronic diseases (Patrick & Erickson, 1993; Sackett & Torrance, 1978; Stewart et al., 1989; Stewart & Ware, 1992). The utility weight for severe dementia was comparable to ratings for other terminal diseases such as renal disease. These ratings provide an indicator of perceived impact of dementia and may assist in evaluating health care delivery. The value of these utilities can be strengthened with replication in broader populations. These utility estimates may provide a mechanism for comparing different disease states and their treatments.

REFERENCES

Albert S. M.,& Sano, M. (1997). *Dementia Utilities Evaluation System (DUES).* Presented at the annual meeting of International Psychogeriatric Society. Jerusalem, Israel.

Fryback, D. G., Dasbach, E. J., Klein et al. (1993). The Beaver Dam Health Outcomes study: Initial catalogue of health state quality factors. *Medical Decision Making, 13,*89-102.

Morris, J. C., Ernesto, C., Schafer, K., Coats, M., Leon, S., Sano, M., Thal, L. J., Woodbuty, P., & the ADCS (1997). Clinical Dementia Rating training and relia-bility in multicenter trials: The ADCS experience. *Neurology, 48,*1508-1510.

Nease, R. F., Tsai, R., Hynes, L. M., & Littenberg, B. (1996). Automated utility assessment of global health. *Quality of Life Research, 5,*175-182.

Patrick, D. L., & Erickson, P.(1993). Health status, quality of life and health related quality of life. *Health status and health policy* (pp. 20-26).New York: Oxford Press

Sackett, D. L., & Torrance, G. W. (1978). The utility of different health states as perceived by the general public. *Journal of Chronic Disease, 31,* 697-704.

Schafer, K., Sano, M., Mackell, J., Ernesto, C., & Morris, J. C. (1996). Clinical monitoring of rating scales in multicenter clinical trials. *Controlled Clinical Trials, 17,* 57S.

Stewart, A. L., Greenfield, S., Hays, R. D. et al. (1989). Functional status and well-being of patients with chronic conditions: Results from the Medical Outcomes Study. *Journal of the American Medical Association, 262*(7), 907-913.

Stewart, A., & Ware, J. E. (1992). *Measuring function and well-being: The medical outcomes study.* Durham: Duke University Press.

Weeks, J. C. (1997). Measuring quality-adjusted survival for cancer therapies. *Risk in Perspective, 5*(10)1-4.

Acknowledgments. The study presented in this chapter was conducted by the Alzheimer's Disease Cooperative Study, funded by the National Institute of Health grant U01-AG10483.

Part III

Behavioral-Observational Models of Quality of Life

7

Observed Affect and Quality of Life in Dementia: Further Affirmations and Problems

M. Powell Lawton, Kimberly Van Haitsma,
Margaret Perkinson, and Katy Ruckdeschel

One reason for wishing to comprehend the emotions being experienced by the person with dementing illness is value based. Dementia patients have the same right that all people have to maximize positive feelings and minimize negative feelings. Simply being able to recognize that they experience good and bad moments will do much to enable caregiving staff and families to respond to the individuality and humanity of the patient with Alzheimer's disease. "The Alzheimer patient is still a person with a past, a present, and a future" is the first lesson caregivers should learn.

A second reason follows from the first. Granting the patient a personality, it follows logically that he or she has likes and dislikes and is capable of communicating them somehow. Our major assertion is that even when cognitive and verbal communicative capacity are greatly reduced, the ability to display preferences and aversions may persist through emotional expression. In many ways, the emotions represent a developmentally early system of both responding to and controlling one's external environment. This suggests that emotion may remain in the repertory of communication skills even when more verbally dependent functions are lost. Comprehending the emotion signals of the person with dementia has two major applications to caregiving. First, caregivers, whether direct-care, family members, or professionals may be guided in their efforts by knowing whether the care receiver likes or dislikes an activity, or the care being provided. The mechanics of better care thus can be shaped by a better "reading" of the person's feelings.

Another important rationale is the way this skill affects the caregiver. Whether a therapist, a CNA, or a family member, the caregiver's morale depends strongly on maintaining a sense of accomplishment or an ongoing demonstration that the effects of one's efforts have an impact on patient well-being. Sensitivity to emotional signals from the care receiver provides highly reinforcing feedback and engenders a sense of agency in a situation which may otherwise erode one's sense of control. The caregiver's behavior can thus grow progressively in the direction of providing more rewards and fewer punishments, with corresponding increased caregiver morale.

The Apparent Affect Rating Scale (AARS) was designed as an observational tool for a research project in which moderately to moderately-severely demented nursing home residents were subjects (one of a set of 10 cooperative research projects funded by the National Institute on Aging to study special care units, Ory, 1994). The research leading up to the design of the AARS is described in Lawton, Van Haitsma, and Klapper (1996). The AARS entails rating three negative emotions (anger, anxiety/fear, and depression/sadness) and two positive emotions (pleasure and interest) over a 5-minute period (other time frames can be specified, such as 2 weeks for related methods such as the Family Questionnaire or the Activity Therapist Questionnaire as described in Lawton et al., 1996). The rater is asked to indicate the amount of time during the interval he or she observed a target resident displaying each of the emotions: Never, less than 16 seconds, 16 to 59 seconds, 1 to 2 minutes, or more than 2 minutes. Raters are provided with descriptions of the signs or indicators of each of the emotions, such as clenched teeth, grimace, shouting, etc. as indicators of anger. The AARS as used in this form is depicted in Figure 7.1.

THE PURPOSE OF THE PRESENT STUDY

A first purpose was to test whether the AARS was sensitive enough to capture intraindividual variations in people's affective expression as they moved from one environmental context to another. The earlier report provided validity-relevant information, which demonstrated that residents' dominant affective states were correlated in meaningful ways with other resident characteristics. For example, aggregated AARS ratings of sadness by research assistants were correlated .25 with Multidimensional Observation Scale for Elderly Subjects (MOSES, Helmes, Csapo, & Short, 1987) depression scores and .21 with the Raskin Depression Scale (Guy, 1976) ratings; AARS Pleasure ratings were correlated .41 with CNA ratings of Sociability and .24 with family members' ratings of Extraversion. These validity measures thus affirmed the ability of the

Resident's Name: _____ Time: _____ Unit: _____ Observer's Name: _____

Date: _____

		9	1	2	3	4	5
		Can't tell	Never	less than 16 secs	16-59 secs	1-2 mins	more than 2 mins
	 Pleasure Signs: Laughing; singing; smiling; kissing; stroking or gently touching other; reaching out warmly to other; responding to music (only counts as pleasure if in combination with another sign). Statements of pleasure.						
	 Anger Signs: Physical aggression; yelling; cursing, berating; shaking fist; drawing eyebrows together; clenching teeth; pursing lips; narrowing eyes; making distancing gesture. Statements of anger.						
	 Anxiety/Fear Signs: Shrieking; repetitive calling out; restlessness; wincing/grimacing; repeated or agitated movement; line between eyebrows; lines across forehead; hand wringing; tremor; leg jiggling; rapid breathing; eyes wide; tight facial muscles. Statements of anxiety/fear.						
	 Depression/Sadness Signs: Cry, frowning; eyes drooping; moaning; sighing; head in hand; eyes/head turned down and face expressionless (only counts as sadness if paired with another sign). Statements of sadness.						
	 Interest Signs: Participating in a task; maintaining eye contact; eyes following object or person; looking around room; responding by moving or saying something; turning body or moving toward person or object.						

FIGURE 7.1 Apparent Affect Rating Scale.

AARS to agree with other modes of assessing people. This between-person validity, which requires the aggregation of multiple observations of the same person in many contexts, represents the less-important of two aspects of validity. The more important aspect is within-person validity, the ability of the AARS to capture changes in a single individual over time and across different contexts. Thus the present report investigated the sensitivity of the AARS in reflecting changes in affect states in single residents as they moved among behavioral contexts that might be expected to elicit different states.

The second purpose was to test the practicability of teaching the use of the AARS to the most important institutional caregiver, the certified nursing assistant (CNA). The first report on the AARS (Lawton et al., 1996) demonstrated the ability of two trained research assistants to agree on observed affect states in residents when they watched the same sequence of behavior. For the five states, kappa ranged from .78 for anxiety to .89 for anger, representing high levels of agreement. The assistants had received considerable training, including multiple feedback sessions in which pairs of ratings were discussed in terms of the reasons for agreement or disagreement. However, one of the ultimate purposes of using the AARS is to enhance the caregiving skills of paid staff or family members. A long-term research need is thus to determine the types and quantity of training necessary for these groups to attain rating expertise comparable to that of the research assistants. Therefore a second purpose of this study was to test how well nursing assistants could utilize the AARS.

Study 1. Validity of the AARS: Sensitivity to Behavioral Context

In order to test the ability of the AARS to discriminate changes in intraindividual affect states, contexts were sought that everyone was likely to experience and for which contrasting affect states might be expected. The four behavior settings chosen for study were:

Morning Care. The period between awakening in the morning and breakfast includes either self-waking or calling by a staff member; going to the toilet or being sent there by a staff member or being cleaned up; washing; and getting dressed, whether by one's own effort or by staff. The activity of staff on residents' behalf may be seen as intrusive, and residents often offer active resistance to staff's efforts. Although some mildly impaired residents did not require staff assistance in completing morning care, staff (most often the CNA) usually were active in choosing clothes, dressing, and helping the resident get cleaned up. Given such general dependence, together with frequent resident resistance to care and resultant intrusion into the resident's personal, physical, and psychological space, and resultant resident resistance to care, it was hypothesized that anger and anxiety would be highest during morning care, and that pleasure would be relatively low and interest high.

Meal Time. Meal time (breakfast or lunch) was similar to morning care in that some residents ate without help, while others required varying amounts of help. Self-feeding was clearly the modal behavior, however. The lesser degree of intrusiveness, plus the intrinsic enjoyment of eating, led to the prediction that pleasure would be high, while anger, anxiety, and sadness would be low. Interest was predicted to be high because of the task demands that focus eyes, hand, and mouth on the process of getting food.

Down Time. As is typical in institutional life, much time is spent with no activity scheduled or expected of the resident. This "down time" may be spent in one's own room, in designated public spaces, or a variety of other locations. In order to standardize across residents, observation times were sought when the person was in a lounge, hall, or other common space and neither appeared to be engaging in activity nor located in a setting where some organized activity was in process. Interest was hypothesized to be least and affect absent more than in the other contexts, as well as relatively low pleasure, anger, anxiety, or sadness: Down time is affectively neutral.

Activity Time. Activity was operationalized as a setting where an organized activity was in process in close enough proximity to the resident to allow participation. Of course, in many such instances there was no participation. Data were missing for a few of the least impaired residents who were mobile on their own and actively avoided organized activity settings. The activity context, as compared to the relatively obligatory contexts of morning care and meal time, represented an opportunity, not a demand. It was predicted that pleasure and interest would be high. Although the negative emotions (anger, anxiety, depression) might be crowded out by the positive emotions, the two-factor conception of emotion (Lawton, 1983; Watson & Tellegen, 1985) would suggest that those negative emotions would be less strongly affected by a putatively positive experience than would the positive emotions.

Although all residents did not receive the full quota, 6 observations were sought for each of the contexts, a total of 24 per subject. A minimum of three per context were required to maintain a resident in the sample. Trained research assistants used the Psion event recorder and The Observer software (Noldus, 1991; Van Haitsma, Lawton, Klapper, & Corn, 1997) as means of rating all behavior that occurred over each 5-minute observation period. The AARS was one of many scales completed during this time. Although the raters were not specifically alerted to the hypotheses regarding affect differences across contexts, they were in a position for their ratings to be influenced by their implicit hypotheses about the type of affect that might be expected to occur in the four contexts. On the other hand, their training emphasized the importance of making the ratings on the basis of the resident's behavior, regardless of context.

Results

Table 7.1 shows the mean affect ratings associated with each context. The multiple AARS scores for each resident in each context were averaged to take account of the varying number of replications. A one-way repeated measures analysis of variance was performed separately for each affect, a rating of no affect, and missing data, with pairwise tests between contexts assessed using the Duncan multiple-range test ($df = 3,75$). In general, the results support the hypotheses, with some exceptions:

Morning Care was, as hypothesized, characterized by greater anger and anxiety than the other contexts. In addition, interest was relatively high (the equal of interest in the meal time context).

The Dominant State during meal time was interest, while other states were generally absent to low duration. Contrary to prediction, pleasure did not typically accompany eating.

Down Time was, as expected, a time of low affective response by all the measures. It was as low as meal time in pleasure, anger, and anxiety, lowest in interest, and most likely to evoke ratings of no affect.

Activity Time was, as predicted, highest in pleasure and not notably lower in the three negative affects than in most of the other settings. Contrary to prediction, interest was relatively low (interest was significantly greater during morning care and meals than during activities). Affect was absent for longer average durations than was true in morning care and meals, but for shorter durations than in down time.

Study 2. Use of the AARS by Certified Nursing Assistants

Exploration of the ability of the CNA to use the AARS was performed in two successive research projects, which will be referred to as (1) minimal training and (2) extended training.

Minimal Training. This research studied 39 nursing home residents on a unit caring for mildly demented residents and 40 residents on a unit of severely demented residents. For the aspect of the research being reported here, observation occasions were arranged so that a trained research assistant and a CNA together observed a single resident for 5 minutes, after which both independently completed the AARS. Half of the observations were made during an activity in which the resident was included (that is, as part of a group or alone, and free to participate but not necessarily actively engaged) and half during "down time," that is, a time when no activity or obligatory task was in progress. Although four such occasions of each kind were sought for each resident, dropouts, missed occasions, difficulty in locating a resident, or difficulty in scheduling a CNA

TABLE 7.1   **Estimated Duration of Affects in Four Contexts**

	Morning Care	Meal	Down-time	Activity	F
Pleasure	1.2[a]	1.1[b]	1.1[a,b]	1.4[c]	3.10***
Anger	1.3[a]	1.0[b]	1.1[b]	1.1[b]	18.03***
Anxiety	2.4[a]	1.3[b]	1.4[b]	1.3[b]	99.35***
Sadness	1.1[a]	1.0[b]	1.1	1.1	4.76**
Interest	4.8[a]	4.9[a]	3.6[b]	4.2[c]	108.44***
No affect	1.4[a]	1.1[b]	2.9[c]	2.2[d]	133.31***
Missing affect	1.0	1.0[b]	1.1[c]	1.0[b]	5.43**

**$p < .01$.   ***$p < .001$.
Note. Values with differing subscripts within a row were significant ($p < .05$ or greater) by the Duncan multiple-range test.

resulted in a total of 128 paired observations being available, with the ratings provided by four research assistants and 15 CNAs.

Training the CNAs. The research assistants met with day-shift CNAs on each of the care units for 30 minutes to introduce the AARS and explain its use. Either the project director or the research assistants explained the goals of the project, then research assistants described the five emotions to be rated and the signs that indicated the presence of those emotions. CNAs were shown how to fill out the AARS and given tips on where they should position themselves during the observations. Each CNA completed a set of practice observations accompanied by one of the research assistants. After this practice session, the RA offered feedback to the CNAs on their ratings. Every attempt was made to assign the same CNA to perform all observations on a single resident. Scheduling and assignment changes forced a number of exceptions to this goal, however, as did the status of the resident, since residents who were sleeping were not observed.

At the time each paired observation was performed, the RA provided brief reminders to the CNA concerning the procedures to be used in observing residents and filling out the AARS form. This typically took no more than 1 or 2 minutes. Each observation occasion was targeted for 5 minutes. The RA and the CNA made independent AARS ratings in the usual manner for the down time and activity. After each session, a second research assistant briefly interviewed the CNA and RA separately regarding their level of confidence in their AARS ratings and the criteria they used in rating the resident's affect.

Results of Minimal Training

Table 7.2 shows two measures of agreement between the RAs and CNAs. Kappa is the only measure that corrects for chance agreement. With the number

TABLE 7.2   Minimal Training: Agreement on Estimated Time Ratings by Research Assistants and Certified Nursing Assistants for Five Affects

	Research Assistant and CNA	
	% Agree[a]	Intraclass Correlation
Pleasure	74	.64
Anger	91	.67
Anxiety	65	.43
Depression	80	.28
Interest	53	.02

[a]An agreement is exact ± 1-point disagreement.

of occasions studied here it is not possible to compute kappas because of the large number of zero-incidence cells. Although the overall percentages of agreement and some of the intraclass correlations portray modest levels of agreement, neither of these measures corrects for chance agreement. Among the affects, the most frequent rating for interest, for example, was a "5" (present for more than 2 minutes), while "1" (never present) was the most common rating for the other four states. Thus, an excess of agreements in the modal category would be expected. One can only conclude that the minimal approach to training CNAs to rate observed emotion in the AARS did not work as well as might be wished.

Enhanced Training. The next research endeavor in this series studied 180 nursing home residents on 8 units who represented a full range of cognitive impairment from mild to severe. This study was designed to examine the impact of CNA-delivered one-on-one interventions on resident quality of life. For the purpose of the present report, research assistant and CNA pairs made AARS ratings independently after observing a resident for a 10-minute period. A total of 96 CNAs and 4 research assistants were involved in making AARS ratings. Each resident was observed 5-8 times with both CNA and RA present, with a mean of 5.91 sessions per resident. Half of the residents were observed while engaged in a one-to-one activity with the CNA and half were observed during "usual care," which typically corresponded to "down time." A total of 890 paired observations (with a few missing individual affect ratings) were recorded with a mean of 9.51 observation sessions per CNA. Training procedures for this study replicated and enhanced the training procedures described in the previous section. The scale was first presented in a group orientation meeting introducing the CNAs to the scale's purpose. A copy of the scale was handed out and the signs of each emotional state were described verbally.

Following this group experience, the CNAs were then reintroduced to the scale in a one-on-one session with a research assistant several days later. The RA and CNA practiced using the scale while watching two to three individuals on the unit for 10-minute periods. In a second one-on-one session, the RA and the CNA observed a 10-minute prescribed interaction between another staff member and a resident from a distance. After this 10-minute session, the CNA completed the AARS form without prompting from the RA. The RA and the CNA then compared their independent ratings and discussed any discrepancies. After several sessions of completing the AARS completely independently, the CNA was again joined for an observation session by a researcher to compare independent, simultaneous ratings and discuss any discrepancies.

Results

Table 7.3 shows three measures of agreement between RAs and CNAs obtained after the enhanced training. In this instance, because of the greater number of ratings, it was possible to calculate weighted kappa, in addition to percent agreement and intraclass correlation. The results of the enhanced training showed a modest increase in the ability of the CNAs to rate observed emotion. When comparing percent agreement and intraclass correlations obtained through enhanced training as compared with minimal training, improvement in every affect category except anger was noted. The most dramatic increase in reliability was noted in ratings of depression and interest. However, as noted previously, neither of these measures of reliability corrects for chance agreement. When a much more stringent test, weighted kappa, was examined, it became evident that much room for improvement still exists. Kappas for the positive emotions, pleasure and interest, showed acceptable levels of reliability. The negative emotions of anger, anxiety, and depression continued to be rated in a fashion indicating that considerable disagreement between CNA and research assistant was still present.

DISCUSSION

Study 1

These results demonstrate that the AARS is capable of distinguishing varying affective states for the same individual in different behavioral contexts. This important aspect of the validity suggests that the AARS would be a viable clinical tool for measuring the outcome of various interventions targeted to a specific individual or group of individuals. For example, knowing that pleasure is very low during meal times suggests that this would be an ideal entry point for interventions designed to enhance pleasurable dining. Enhancements are as simple as improving the food or as elaborate as a total environmental redesign (colors, textures, external views, warmer lighting, tablecloths,

Table 7.3   Enhanced Training: Agreement on Estimated Time Ratings by Research Assistants and Certified Nursing Assistants for Five Affects

Affect	Weighted Kappa	% Agree	Intraclass r
Pleasure	.66	84	.87
Anger	.37	90	.62
Anxiety	.40	79	.67
Depression	.29	86	.53
Interest	.58	87	.85

Note ñ Number of rating pairs ranges from 858 to 882.

nondisposable silverware and plates, and so on). The affective response of an individual selected to receive such an intervention could be tracked using the AARS during mealtimes. The targeted outcome of the intervention would be increased pleasure within a specified time period. Feedback to staff regarding the person's progress (or lack thereof) could be provided in the form of a graph, which could be used by the care planning team in making any needed adjustments to the intervention process.

Anxiety is substantially elevated during morning care. Although this association is easy to validate through clinical observation, demonstrating through hard data what a marked effect occurs during this period may be useful in staff training. One use might be in open discussion when staff is encouraged to speculate about the several possible reasons for agitation at that time. "Down time" was documented as just that: Almost all affect ratings were significantly lowest during this period. The results for times when activities were being conducted are the most provocative. The purpose of activity programming is to capture interest and ideally to evoke positive affect. Although the effect for pleasure was significant, the effect size was low, and interest was notably lower than in morning care and at meal time. A major reason for the low measure impact of activity is that this behavior setting represents a context with which the person may or may not be subjectively or behaviorally engaged. In contrast, morning care and meals are completely certain to have engaged the attention of most people at most times. Washing, dressing, grooming, and eating demand cognitive and behavioral focusing. It would, indeed, be surprising if interest was not evident almost all the time. Activities, on the other hand, are usually group-focused. The hope is that being able to watch an activity, or better yet, being able to persuade the attendee to participate, will engage the patient actively. Yet we know clinically that such expectations are difficult to achieve. Few activities succeed in gaining the attention of all who are physically proximate to the activity, and of all whose attention is gained, only a fraction may respond emotionally. Thus the results reflect especially the difference between near-100% attention to the two ADL tasks as compared to the only partial relevance of the activity context to many participants. In terms of the purpose of the study, however, the validity of the measure itself seems strongly affirmed. Future intervention research could clearly find the AARS useful as an assessment device for evaluating activity programs. In fact, the AARS would be useful at two levels. The first is at the individual level when an activity is presented to a single individual in such a way as to be very likely to evoke his or her focus of attention. The critical test in this instance would be the quality of the affect, or the percentage of the time when interest is evoked. The second level is represented by the present procedure, where the outcome is the proportion of all present individuals who are engaged or display affective responses. Different activities or variations in how the activity is conducted could easily be compared in an experimental design.

Study 2. Suggestions for Enhanced Training in Using the AARS With CNAs

These studies demonstrate that our enhanced training given to CNAs, as contrasted with minimal training, was sufficient to produce only modest increases in the reliability of ratings using the AARS. Building on what we have learned, we have continued to explore ways to intensify the training given to CNAs in the use of the AARS. Specifically, we suggest that enhanced training for CNAs focus on increasing the opportunities for exposure to the concept of rating observed emotion, practice in a variety of "real life" situations, and increased feedback targeted to areas of particular difficulties in using the rating scale. This training can be done by a researcher, social worker, nurse educator, etc. For the rest of this section, the individual doing the training will simply be referred to as the trainer.

Exposure to the concept of rating observed emotion can be increased in several ways. Rating emotion is an extremely complex task that appears deceptively simple. In the initial group session, CNAs are introduced to the scale's purpose and a copy of the instrument is distributed. The signs of each emotional state should be described verbally and demonstrated. This exercise can be made a fun experience by having the trainer demonstrate the signs of emotion in an exaggerated fashion and asking people to take turns doing the same as each sign of emotion is read. This allows the group not only to have fun, but also to observe the signs of emotion in others, albeit in an exaggerated form. The efficacy of such an exercise would be fortified by viewing a 22-minute commercially available videotape, "Recognizing and Responding to Emotion in Persons with Dementia" (Terra Nova, 1998). This video exposes the viewer to the signs of each emotion as expressed by persons with dementia in various situations. The tape highlights difficulties in distinguishing one emotion from another, in detecting the subtle signs of some emotional states, and in distinguishing emotional states from an individual's usual or "baseline" facial expression, e.g., someone whose wrinkled face makes them look sad all the time. At the end of the tape, the trainer leads the group through a series of discussion questions. This exercise represents yet another opportunity to reinforce the signs of each emotion and the words that are used to describe them on the scale.

Following this group experience, the CNAs are reintroduced to the scale in a one-on-one session with a trainer several days later. The trainer and CNA practice using the scale while watching three to four individuals on the unit for 5- to 10-minute periods. This procedure is the same as described in the previous training sections, except that now it is recommended that the trainer point out signs of emotion as they occur in the moment and clarify the meaning of each sign even if it does not occur. For example, a sign of pleasure, "touching with an approach manner," or anger, "narrowing of eyes," is demonstrated by the trainer, even if the sign does not occur during the observation session. Again, this offers another opportunity for the CNA to observe rarely occurring emotions, even if it is in an artificial context. During this session several issues in using the AARS may arise. First, while the majority of the CNAs readily understand the criteria and mechanics of the rating scale, some CNAs have difficulty estimating the duration of the emotional response. Within a research context, this problem can be addressed by having the researchers count off the intervals of time during the observation period.

Second, it is important in this one-on-one session to emphasize that the rating must be based on the emotions observed during the current session, rather than responding according to the resident's "typical" emotion or the context within which the observation is taking place. That is, if a pleasant, lively event such as a birthday party were under way in another part of the room, the trainer should point out that a resident would not necessarily experience a positive emotion just by being in a positive social context.

Third, interest has proven to be a challenging emotion to rate for very severely cognitively impaired individuals. The hallmark of this emotion is generally considered to be visual tracking and angle of gaze (Lawton, Van Haitsma, & Klapper, 1996). However, severely demented individuals often may have a fixed gaze or sit with their eyes closed, but nonetheless respond to their environment, indicating a subtle form of engagement with the world around them. The resident may move in response to a CNA question by nodding, raising eyebrows, or reaching out a hand. In a similar vein, the resident may respond to the CNA by increasing the rate or volume of incoherent speech, perhaps indicating an attempt to communicate with the CNA. As a result of our research experience, these criteria have been added to the AARS to make it more sensitive to emotional expression in the most severely demented individuals.

In a second one-on-one session, the trainer and CNA observe a prescribed interaction between another staff member and a resident from a distance. Ideally, the resident selected for this session should be an emotionally expressive person who will provide the opportunity to observe a range of emotional signs. After this 5-minute session, the CNA completes the AARS form without prompting from the trainer. The trainer and the CNA then compare their independent ratings and discuss any discrepancies in the ratings. It is important that the trainer discuss discrepancies in a sensitive manner with the CNA. The trainer's job at this level of training is to uncover the reasons for differences in ratings. Did the CNA see something that the trainer missed? Is the CNA attributing the sign of one emotion to another emotion category? The trainer's manner in leading this discussion will significantly impact the CNA's receptivity to learning to use the scale.

Periodic follow-up sessions with the CNA are important to check for the development of "observer drift" or the tendency for raters to develop idiosyn-cratic interpretations of some emotional signs, or to begin using criteria which are not explicitly listed on the AARS form. Typically, the first follow-up session should occur within 2 weeks of beginning independent ratings, and then quarterly thereafter.

It has been our experience that the majority of raters can benefit from this enhanced training procedure. However, there is clearly a subset of individuals for whom the ability to accurately perceive observed emotion is significantly impaired. For these individuals, training appears to have little or no effect on enhancing their skill in rating observed emotion. From a research perspective, difficulties in obtaining reliable ratings of observed emotion are easily rem-edied by identifying these poor raters from the outset and removing them from the rating pool. From a clinical perspective, the inability to reliably rate observed emotion has significant clinical implications for the quality of caregiving. Do persons who have difficulty perceiving observed emotion have more problems in interacting with persons with dementia? In missing emo-tional cues, do they find themselves trying to manage behavioral difficulties that others who are more skilled do not encounter? Do they leave their jobs at a higher rate than those more skilled at reading nonverbal emotional expres-sions? The answers to these questions and others would be very relevant to the selection and training of staff who deliver care to persons with dementia.

From a long-range perspective, it is desirable that training staff to observe emotion in persons with dementia should be extended over time, rather than being done in one teaching sequence. We suggest that every in-service training program (for professional staff as well as for CNAs) could benefit from including displayed emotion and its meaning as one of its topics. This could be a continued theme in such training over time. Further, the care planning conference is another context during which such training could be fruitfully introduced, assuming the CNAs are present and active during these meetings. Once the observation of emotion is established as an ongoing feature of training and care, staff will become increasingly adept at using such informa-tion to improve quality of care. As will be seen in the next section, the emotions observed during everyday care may be used in planning future care and activities. The care planning conference is a perfect setting in which to embed such training.

In summary, the ability to discern emotional expression accurately and then to use this information in formulating a plan of care is an extremely complex task that requires considerable interpersonal skill and practice. Future research is needed to determine ways of detecting persons who are skilled in this ability, how to effectively train persons who are not as skilled in reading emotion, and optimal methods for incorporating observed emotion into the plan of care for persons with dementia.

CONCLUSION

The demonstrated contextual differences have implications for service. Direct-care staff, when being trained on tasks involving physical activities of daily living (ADLs), should be thoroughly oriented to the empathetic approach. If they are asked to look at the resident for nonverbal signs of anger and anxiety, such recognition may heighten their awareness of the distress associated with ADL care. Having become sensitized to the signs of distress, the next step is to get staff to use the information to guide their approach; for example, to use more supportive talk, eye contact with a smile, a slower motion, or more waiting for the patient to make the first move. Staff then can see whether the change is in their behavior or is accompanied by a change in the expressed emotion of the resident. Similar reasoning applies to eating: encourage the staff person to observe the resident, and then to experiment with his or her assistive behavior, to try to enhance the pleasure associated with eating.

Usable information regarding people's emotion states is conveyed by facial expression and other nonverbal behavior. Although dementing illness introduces barriers to the comprehension of such information, research to date supports the idea that it is worthwhile to look for such information in both clinical and research contexts.

The research reported in this article, while providing encouragement regarding the value of close observation of people with dementing illness, also sounds a cautionary note regarding how much return we can expect from a given investment in staff training and practice. "Reading" the nonverbal signs of emotion is not a familiar process. Successful reading demands learning and practicing a technology, and a continuous process of quality improvement through comparing different raters' judgments, discussing them, and revising in light of the discussion. In short, sensitization to and expertise in evaluating resident affect states and using these evaluations in treatment are a time-extended process. It is thus little wonder that two forms of brief training of CNAs to perform affect ratings resulted in less than completely affirmative results. There was enough agreement to make the training seem worthwhile to continue. The sheer amount of training and the time over which the training was spread were insufficient to allow the complete assimilation of the material. Additional study is needed to determine how much training is necessary, the limits of agreement that can be attained, and the even more challenging task of putting this technology into practice as a means of elevating the quality of life of people with dementing illness.

The sensitivity of emotion ratings to the pull of environmental context argues for the usefulness of the technique as a research tool. The type of validation data provided here needs to be replicated in a research design where raters are not aware of the context. Theoretically, such a study could be done with videotape recordings rated by trained judges not involved in the original scene. Our research obtained such data, but there are major problems involved in making the videotape to exclude all contextual cues. In the absence of such an ideal research procedure, training which encourages raters to focus on behavior and excludes context has an excellent chance of generating data relatively free of bias.

REFERENCES

Guy, W. (1976). *ECDEU Assessment manual for psychopharmacology.* Rockville, MD: U.S. Department of HEW.

Helmes, E., Csapo, K. G., & Short, J. A. (1987). Standardization and validation of the Multidimensional Observation Scale for Elderly Subjects (MOSES). *Journal of Gerontology, 4,* 395-405.

Lawton, M. P. (1983). Environment and other determinants of well-being in older people. *The Gerontologist, 23,* 349-357.

Lawton, M. P., Van Haitsma, K. S., & Klapper, J. A. (1996). Observed affect in nursing home residents. *Journal of Gerontology: Psychological Sciences, 51B,* P3-P14.

Noldus, L. P. (1991). The observer: A software system for collection and analysis of observational data. *Behavioral Research Methods, Instruments and Computers, 23,* 415-429.

Ory, M. G. (1994). Dementia special care: The development of a national research initiative. *Alzheimer Disease and Associated Disorders, 8* (Suppl. 1), S389-S404.

Terra Nova (1998). Recognizing and responding to emotion in persons with dementia. Training videotape distributed by Terra Nova Films (800) 779-8491, 9848 South Winchester Ave., Chicago, IL 60643. Produced by the Philadelphia Geriatric Center.

Van Haitsma, K., Lawton, M. P., Klapper, J. K., & Corn, J. (1997). Methodological aspects of the study of streams of behavior in elders with dementing illness. *Alzheimer's Disease and Associated Disorders, 11,* 228-238.

Watson, D., & Tellegen, A. (1985). Toward a consensual structure of mood. *Psychological Bulletin, 98,* 219-235.

Acknowledgment. The authors of this chapter wish to gratefully acknowledge the support of the following grant agencies which made the report possible: A stimulation-retreat program for moderately demented nursing home residents. UAG-10304 National Institute on Aging. Emotion in Dementia: Its measurement and comprehension by care-givers. TRG-90-001 Alzheimer's Association. Individualized positive psychological intervention: Impact on staff and demented nursing home residents. TRG-006 Alzheimer's Association/Tacrine Fund Pilot Research Grant.

8

A Model of Psychological Well-Being in Advanced Dementia

Ladislav Volicer, Ann C. Hurley, and Lois Camberg

Several diseases cause development of a progressive dementia, characterized by memory deficit and other cognitive dysfunctions. The most common of these diseases are Alzheimer's disease, vascular dementia, fronto-temporal dementia (including Pick's disease) and dementia with Lewy bodies (Klein & Kowall, 1998). Individuals suffering from dementia may have more than one type of the pathological changes characterizing these diseases when their brains are examined after death. There may be different clinical manifestations of the symptoms of dementia depending on the pathological changes in the brain or different trajectories in the progressive decline, but one uniform feature across all the dementias is the lack of an effective treatment that would prevent or reverse any of these diseases.

Cognitive dysfunctions caused by dementia include impairment of speech and comprehension, inability to use tools, and impairment of judgment. These dysfunctions greatly limit the person's ability to engage in independent activities that he/she might have enjoyed before the development of dementia. Dysfunctions also limit the person's independence in activities of daily living, initially with more complex activities such as balancing a checkbook or using a television, but later with basic activities such as dressing, bathing, and eating. Because persons with advanced dementia cannot engage in independent activities, they are at a risk of social isolation, boredom, and may develop associated dysfunctional behaviors, such as restlessness and agitation (Volicer, Hurley, & Mahoney, 1998a).

Promoting psychological well-being is a goal of care in dementia as it is in many chronic diseases which cannot be completely cured. Psychological well-being is uniquely personal and subjective and is usually determined from reports of the individual regarding his/her life enjoyment and satisfaction. It is not possible to use this method with persons who have advanced dementia, because of their speech and short-term memory impairments. Persons with advanced dementia live in the "here and now" and do not remember even the most enjoyable activities such as having a special meal or a visit from relatives.

This paper proposes a conceptual model of psychological well-being in persons with advanced dementia. Methods for the measurement of the psychological well-being, and some interventions which improve psychological well-being of demented individuals, are also described.

COMPONENTS OF PSYCHOLOGICAL WELL-BEING

Psychological well-being of persons with advanced dementia, who cannot report their feelings because of aphasia, has to be evaluated by observing the person's mood and behaviors. In persons with advanced dementia, mood states are a very important indicator of psychological well-being because of the inability to remember and plan for the future. Healthy individuals may be willing to suffer through a period of impaired mood, knowing it is transient and can be overcome to achieve a long-term goal that would significantly improve their psychological well-being. Persons with advanced dementia are not able to comprehend such reasoning and their psychological well-being is more dependent on their momentary mood state.

Happy-Sad Mood. Happy and sad moods are two aspects of the spectrum of emotions that can be evaluated by observing facial expression. Darwin (1955) stated that facial expression is the language of emotions and that there is an evolutionary biological basis for the expression of emotions in man. Corroboration of this hypothesis, that facial expressions communicate emotions, was provided by Adelmann and Zajonc (1989) in a review of the theoretical and empirical literature of emotional facial action in which the correspondence between specific affective self-reports and facial patterns of the corresponding emotion was identified. Spontaneous expression of emotions is essentially invariant over the life span (Izard & Dougherty, 1982). For normal individuals, Russell (1997) arranges the spectrum of emotions around a circle in which the emotions are grouped according to their similarities and opposites (Figure 8.1).

The rating of facial expressions was also found to be applicable to Alzheimer patients (Mace, 1989), even though their facial expressions are sparse and not always clear (Asplund, Jansson, & Norberg, 1995). Smiling is the simplest and most easily recognized expression of emotion (Ekman & Friesen, 1975) and easily recognizable shapes of the mouth can depict happy and sad moods. Sad mood is one of the symptoms of depression which is required for diagnosis of depression according to DSM-IV (1994). Episodes of sad mood are very common in demented individuals. A study of 175 community-living demented individuals found that sad mood or loss of interest was present in 97% of participants, and that the vegetative symptoms of depression were also very common (Merriam, Aronson, Gaston, Wey, & Katz, 1988). Eighty-six percent of these individuals had both sad mood and vegetative symptoms and therefore fulfilled the criteria for the diagnosis of depression.

Engagement—Apathy

Inability to initiate meaningful activities, manifested as engagement with the environment, is one of the main consequences of dementia (Volicer et al., 1998a). This inability may lead to several negative consequences, such as apathy, agitation, and depression. Patients who are not provided with a meaningful activity often sit motionless, staring into space with a vacant expression. They show indifference and emotional disengagement.

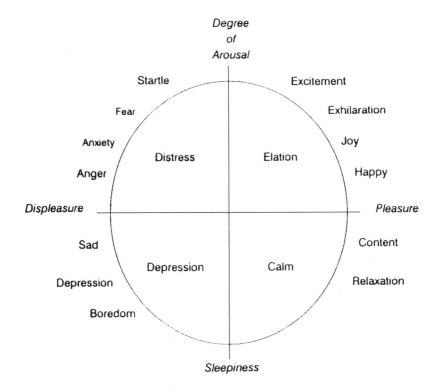

FIGURE 8.1 A circumplex for emotions (reprinted from Russell, 1997). Copyright © 1997 by the American Psychological Association. Reprinted with permissions.

Apathy is a very common symptom and was observed in 80% of community-dwelling outpatients (Craig et al., 1996). Although apathy was modestly correlated with dysphoria, the brain blood flow changes were different in these two conditions. Apathy was associated with severe prefrontal and anterior temporal hypoperfusion while dysphoria was not related to blood flow variation (Craig et al., 1996). The distinction between apathy and sad mood/depression was also supported by the lack of correlation between apathy and depression subscores of the Neuropsychiatric Inventory (Levy et al., 1998). In addition, these authors found that the relationship between apathy and depression varies across different diagnoses of dementing illnesses. However, the "loss of interest" symptom is used by different investigators to be an indicator of either apathy or depression, and these conditions may coexist in the same individual.

Agitation—Calm

Agitation is reported to be one of the most common problem behaviors in demented individuals. However, the definition of agitation is not uniform in all studies. Cohen-Mansfield (1988), who reported that two agitated behaviors occur at least once a week in 87% of demented nursing home residents, included verbal and physical aggression under agitation. Other investigators called these behaviors aggressiveness or combative behaviors and reported their occurrence mostly within the context of personal care (Ryden, Bossenmaier, & McLachlan, 1991). We prefer to use the term, resistiveness-to-care, for problem behaviors that occur during contact with the caregivers because this behavior is invoked by the caregiving encounter although the underlying cause is patients' confusion and misperception. When care has to be provided and patients cannot understand what is happening, they often resist caregiving efforts as a matter of self-defense. If caregivers persist on providing care despite clues that the patient may be bothered by what the caregivers are doing to them, patients may strike out to protect themselves.

We reserve the term agitation to mean problem behaviors that occur without external stimulation. The distinction between agitation and resistiveness is supported by finding that resistiveness preceded aggressive behavior (Bridges-Parlet, Knopman, & Thompson,1994) and by factor analysis of the RAGE scale in which the item "being uncooperative or resisting help" loaded only weekly on the agitation factor (Patel & Hope, 1992). Using the patient-centered approach, agitation may be defined as those patient behaviors that:

1. communicate to others that the patient is experiencing an unpleasant state of excitement,
2. are observable without subjective interpretation,
3. are not strictly behaviors that are invoked by caregiving activities,

4. are unrelated to a known physical need of the patient that can be remedied,
5. are without known motivational intent (Hurley et al., 1998).

In an absence of agitation, patients may be considered to be calm. Yet, it is sometimes difficult to distinguish calm from apathy or withdrawal. Often, caregivers must prioritize their time to manage first those problematic behaviors that might cause injury to the person or to others near the person, leaving those behaviors that signal that the person is experiencing a negative, although not disruptive behavior, untreated.

MODEL OF PSYCHOLOGICAL
WELL-BEING IN DEMENTIA

Normal individuals have the capacity to express a variety of mood states summarized by the circumplex model of emotions shown in Figure 8.1 (Russell, 1997). Emotions are arranged around a circle according to their similarities (fear, anxiety, anger) and relationships to the poles of positive or negative degree of arousal and pleasure. Opposite emotions are placed on the opposite sites of the circle (boredom and exhilaration). This circle can be divided into four quadrants: distress, elation, depression, and calm.

Lawton (1983) who studied cognitively intact individuals pioneered the analysis of psychological well-being in the elderly. Lawton postulated a two-factor model of psychological well-being that consists of "Positive Affect" which includes happy, interested, energetic, content and warm hearted, and "Negative Affect" which includes sad, annoyed, worried, irritated and depressed (Lawton et al., 1992). In the cognitively intact elderly, Positive Affect was related to high levels of leisure activity participation and Negative Affect was more inwardly oriented (Lawton, 1994). In applying this research to demented individuals, Lawton and his colleagues decreased the number of items from the original 10 to 6, because those subjects were not able to provide subjective reports and observers were not able to distinguish subtle differences in behavioral signs (Lawton, VanHaitsma, & Klapper, 1996).

An observation study of 57 demented nursing home residents who exhibited either agitation or withdrawn behavior showed that it is possible to recognize not only Positive and Negative Affect but six indicators of emotional state and psychological well-being: happy, engaged, calm, sad, withdrawn, agitated. These indicators can be seen as opposite poles of three continua which can be empirically measured. The first continuum ranges from Happy to Sad, and may be recognized by an individual's facial expression. The second continuum ranges from Calm to Agitated and is expressed by body movements and vocalization. The third continuum ranges from Engaged to Apathetic and can be measured by the degree of an individual's involvement with the environment.

Using these six indicators, we can characterize an individual with the optimal degree of psychological well-being as a person who is observed to be happy, calm, and engaged with the environment. Conversely, agitation, unhappiness, and apathy indicate the absence of psychological well-being.

As dementia progresses, individuals lose their ability to cognitively process their mood states and express emotions verbally, and resort to other mechanisms, primarily nonverbal means of communication. Thus, anger can be expressed as combative behavior during care, and boredom as agitation and repetitive crying out. The decreased ability to handle and express emotions can be depicted as a cone with the base made of the normal circumplex of emotions. With the progression of dementia, the range of and capacity to express emotions become more restricted. Eventually, in a terminal stage of dementia, the individual may lose most of the contact with the environment and become unable to express emotions (Figure 8.2).

By placing "withdrawn," "sad," and "calm" closer together, this model takes into consideration that it is more difficult to distinguish these conditions than "agitated," "happy," and "engaged." The "outwardly" expressed characteristics-—agitated, engaged, and happy—are more readily recognizable by well-accepted markers such as restlessness, talking, and smiling than are the

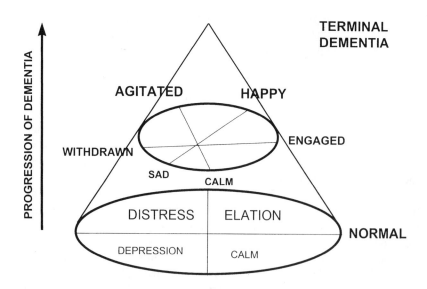

FIGURE 8.2   Model of the effect of the dementing process on psychological well-being. Base of the cone is the normal circumplex of emotions, which is increasingly restricted by progression of dementia.

"internal" characteristics—apathetic, calm, and sad. A question not yet answered is "to what degree can apathetic be distinguished from calm or sad when an individual indeed feels 'sad' but is not expressing it?" The degree of confidence in evaluating a psychoemotional state is greater when the person with advanced dementia exhibits outward behavior that is commonly known to spring from a specific internal feeling.

Another characteristic of this model is the close proximity of "agitated" and "withdrawn." Mega, Cummings, Fiorello, and Gornbein (1996) observed agitation in 60% of Alzheimer patients, whereas apathy was observed in 72% of them. This indicates that agitation and apathy often occur in the same individuals who switch from agitation to apathy and back. This oscillation makes the pharmacological treatment of agitation especially difficult because the sedative side effects of medications used to treat agitation may increase apathy and withdrawal (Volicer et al., 1998a).

METHODS FOR MEASURING PSYCHOLOGICAL WELL-BEING IN DEMENTIA

Caregivers need to be able to assess the psychological well-being of persons with advanced dementia to know when to provide and how to evaluate the efficacy of interventions to enhance psychological well-being. Psychological well-being has both positive and negative aspects. Optimal psychological well-being is a state with maximal positive aspects and minimal or absent negative aspects. Positive aspects of psychological well-being in persons with advanced dementia are evaluated less frequently than are negative aspects. Negative aspects are often the targets of a therapeutic intervention and there are many psychometrically acceptable instruments for their assessment. However, evaluation of a therapeutic intervention should include effects on both positive and negative aspects to obtain the true therapeutic value of the intervention. The lack of adequate instruments to measure positive aspects of well-being in persons with advanced dementia may be a contributing factor to the focus on negative aspects.

Mood

Mood state is usually rated according to a subject's report. Such a report, unfortunately, cannot be obtained from an individual with severe dementia. However, we can estimate an individual's mood from facial expressions. We asked raters to observe the residents and assign scores based on their mouth shape using 1 to indicate frown, 2 to indicate neutral expression, and 3 to indicate smile. These scores were then compared with scores on other observation measures: engagement and agitation.

This method of evaluation, which we call FACE (Figure 8.3), was found to have good rater reliability with a mean kappa of .927 (*SD* .167). The positive correlations

FACE MOOD EVALUATION

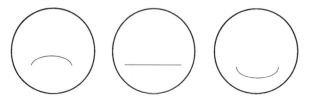

FIGURE 8.3   FACE instrument for measuring mood by observation.

between FACE and measures of engagement and the negative correlation between FACE and agitation-supported validity of FACE evaluation. However, these three measures also showed a degree of independence. When agitation was statistically controlled, the correlation between FACE and engagement measures decreased. Similarly, when engagement was controlled the correlation between FACE and agitation decreased significantly. These results support the conceptual distinction of FACE from other indicators of psychological well-being.

Lawton's Positive Affect scale for demented individuals could also be considered a measure of mood. However, we found that for one of the items, Contentment, we were unable to achieve good reliability during observer training. The remaining two items, Pleasure and Interest, were highly correlated with each other but the correlation was abolished by controlling for engagement, while it was unaffected by controlling for observed mood (FACE). This indicates that these items do not measure mood in the way FACE does. In addition, a multidimensional scaling analysis (Young, Takane, & Lewyckj, 1980) located Positive Affect and Engagement-VAS in the same area. These results provide empirical support for the notion that the two Positive Affect items measure mainly the degree of engagement.

Engagement

Engagement may be evaluated by a report of the caregiver (proxy) or directly by an observation of the subject. We used both methods, proxy evaluation by two mood items from the MOSES (Helmes, Csapo, & Short, 1987) and direct observation using a visual analogue measure (Engagement-VAS). Observed engagement was significantly correlated with caregiver (proxy) reports. Engagement was negatively correlated with agitation and positively correlated with FACE. When FACE was controlled for statistically, the correlation between engagement and agitation was abolished, providing empirical support that engagement and agitation are two different concepts.

Agitation

We failed to find a scale that would measure agitation with the conceptual distinction from related concepts as defined in the previous section. Therefore, we developed a scale to measure agitation by direct patient observation. As the first step in the development of this scale we constructed a typology of observed indicators of the concept of agitation according to different types of body motions and noise (Figure 8.4). Body motions were separated into whole body motions and partial body motions. The individual can exhibit whole body motion either by moving around (not in place) or by stationary behaviors which can be exhibited even by patients who are unable to ambulate or are restricted from ambulation. Partial body movements were divided into head and extremities movements. It is possible to distinguish movements of face and mouth which are either self-contained or affect the environment. Similarly, movements of the extremities could be either restricted to the person alone, or involve elements of environment (e.g., furniture). Noise can be classified into verbal and nonverbal utterances. Both of these noises can be either intermittent or continuous.

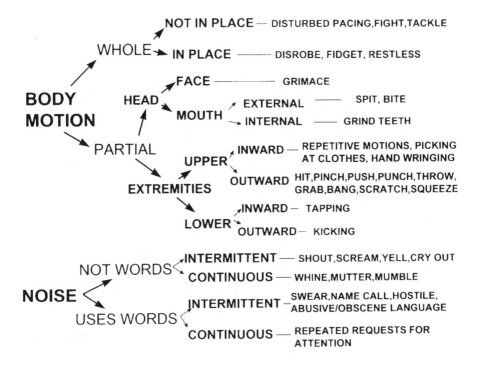

FIGURE 8.4   Types of body motions and noise included in agitated behavior.

Based on this classification, we have recently developed and tested a Scale for the Observation of Agitation in persons with Dementia (SOAPD) (Hurley et al., 1998) which evaluates the degree of agitation by rating the duration of body movements or vocalizations during a 5-minute observation period. For two items, intensity of the behavior is also rated (Table 8.1). The items' scores are multiplied by a weight factor, which was determined by the magnitude estimation process (Sennott-Miller, Murdaugh, & Hinshaw, 1988). The final score is computed by adding the weighted scores. A panel of experts supported content validity of this scale and empirical testing provided evidence of concurrent and construct validity.

INTERVENTIONS FOR IMPROVEMENT OF PSYCHOLOGICAL WELL-BEING IN DEMENTIA

The best way to achieve optimal psychological well-being is to provide appropriate and meaningful activities for the demented individual. Because the individual with advanced dementia cannot initiate such an activity alone, caregiver involvement is required. Activities have to be tailored to the remaining strengths and abilities of the individual, and take into consideration life history, premorbid likes and dislikes, and present preferences.

General Strategies

Engagement of the individual should not be restricted to only those short-time periods when special programs may be carried out. Instead, demented individuals should become involved in all aspects of daily living that surround them, even housekeeping and mundane chores, such as folding laundry, stuffing envelopes, or rearranging the furniture (Simard, 1999). Such an involvement may require more time and effort from the caregivers. However, it also provides an opportunity for a wide range of staff, including housekeepers, kitchen personnel and clerks to get involved with demented residents. A sheltered workshop can also be used to provide activities for demented outpatients attending a day care program.

Maintenance of mobility is very important for preservation of psychological well-being. Progression of Alzheimer's disease results in gait disturbances and the inability of demented individuals to recognize obstacles in their way. Therefore, it may be unsafe for them to walk unassisted. Physical therapy and assistance of other staff are helpful in maintaining ambulation but require significant resources. Use of assistive devices, such as a Merry Walker, can help in maintaining ambulation at a lower cost (Trudeau, Biddle, & Volicer, 1997).

Environmental modifications are also very important for psychological well-being. Modifications should take into consideration concerns for safety of the demented individuals. Exits have to be secured to prevent elopement and a safe path for wandering should be provided. The environment should be made home-like by including kitchens and living rooms resembling rooms found at

TABLE 8.1   Scale to Observe Agitation in Persons With Dementia

Item	Intensity	Short	Duration Medium	Long
Total Body Movements	N.A.	188.9	377.8	566.7
Up and Down Movements	N.A.	194.2	388.4	582.6
Repetitive Motions in Place	mild	37.3	74.6	111.9
Repetitive Motions in Place	moderate	98.7	197.4	296.1
Repetitive Motions in Place	extreme	191.7	383.4	575.1
Outward Motions	mild	36.5	73.0	109.5
Outward Motions	moderate	100.0	200.0	300.0
Outward Motions	extreme	236.3	472.6	708.9
High Pitched or Loud Words	N.A.	262.4	524.8	787.2
Repetitive Vocalization	N.A.	179.6	359.1	538.8
Negative Words	N.A.	229.0	458.0	687.0

The numbers are weights assigned to each behavior by the Magnitude Estimate Method (Sennott-Miller et al., 1988). The score is calculated by adding weights for all behaviors observed during the 5-minute observation period. N.A. = not applicable.

home, but also "Alzheimer friendly" by removing objects which would be dangerous for demented individuals. A study comparing environmental characteristics and level of residents' agitation found that the level of agitation was higher in units with low light levels, an institutional environment with low similarity to a home, unclean halls, poorly maintained public areas and bedrooms, presence of odors of urine and feces in public areas, and the absence of a public kitchen for activities and family use (Sloane et al., 1998).

Specific Approaches

Engagement may be increased by an individual interaction, individual or group-structured activities, or by providing environmental stimulation. Some patients enjoy watching TV or listening to music, while others may benefit from a Simulated Presence Therapy (SPT) (Woods & Ashley, 1995). SPT consists of an audiotape which provides a one-sided conversation similar to a telephone call. This conversation uses remaining long-term memories to engage the patient in a conversation. Using headphones and an autoreverse portable tape player, some patients respond positively by interacting repeatedly with the tape. Due to short-term memory loss, patients forget the conversation so that each repeat is a new experience for them.

Music can also be combined with a visual display which attracts the attention of residents with even very advanced dementia. A stimulating environment, called Snoezelen, was originally developed for children with developmental deficits but may be also used for demented individuals (Pinkney & Barker, 1994). A combination of relaxing music with display of moving colored images provides both relaxation which may decrease agitated behavior (Volicer, Mahoney, & Brown, 1998b) and a gentle stimulation preventing withdrawn behavior.

The effects of increased engagement, provided by activity programming, were studied in 81 residents of a community nursing home (Rovner, Steele, Shmuely, & Folstein, 1996). Participants were randomly assigned to an intervention and control group. The intervention consisted of activities in a special room for 5 hrs/day, establishment of psychotropic drug management guidelines, and educational rounds. After 6 months, participants in the experimental group exhibited fewer behavior disorders, received less antipsychotic medication, and were less likely to be restrained than those in the control group. Depressed mood can also be improved by providing meaningful activities. Merriam and colleagues (1988) found that caregivers of community-living demented individuals reported that they could improve symptoms of depression in 90% of the patients by providing distraction or cheering them up.

Some individuals with advanced dementia might not be able to benefit optimally from activity programs because of depression or delusions. In that case, skillful pharmacological management may remove excess disability and allow achievement of the highest quality of life possible. Drug therapy is especially useful in patients who are depressed. Although double-blind studies are lacking, antidepressants (especially selective serotonin reuptake blockers) are used widely in demented depressed patients and are effective in improving mood and food intake even in late stages of dementia (Volicer, Rheaume, & Cyr, 1994).

REFERENCES

Adelmann, P. K., & Zajonc, R. B. (1989). Facial efference and the experience of emotion. *Annual Review of Psychology, 40,* 249-280.

Asplund, K., Jansson, L., & Norberg, A. (1995). Facial expressions of patients with dementia: A comparison of two methods of interpretation. *International Psychogeriatrics, 7,* 527-534.

Bridges-Parlet, S., Knopman, D., & Thompson, T. (1994). A descriptive study of physically aggressive behavior in dementia by direct observation. *Journal of the American Geriatrics Society, 42,* 192-197.

Cohen-Mansfield, J. (1988). Agitated behavior and cognitive functioning in nursing home residents: Preliminary results. *Clinical Gerontologist, 7(3/4),* 11-22.

Craig, A. H., Cummings, J. L., Fairbanks, L., Itti, L., Miller, B. L., Li, J., & Mena, I. (1996). Cerebral blood flow correlates of apathy in Alzheimer disease. *Archives of Neurology, 53*(11), 1116-1120.

Darwin, C. (1955). *The expression of the emotions in man and animals.* New York, NY: Philosophical Library.

Ekman, P., & Friesen, W. V. (1975). *Unmasking the face.* Englewood Cliffs, NJ: Prentice-Hall.

Helmes, E., Csapo, K. G., & Short, J. A. (1987). Standardization and validation of the Multidimensional Observation Scale for Elderly Subjects (MOSES). *Journal of Gerontology, 42,* 395-405.

Hurley, A. C., Volicer, L., Camberg, L., Ashley, J., Woods, P., Odenheimer, G., Ooi, W.L., McIntyre, K., & Mahoney, E. (1999). Measurement of observed agitation in patients with Alzheimer's disease. *Journal of Mental Health and Aging,* in press.

Izard, C. E., & Dougherty, L. M. (1982). Two complementary systems for measuring facial expressions in infants and children. In C. E. Izard (Ed.), *Measuring emotions in infants and children* (pp. 97-126). Cambridge: Cambridge University Press.

Klein, A., & Kowall, N. (1998). Alzheimer's disease and other progressive dementias. In L. Volicer & A. Hurley (Eds.), *Hospice care for patients with advanced progressive dementia* (pp. 3-28). New York, NY: Springer Publishing Company.

Lawton, M. P. (1983). The varieties of well-being. *Experimental Aging Research, 9,* 65-72.

Lawton, M. P. (1994). Personality and affective correlates of leisure activity participation by older people. *Journal of Leisure Research, 26,* 138-157.

Lawton, M. P., Kleban, M. H., Dean, J., Rajagopal, D., & Parmelee, P.A. (1992). The factorial generality of brief positive and negative affect measures. *Journal of Gerontology: Psychological Sciences, 47*(4), P228-P237

Lawton, M. P., Van Haitsma, K., & Klapper, J. (1996). Observed affect in nursing home residents with Alzheimer's disease. *Journal of Gerontology, Series B: Psychological Sciences and Social Sciences, 51B,* P3-P14

Levy, M. L., Cummings, J. L., Fairbanks, L. A., Masterman, D., Miller, B.L., Craig, A. H., Paulsen, J. S., & Litvan, I. (1998). Apathy is not depression. *Journal of Neuropsychiatry, 10*(3), 314-319.

Mace, N. (1989). A new method for studying the patient's experience of care. *American Journal of Alzheimer's Care, 4(5),* 4-6.

Mega, M. S., Cummings, J. L., Fiorello, T., & Gornbein, J. (1996). The spectrum of behavioral changes in Alzheimer's disease. *Neurology, 46,* 130-135.

Merriam, A. E., Aronson, M. K., Gaston, P., Wey, S. L., & Katz, I. (1988). The psychiatric symptoms of Alzheimer's disease. *Journal of the American Geriatrics Society, 36,* 7-12.

Patel, V., & Hope, R. A. (1992). A rating scale for aggressive behavior in the elderly—the RAGE. *Psychological Medicine, 22,* 211-221.

Pinkney, L., & Barker, P. (1994). Snoezelen—an evaluation of a sensory environment used by people who are elderly and confused. In R. Hutchinson & J. Kewin (Eds.), *Sensations & disability.* Chesterfield, UK: ROMPA.

Rovner, B. W., Steele, C. D., Shmuely, Y., & Folstein, M. F. (1996). A randomized trial of dementia care in nursing homes. *Journal of the American Geriatrics Society, 44,* 7-13.

Russell, J. A. (1997). How shall an emotion be called? In R. Plutchik & H. R. Conte (Eds.), *Circumplex models of personality and emotions* (pp. 205-220). Washington, DC: American Psychological Association.

Ryden, M. B., Bossenmaier, M., & McLachlan, C. (1991). Aggressive behavior in cognitively impaired nursing home residents. *Research in Nursing & Health, 14*(2), 87-95.

Sennott-Miller, L., Murdaugh, C., & Hinshaw, A. S. (1988). Magnitude estimation: Issues and practical applications. *Western Journal of Nursing Research, 10,* 414-424.

Simard, J. (1999). The lifestyle approach. In L. Volicer & L. Bloom-Charette (Eds.), *Enhancing quality of life in advanced dementia.* Washington, London: Taylor & Francis.

Sloane, P. D., Mitchell, C. M., Preisser, J. S., Phillips, C., Commander, C., & Burker, E. (1998). Environmental correlates of resident agitation in Alzheimer's disease special care units. *Journal of the American Geriatrics Society, 46*(7), 862-869.

Trudeau, S. A., Biddle, S., & Volicer, L. (1997). Enhanced ambulation and quality of life in persons with late stage Alzheimer's disease. *The Gerontologist, 37*(1), 185-186.

Volicer, L., Hurley, A. C., & Mahoney, E. (1998a). Behavioral symptoms of dementia. In L. Volicer & A. Hurley (Eds.), *Hospice care for patients with advanced progressive dementia* (pp. 68-87). New York: Springer Publishing.

Volicer, L., Mahoney, E., & Brown, E. J. (1998b). Nonpharmacological approaches to the management of the behavioral consequences of advanced dementia. In M. Kaplan & S. B. Hoffman (Eds.), *Behaviors in dementia: Best practices for successful management* (pp. 155-176). Baltimore, MD: Health Professions Press.

Volicer, L., Rheaume, Y., & Cyr, D. (1994). Treatment of depression in advanced Alzheimer's disease using sertraline. *Journal of Geriatric Psychiatry and Neurology, 7,* 227-229.

Woods, P., & Ashley, J. (1995). Simulated presence therapy: Using selected memories to manage problem behaviors in Alzheimer's disease patients. *Geriatric Nursing, 16,* 9-14.

Young, F. W., Takane, Y., & Lewyckyj, R. (1980). ALSCAL: A multidimensional scaling package with several individual differences options. *American Statistician, 34,* 117-118.

Acknowledgments. The chapter authors appreciate the significant contributions of Patricia Woods and Jane Ashley to data collection, of Dr. Kevin McIntyre to concept development, and of Dr. Wee Lock Ooi to data analysis.

Part IV

Applications of Quality of Life Measures to Care of People With Alzheimer's Disease

9

Measurement of Depression and Depression Recognition Among Individuals With Cognitive Impairment

Jeanne Teresi, Robert Abrams,
and Douglas Holmes

BACKGROUND

Two articles in this issue (Lawton, Van Haitsma, Perkinson, & Ruckdeschel, 1999; Volicer, Hurley, & Camberg, 1999) focus on the assessment of affect and psychological well-being among individuals with dementia; both articles address the complexities encountered in such assessment. Equally important, but probably even more fraught with difficulty is the assessment and diagnosis of depression. Diagnoses are important for several reasons: the epidemiology and etiology of a disease process can be studied only when linked to a classification based on standard, accepted criteria; medications and other treatments are effective only when applied to a well-defined disease; and reimbursement is frequently linked to a diagnosis. Yet, studies of depression in nursing homes frequently do not document the diagnostic processes undertaken and do not present data which identify or characterize those who could not be diagnosed due to impairment of consciousness. In our view, it is not possible to diagnose clinically all chronically impaired individuals for depression because of communication disorders that are prevalent among this population. Yet, many protocols, developed for use among community-resident elderly, are heavily reliant upon measures that require ability to self-report symptoms. This article describes a protocol developed to document the depression diagnostic process, one that allows the designation "not diagnosable." In addition to the depression measures that do not rely entirely on self-report, the protocol includes a Staff Depression Recognition measure. This new protocol is compared with a traditional depression protocol. Accompanying psychometric data, based on a sample of approximately 319 nursing home residents, are presented.

Depression among persons with cognitive impairment in long-term-care settings has been inadequately studied. The National Institutes of Health (1991) Consensus Statement on Diagnosis and Treatment of Depression in Late Life observed that "the prevalence of major depression in nursing home populations is high and is generally unrecognized and untreated." The report added: "Training programs for care providers, including nursing staff and 'hands on' staff, in both community and institutional settings must be directed at identification of the behavioral manifestations of depression and improvement of the care provided."

Conceptual Orientation. Depression—because of its wide prevalence and its negative impact on quality of life—constitutes one of the most important psychiatric disorders in late life. Prevalence estimates vary considerably, depending upon definition and assessment methodology, with studies using formal diagnostic criteria yielding lower ratios (Roberts, Kaplan, Shema, & Strawbridge, 1997). Our position is that, for practical purposes, depression among nursing home residents should be taken to include not only syndromes which meet specific DSM diagnostic criteria but also a wider spectrum of depressive symptomatology, such as minor depressions which themselves account for considerable suffering and are likely to respond to contemporary treatments. Our position is supported by findings which suggest that elderly persons with dementia may have treatable depression syndromes characterized by somatic symptoms poorly captured by DSM nosology. Also, sad affect or melancholia per se may be less prominent than in younger or cognitively intact patients; and the transience of affective symptoms—often they appear intermittently—may be yet another way in which depressed, demented chronic care residents are disqualified from DSM major depression diagnoses (Alexopoulos & Abrams, 1991; Abrams & Alexopoulos, 1994).

Another important assessment issue is the definition of and relationship among psychological well-being, affect, and depression in long-term-care populations. A detailed discussion of the relationship between personality, emotion, affect, depression and psychological well-being and their state and trait aspects is beyond the scope of this paper; however, we will briefly discuss some concepts of relevance to the conceptual orientation of the work presented here.

Affect has been considered a personality construct with two orthogonal components: positive affect (PA) and negative affect (NA) (Watson & Tellegen, 1985). The concept of negative affectivity (Watson & Clark, 1984) has been defined as a propensity to report dissatisfaction and distress, regardless of external reality. The concept has been measured by scales which relate to self-reported pessimism, self-blame, worry, lack of self-confidence and dissatisfaction. Positive affect has been characterized as happiness, contentment, high energy, and interest. Various psychometric analyses have been performed, examining the first and second order factor structure of positive and negative affect measures (e.g., Hockwarter, Harrison, & Amason, 1996; Huelsman, Nemanick, & Munz, 1998; Roesch, 1998). A circumplex model positing the constructs as negatively correlated but relatively independent has been tested by Lawton and colleagues (Lawton, Kleban, Rajagopal, Dean, & Parmelee, 1992) on scales used to assess PA and NA among the elderly. Other studies have examined the state and trait components of affect (Hamid & Cheng, 1996). Most studies have been conducted using student samples.

Although some work (Lawton, Winter, Kleban, & Ruckdeschel, 1999) has shown the concepts of affect and depression to be distinctly different in nondemented populations, with different relationships of each to quality of life variables such as activity participation, the distinction has been blurred when applied to the more severely cognitively impaired. In related work, Volicer and colleagues (1999) found that they were unable to distinguish positive affect, as measured by pleasure and interest using the Positive Affect Scale (Lawton, VanHaitsma, & Klapper, 1996), from engagement, measured as a component of psychological well-being. While Lawton and colleagues (Lawton, Parmelee, Katz, & Nesselroade, 1996) include depression as a component of negative affect, they show that the NA factor is not synonymous with a clinical diagnosis of depression.

An important issue is whether affect is a state or trait, or both. Generally, related work in elderly chronic care populations investigates affect as a state. Affect as measured in a nursing home setting is considered as a state, perhaps in part because emotional lability is often a feature of dementing illness. However, the question remains as to whether consistent affective patterns observed over time might provide evidence of a trait, more akin to a personality trait, e.g., those with consistent negative affect might be those who had a life-long pattern of behaviors, characterized as "pessimistic." While most evidence indicates that premorbid personality styles do not predict changes with dementia, premorbid personality may affect other psychiatric symptoms in dementia (Abrams, 1996). One state-trait hypothesis is that trait measures of affect will be more highly correlated with measures of personality than with state measures. However, major depression and subsyndromal depression symptoms such as loss of interest occur in dementia and can be difficult to distinguish from personality and cognitive changes (Abrams, 1996).

Analytically, different longitudinal patterns of relationships are expected, depending upon whether a state or trait is measured. However, the distinction between states and traits, and the analytic evidence for the presence of each is complex (see Aldwin & Levenson, 1994; Hertzog & Nesselroade, 1987; Kenny & Zautra, 1995; Teresi & Holmes, 1994). Intraindividual differences are key to the measurement of states and to the determination of whether a construct is a trait or state (stable or not). Yet much of the literature focuses on nomothetic descriptors of interindividual differences (means and correlations.)

In one of the few studies of intraindividual differences, Lawton and colleagues (Lawton, Parmelee, Katz, & Nesselroade, 1996) examined the longitudinal pattern of affective states among depressed and normal elderly. Measuring positive and negative affect daily for 1 month, the authors found that compared to those who were normal, those with major depression were characterized by higher but more variable NA. Not all days were bleak. On the other hand, a hallmark of those with major depression was persistent lack of PA. Those with minor depression were variable in both PA and NA.

Returning to the issue of the nature of affect, Lawton (in press) views affective states as encompassing both mood (a more stable component) and emotion (a more transient component). Personality, a trait, and depression, which has both state and trait features, can influence affect. Our view is that major depression is a latent trait in that the underlying attribute is defined by relatively immutable etiologic factors: genetic, biologic, and physiologic. Moreover, by definition, the depressive symptoms must be present for at least some specified time to meet criteria, producing an element of stability. However, consistent with Lawton and colleagues (1996), findings that indicators of negative affect can vary among depressed individuals on a daily basis, we view negative affective symptoms (which may be caused by depression or by negative events) as more state-like in that different indicators may change in response to external stimuli. On the other hand, positive affect may be a more stable or trait-like construct, although evidence suggests that certain aspects of PA are amenable to change based on environmental interventions (Lawton et al., 1998). We conceptualize affect as a construct which is correlated with but distinct from major depression. However, the operationalization of each, when applied to a long-term-care population where cognitive impairment precludes self-report, may result in a blurring of the constructs.

Depression Recognition Among Staff. Evidence supports the contention that depression often is not recognized as such by nursing home staff. Rovner et al. (1991) found that fewer than 25% of depressed residents were recognized as depressed and treated for depression by nursing home physicians. The inconsistent, transient expressions of sad affect seen in many individuals with combined depression and dementia (Alexopoulos & Abrams, 1991) may account for some of the disparity. Another possible explanation is that staff members view states of unhappiness or demoralization as being troublesome conditions which do not, however, merit specific psychiatric intervention. This attitude, taken in the context of low reimbursement rates for mental health care, has contributed at least partially to the failure to diagnose psychiatric disorders, underlining the need for depression recognition measures that can be used by staff for identification of people who may be in need of psychiatric assessment.

Depression Assessment Among Communication Impaired. Communication problems can render individuals with severe dementia unratable with traditional instruments (see Katz & Parmelee, 1996). Although few studies have addressed the difficulty of assessing all individuals with dementia, several investigators have developed individual scales measuring depression in dementia; see, for example, the work of Alexopoulos, Abrams, and their associates (1988) and Greenwald and colleagues (1991). Others have attempted to assess affective disorder among individuals with cognitive impairment (Toner, Teresi, Gurland, & Tirumalasetti, 1999). Lawton and colleagues (1996) and Shue and colleagues (1996) have developed measures that permit assessment of affect in later-stage Alzheimer's disease patients. (For a review of several of these measures, see Katz & Parmelee, 1996.) These measures allow evaluation and treatment of individuals who heretofore might have been assessed inadequately, if at all.

METHODS

A measurement protocol was developed for diagnosis of depression among individuals with dementia. The protocol includes a standardized form for reviewing charts, the Diagnostic Impression Worksheet, a Staff Depression Recognition measure, and several depression screening and diagnostic measures. Three psychiatrists rated each of 44 subjects with respect to the psychiatric assessment measures (see Table 9.1); the remaining study participants were diagnosed by one psychiatrist. This procedure involved the psychiatrist completing a chart review and all of the psychiatric rating scales described below, except for the Staff Depression Recognition measure and a separate Affect Observation scale. Other (staff and resident) measures were collected by master's- or bachelor's-level research assistants.

Measures were subjected to two types of reliability analyses: internal consistency and interrater agreement. Because depressive symptomatology can be regarded as a state rather than a trait, test-retest estimates of reliability were not computed. Cronbach's alpha was used to estimate internal consistency and the intraclass correlation coefficient (ICC) (Bartko, 1966) to estimate interrater reliability of the diagnostic scales. Design was taken into account in selecting the ICC formula (Fleiss, 1986). For continuous items, the intraclass correlation coefficient was computed using a fixed effect model. The fixed effects model was chosen because the study design stipulated that the same raters perform all subject assessments. Rater bias was examined by determining whether or not psychiatrists differed in mean levels on response categories. Agreement across the three psychiatrists on measures of depressive symptomatology and overall depression was examined using kappas (Cohen, 1960) and maximum kappas (Dunn, 1989) for binary and nominal items. Positive, negative and overall agreement across raters (Cicchetti & Feinstein, 1990) was also examined. The proportion positive is $2a/f_1 + g_1$, where a is the number of positive agreements and f_1 and g_1 are the marginal positive totals. Maximum kappa is defined as:

$$max(\kappa) = (\text{max agreement} - \text{expected agreement}) / (n - \text{expected agreement}),$$

where: max agreement $= \Sigma \min (n_{i+}, n_{+i})$.

Caution should be exercised when interpreting reliability coefficients (see Teresi and Holmes, 1994, 1997, for a discussion). For example, kappa or weighted kappa (Cohen, 1960; Fleiss & Cohen, 1973), used to estimate interrater agreement for nominal data, are affected by the baserate of the condition being assessed (Kraemer, 1979; Spitznagel & Hezer, 1985; Thompson & Walter, 1988). Feinstein and Cicchetti (1990), show that marginal totals can affect both the maximum value of P_o (observed total agreement) and P_e (the correction factor for chance agreement calculated using marginal probabilities). Generally, kappas are lower when the baserates are smaller (low exposure rates) and positive agreement is low. For this reason, kappa together with proportion positive and proportion negative has been proposed for use by Cicchetti and Feinstein (1990) to characterize agreement. Because the value of kappa is constrained by the marginal probabilities, maximum kappa was calculated to provide a guideline against which to judge the value of the observed kappa. Turning to analysis of variance methodology applied to continuous ratings, a similar problem is observed; the between-subject (subject to subject) variation can be low, resulting in a smaller numerator in calculation of statistics such as the ICC (see Bartko, 1994). Therefore, the item-level interrater reliability data in particular must be interpreted with caution; however these data are presented as guidelines in identifying low-prevalence items for which agreement is more difficult to achieve, as well as items for which agreement is marginal or poor.

Psychiatric Assessment

Cornell Scale for Depression in Dementia. The Cornell Scale for Depression in Dementia (Alexopoulos et al., 1988a) is a 19-item scale that reflects 4 constructs: Mood and Related Signs; Behavior Disturbance; Cyclic Function and Ideational Disturbance, plus three items measuring Physical Signs. Items are measured on a 3-point continuum: "absent"; "mild or intermittent"; "severe." There is also a code for "unable to evaluate." A typical item measuring the construct "mood-related signs" is "sadness: sad expressions, sad voice, tearfulness." Another typical item measuring the construct "mood-related signs" is "anxiety: anxious expression, ruminations, worrying." For the current application, the Cornell format was modified to permit independent scoring and coding of each item three times—once based on direct resident assessment (if possible); a second, based on informant assessment and the third based on rater opinion (consensus).

The internal consistency of the Cornell in one study was .84 (Alexopoulos et al., 1988); the rank order correlation between the Cornell and Depression RDC subtypes was .83. The internal consistency estimates for the current sample were .71 for the informant items, .84 for the resident items and .79 for the consensus items. The parallel interrater reliability estimates were .54, .88, and .68, respectively (see Table 9.1). For both forms of reliability, the informant version was least reliable. Examination of item level data provides some additional information about the functioning of the scales.

(a) Informant: Raters differed in terms of average response category levels on two items: 'irritability,' ($F = 3.19, p \leq .05$), and 'suicide,' ($F = 4.24, p \leq .05$), although the intraclass correlation coefficient for both items was acceptable ($R = .70$, and .76, respectively). Intraclass correlation coefficients (R) ranged from 0 to .90; low values were observed for items of low prevalence, for example 'early morning awakenings.'

(b) Resident: Raters differed on average levels on three items: 'agitation,' ($F = 4.91, p \leq .01$); 'multiple physical complaints,' ($F = 4.95, p \leq .01$); 'multiple awakenings during sleep,' ($F = 4.61, p \leq .01$). The intraclass correlation coefficient was high only for the latter ($R = .79$). Intraclass correlation coefficients ranged from .35 to .96; R was particularly poor (.35) for one item, 'irritability.'

(c) Rater Opinion-Consensus: Raters differed on average levels on four items: 'anxiety,' ($F = 3.03, p \leq .05$; 'sadness,' ($F = 6.67 p \leq .01$); 'agitation,' ($F = 4.25, p \leq .05$); 'lack of energy,' ($F = 4.96, p \leq .01$); 'diurnal variation of mood,' ($F = 5.07, p \leq .01$). The intraclass correlation coefficient for these four items ranged from .25 to .75. The item with the lowest prevalence, 'diurnal variation of mood,' yielded the lowest R (.25); intraclass correlation coefficients for the rest of the items were adequate, ranging from .59 to .83.

Feeling Tone Questionnaire (FTQ). The FTQ was developed for use in a cross-national study of institutionalized persons (Gurland et al., 1979); psychometric properties are reported by Toner, Teresi, Gurland, & Tirumalasetti (1999). The measure contains 16 questions asked directly of the resident. Typical items are: "Are you feeling well?"; "Are you feeling happy today?"; "Do you feel lonely?"; "Do you have a good appetite?"; "Do you sleep well?" Each item is coded "non-deviant" "deviant" or "equivocal (sometimes, it depends)," and the response rated for affect using a 5-point continuum from 1—"laughs, praises, enthusiastic, emphatically positive" to 5—"extreme negative—cries, groans, curses, is emphatically negative". Three scales are scored: Response, Affect, and Total. The FTQ has been used among several samples

TABLE 9.1   Summary of Internal Consistency and Interrater Reliabilities for Depression Measures

Scale Name	Mean	S.D.	a	# of Items	N	R ICC	F	N
Diagnostic								
Direct								
Major	1.96	2.08	.74	9	182			
Minor	3.51	3.53	.84	17	184			
Nurse								
Major	1.87	1.62	.59	9	258			
Minor	3.24	2.94	.77	17	205			
Psychiatrist								
Major	2.35	1.90	.67	9	268	.90	4.23[a]	39
Minor	4.06	3.32	.81	17	266	.82	.06	41
Hamilton	7.04	7.59	.88	25	116	.93	7.39	23
Cornell								
Informant	4.93	4.72	.71	19	254	.54	0	44
Resident	4.29	5.01	.84	19	186	.88	.25	43
Consensus	4.87	4.85	.79	19	237	.68	1.13	42
FTQ								
Total	49.43	12.46	.91	32	200	.70	6.16	32
Response	6.93	5.18	.78	16	212	.76	12.53	31
Affect	43.12	9.61	.94	16	215	.68	33.19	34
SCID								

of nursing home residents (Holmes et al., 1990; Teresi et al., 1993; Teresi, Holmes, & Monaco, 1993), where reliabilities were in the .90s. The three FTQ scales had alphas of .78 for the Response scale, .94 for Affect, and .91 for the Total scale for this sample. Interrater reliability coefficients were .68, .76, and .70. The individual items for the FTQ subscales were tested for interrater reliability; generally, the individual response was less reliable than the affect rating. The FTQ was completed by psychiatrists at the time of the psychiatric assessment, and independently by research staff within 1 month of this evaluation.

   a. Affect Rating Subscale: Differences across raters on average levels of the items were not significant. The intraclass correlation coefficients were good for all items ($R = .72-.97$).

   b. Response Subscale: Raters differed on average levels on four items of the FTQ-Response subscale: 'feeling bored,' ($F = 3.14, p \le .05$); 'feeling helpful,' ($F = 4.83, p \le .01$); 'anybody nasty,' ($F = 3.55, p \le .01$); sleeps well,' ($F = 3.37, p \le .01$). The intraclass correlation coefficient (R) ranged from .35 to .73. R was poor (less than .50) for 8 items.

Hamilton Depression Rating Scale (Hamilton, 1960). The Hamilton Depression Rating Scale contains 24 items, most of which are rated on a 4-point continuum from "absent or no difficulty" to the most severe level of disorder. Typical items are "depressed mood"; "suicide"; "insomnia"; "agitation"; "somatic symptoms"; "diurnal variation." A typical response continuum for "depressed mood (sadness, hopelessness, helpless, worthless)" is '0' absent; '1' feeling states indicated only in questioning; '2' feeling states spontaneously reported verbally; '3' communicates feeling states nonverbally, i.e., through facial expressions, positive voice and tendency to weep; '4' resident reports virtually only those feeling states in his spontaneous verbal and nonverbal communication. A typical response continuum for "retardation (slowness of thought and speech, impaired ability to concentrate, decreased motor activity)" is '0' normal speech and thought; '1' slight retardation at interview; '2' obvious retardation at interview; '3' interview difficult; '4' complete stupor. Interrater reliabilities for nursing home populations range from .96 to .98. In the current study sample the scale had an alpha of .88, and an interrater reliability estimate of .93. Noteworthy is the fact that the Hamilton Depression Rating Scale could only be completed for 116 of 319 respondents, and 23 of 44 possible interrater reliability subjects.

   The items for the Hamilton scale were tested for interrater reliability; significant differences were observed among the raters' average levels for 4 items ($F = 3.32-5.80$). The intraclass correlation coefficient (R) for these 4 items ranged form .40 to .80; R was best for items such as: 'depressed mood,' and 'insight,' ($R = .86$, and .80, respectively). Intraclass correlation coefficients for the rest of the items ranged from .44 to .92; items with low prevalence yielded low R.

Structured Clinical Interview for DSM-III-R Personality Disorders (SCID).
The SCID (Spitzer, Williams, Gibbon, & First, 1989) was the research diagnostic tool attempted for use in making the DSM-III-R diagnosis for major depression and dysthymia. (The study was conducted during the transition period between DSM III and DSM IV; DSM-IV criteria were not available at the time of the study initiation.) Other direct assessment measures (FTQ, Cornell) were used as the research diagnostic tool for residents with severe cognitive and/or communication disorder. Because our experience with depression measures had shown that extremely demented individuals have impairments in attention so severe that they cannot report their own depression, we had developed criteria with which to determine potential capability for response to this measure. For example, one requirement for major depression is that at least 5 of 9 symptoms were present during the same 2-week period and that they represent a change from previous function. A typical item is "In the past month has there been cal Signs. Items are measured on a 3-point con inuum: "absent"; "mild or intermittent"; "severe." There is also a code fo "unable to evaluate." A typical item measuring the construct "mood-re ated signs" is "sadness: sad expressions, sad voice, tearfulness." Another typic l item measuring the construct "mood-related signs" is "anxiety: anxious ex ression, ruminations, worrying." For the current application, the Cornell format was odified

permit independent scoring and coding of each item three times—once based on direct resident assessment (if possible); a second, based on in ormant assessment and the third based on rater opinion (consensus). The int rnal consistency of the Cornell in one study was .84 (Alexopoulos et al., 1988) the rank order correlation between the Cornell and Depression RDC subtypes wa .83. The internal consistency estimates for the current sample were .71 for t e informant items, .84 for t

e resident items and .79 for the consensus items. The parallel inter ater reliability estimates were .54, .88, and .68, respectively (see T- able 9.1). For both forms of reliability, the informant version was least reli ble. Examination of item level data provides some additional information about t e functioning of the scales. (a) Informant: Raters differed in terms of a erage response category levels on two items: 'irritability,' (F = 3.19, p ≤ . 5), and 'suicide,' (F = 4.24, p ≤ .05), although the intraclass correlation coeff cient for both items was acceptable (R = .70, and .76, respectively). Intraclass correlation coefficients (R) ranged from 0 to .90; low values were observ d for items of low prevalence, for example 'early morning awakenings.' (b) Res dent: Raters differed on average levels on three items: 'agitation ' (F = 4.91, p ≤ .01); 'multiple physical complaints,' (F = 4.95, p ≤ . 1); 'multiple awakenings during sleep,' (F = 4.61, p ≤ .01). The intraclass correla ion coefficient was high only for the latter (R = .79). Intraclass correlation coefficients ranged from .35 to .96; R was particularly poor (.35) for one it m, 'irritability.' (c) Rater Opinion-Consensus: Raters differed on average levels on four items: 'anxiety,' (F = 3.03, p ≤ .05; 'sadness,' (F = 6.67 p ≤ .0); 'agitation,' (F = 4.25, p ≤ .05); 'lack of energy,' (F = 4.96, p ≤ .01); diurnal variation of mood,' (F = 5.07, p ≤ .01). The intraclass correlation coeffi ient for these four items ranged from .25 to .75. The item with the lowest prevalence, 'diu

nal variation of mood,' yielded the lowest R (.25); intraclass correlation coefficients for the rest of the items were adequate, ranging from .59 to . 3. Feeling Tone Questionnaire (FTQ). The FTQ was developed for use in a c oss-national study of institutionalized persons (Gurland et al., 1979); psy hometric properties are reported by Toner, Teresi, Gurland, & Tirumalasetti (1999). The measure contains 16 questions asked directly of the resident. T- ypical items are: "Are you feeling well?"; "Are you feeling happy today?" "Do you feel lonely?"; "Do you have a good appetite?"; "Do you sleep well?"- Each item is coded "non-deviant" "deviant" or "equivocal (sometimes, it depe ds)," and the response rated for affect using a 5-point continuum from 1—"laughs praises, enthusiastic, emphatically positive" to 5—"extreme negative—crie , groans, curses, is emphatically negative". Three scales are scored: Response,- Affect, and Total. The FTQ has been used among several samples of nursing home re idents (Holmes et al., 1990; Teresi et al., 1993; Teresi, Holmes, & Monaco, 199), where reliabilities were in the .90s. The three FTQ scales had alphas of .7 for the Response scale, .94 for Affect, and .91 for the Total scale for this samp e. Interrater reliability c

efficients were .68, .76, and .70. The individual items for the FTQ su- bscales were tested for interrater reliability; generally, the individual resp nse was less reliable than the affect rating. The FTQ was completed by psy hiatrists at the time of the psychiatric assessment, and independently by resea ch staff within 1 month of this evaluation. a. Affect Rating Subscale: D fferences across raters on average levels of the items were not signi- ficant. The intraclass correlation coefficients were good for all items (= .72-.97). b. Response Subscale: Raters differed on average levels on fou items of the FTQ-Response subscale: 'feeling bored,' (F = 3.14, p ≤ .0); 'feeli

helpful,' (F = 4.83, p ≤.01); 'anybody nasty,' (F = 3.55, p ≤ .01); s eeps well,' (F = 3.37, p ≤ .01). The intraclass correlation coefficient (R) ranged from .35 to .73. R was poor (less than .50) for 8 items. Hamilton Depr ssion Rating Scale (Hamilton, 1960). The Hamilton Depression Rating Sca e contains 24 items, most of which are rated on a 4-point continuum from "abs nt or no difficulty" to the most severe level of disorder. Typical items ar "depressed mood"; "suicide"; "insomnia"; "agitation"; "somatic symptoms"; diurnal variation." A typical response continuum for "depressed mood (sadness, ho elessness, helpless, worthless)" is '0' absent; '1' feeling states indicated only n questioning; '2' feeling states spontaneously reported verbally; ' ' communicates feeling states nonverbally, i.e., through facial expression , positive voice and tendency to weep; '4' resi

*ent reports vir*tually only those feeling states in his spontaneous verba
and nonverbal communication. A typical response continuum for "retardation
slowness of thought and speech, impaired ability to concentrate, decreased
motor activity)" is '0' normal speech and thought; '1' slight retardation at
interview; '2' obvious retardation at interview; '3' interview difficult; '4' comp
ete stupor. Interrater reliabilities for nursing home populations range fro
.96 to .98. In the current study sample the s
le had an alpha of .88, and an interrater reliability estimate of .93. No
eworthy is the fact that the Hamilton Depression Rating Scale could only
be completed for 116 of 319 respondents, and 23 of 44 possible interrater rel
ability subjects. The itemsfor the Hamilton scale were tested for interr because
data were not recorded in the charts for about half of the items.

(e) Medical/Doctor Notes: Negative agreement among all raters for the
chart medical notes assessment ranged from 0 to .82. Positive agreement
ranged from .25 to 1.00. Overall agreement ranged from .17 to 1.00. Due to
missing data negative agreement was computed for 9 items, positive agreement
was computed for 14 items, and overall agreement was also computed for 14
items. Estimable kappas ranged from .33 to 1.00; again the *n* was small due to
missing data, rendering the analyses unstable.

(f) Occupational/Recreational Notes: Negative agreement among all raters
for the occupational/recreational notes assessment ranged from 0 to .75.
Positive agreement ranged from 0 to 1.00. Overall agreement ranged from .25
to .59. Due to missing data negative, positive, and overall agreement was only
computed for 6 items. Estimable kappas ranged from 0 to 1.00.

(g) Final Psychiatric Opinion: Negative agreement among all raters for the
final psychiatric opinion ranged from .57 to .90 (.67 to .95 for raters 1 and 2;
.72 to .95 for raters 1 and 3, and .65 to .91 for raters 2 and 3). Negative
agreement for 25 out of the 26 items was above 60%. Positive agreement
ranged from 0 to .84. Positive agreement was above 60% for only 7 out of the
26 items overall, but varied across rater pairs from 15 to 18 out of 26 items.
Overall agreement ranged from .47 to .86 across all raters (.64-.86, .67-.90,
.60-.88 across rater pairs); overall agreement was 60% or higher for 22 out of
the total 26 items.

Low prevalence items, such as: 'feelings of inadequacy,' 'self pity,' and
'somatic concern,' yield low positive agreement. Items with adequate overall,
positive, and negative agreement across raters (agreement was higher than .60)
were likely to be clinically anchored items such as 'depressed mood,' 'psychomotor agitation,' 'weight changes,' 'illness leading to depression', 'diminished ability to think', and 'thoughts of death.'

The kappas ranged from .06 to .83. Low prevalence items, like 'demanding,'
'feelings of inadequacy,' 'feelings of self reproach,' 'self pity,' and 'somatic
concern' yielded low, possibly unstable kappas. Larger discrepancies between
observed and maximum kappas were observed for those items with lower

symptom prevalence. Nineteen out of the 26 items yielded kappas between the range of .40 and .60, three items yielded kappas of less than .40. Maximum kappas ranged from .37 to 1.00; 21 were higher than .60.

DSM-III-R. The use of a standardized assessment and method of recording data related to each symptom used in the DSM-III-R diagnosis assisted in the diagnostic process. Despite this methodology it was not possible to diagnose everyone because of the severe cognitive deficits evidenced by residents with end stage dementing illness. Those who could not be diagnosed were given a missing data code for the Diagnostic Impression Worksheet variables and for diagnosis.

The final diagnosis for major depression, and the final diagnosis for minor depression items were tested for interrater reliability. Weighted kappa, calculated across all diagnostic categories ('none,' 'possible,' 'probable,' and 'definite') and all three raters, was .68 for major depression and .66 for minor depression; maximum kappas ranged from .78 to .95 across rater pairs, indicating that agreement could have been higher. However, considered another way, dichotomizing the major depression diagnosis to: "not present/ possible" vs. "probable/definite" yielded kappas across rater pairs of .80. .83 and .76; maximum kappas were 1.00, .83 and .76, respectively. For minor depression the kappas across the three combinations of rater pairs were: .93, .66, .76; the maximum kappas were .93, .83 and .76. Generally, kappas and maximum kappas were the same, indicating little or no room for improvement in agreement, given the observed marginals.

Staff Depression Recognition Measures

Depression Recognition Congruence refers to the degree of congruence between staff and resident, staff and diagnostic evaluation, and resident interview and diagnostic evaluation, with regard to (a) individual depressive symptomatology, and (b) depressive syndrome classification. Depression recognition congruence was measured in two ways: by using a simple yes/no item asked of staff, e.g., "Would you say _____ is currently depressed?" and by calculating congruence deviations based on a symptom scale (see below).

The aide, nurse, and social worker who were most involved with each resident's care were each asked a series of questions about the possible presence of symptoms of depression. Respondents were asked to rate the symptoms with respect to presence, absence or nonrateability (usually due to severe communication disorder). These items were from the SHORT CARE Depression Scale.

The SHORT-CARE Depression scale (Gurland et al., 1977, 1978; Gurland, Golden, Teresi, & Challop, 1984) is a direct outgrowth of the Geriatric Mental State Schedule (GMS) Depression Scale (Copeland et al., 1976; Gurland et al., 1976); however, in addition to being shorter, it was designed for administration by nonclinically trained staff. The measure was developed using a cross-national (New York and London) sample, and had an internal consistency reliability of .87 for both samples (Golden, Teresi, & Gurland, 1984). In a subsequent study (Gurland et al., 1988), the interrater reliability coefficient, using a sample of 13 raters rating 8 videotapes, was .94. Internal consistency reliabilities ranged from the .70s to the .90s across other community and institutional samples on which the CARE Depression scale has been used; the variability is due in large part to the base rate of depression in the population studied, with higher coefficients corresponding to higher base rates of depression. In one institutional sample the scale had an alpha of .90 at initial interview and .89 at follow-up (Teresi, Holmes, & Monaco, 1993). Typical items are: "Feeling sad or depressed during the past month," "Bothered or depressed by current loneliness," "Admits to having been more irritable (angry) than usual lately," "Poor appetite in the absence of obvious medical cause and without nausea," "Less interest or enjoyment in activities," "Lies awake with anxious or depressed feelings and thoughts," "Has cried during the past month." Respondents are also asked to respond to an anchored 4-point global rating of happiness level.

The concurrent validity of the CARE Depression scale is high (correlation of .75 with diagnosis) (Teresi, Golden, & Gurland, 1984); other validation data (with psychotropic medications, follow-up depression, morbidity) is also good. (Gurland, Golden, Teresi, & Challop, 1984; Teresi, Golden, & Gurland, 1984). The SHORT-CARE Depression Scale includes supplemental diagnostic items which correspond to DSM criteria, and cut scores have been developed for classification of depression (Spagnoli, Foresti, MacDonald, & Williams, 1986). Mann, Graham and Ashby (1984) found that, among institutional samples, a cutting score of 7 on the SHORT-CARE yielded the highest sensitivity and specificity with regard to diagnosis of clinical depression severe enough to require further assessment and/or intervention. Kay et al. (1985) compared rates of depression in Australia using different diagnostic techniques: SHORT-CARE diagnostic criteria, the GMS, and DSM-III criteria; he found fairly good convergence across the three methods. The SHORT-CARE Depression Scale does not permit distinctions among subtypes of depression, e.g., bipolar disorder. Such diagnostic distinctions were not attempted for staff members because (a) the prevalence of bipolar depression is not very high among the elderly, (b) staff were not expected to be able to recognize subtypes of depression, e.g., dysthymia vs. major depression, and (c) diagnostic categories, per se, were not of interest because the focus was on identification of depressive states requiring some form of further intervention.

The Short-Care Direct Resident Assessment Depression Scale was modified for use as a staff depression recognition measure in the current study by altering the stem of the question, e.g., "Has s/he felt sad and depressed during the past month"; the measure contains 29 items asked of the resident or of three possible categories of staff members: social workers, nurses, and nurse's aides. The Direct Resident Assessment had an internal consistency of .86. The Staff Assessment had an internal consistency of .96 for social workers, .91 for nurses, and .93 for nurse's aides. The resident-version of the SHORT-CARE was completed by only 58 residents; most were unable to complete the measure because of cognitive impairment.

Psychiatrists and staff each rated the same symptoms in terms of whether each was present, absent or nonrateable. The correlations among the different versions of the scale are shown in Table 9.3. In addition to the prorated score (used in the correlations in Table 9.3), recognition measures were calculated. Each prorated score was converted to a standard (z) score so that all were on the same metric. Next, the aide score, the nurse score, and the social worker score were subtracted from the psychiatrist z score. Underrecognition was defined as a difference score between psychiatrist scales and staff scales of one or more standard deviations above the mean score. Overrecognition was defined as minus one or more standard deviations from the mean. A zero score plus or minus one standard deviation was defined as congruence between the psychiatric rating scale and the staff rating scale. Thus a positive z score was indicative of the psychiatrist rating more symptoms present (staff underrecognition) and a negative z score was indicative of the staff rating more symptoms (overrecognition).

Rater Observation of Affect

Not a part of the protocol but also included in this study was a rating of affect obtained through observations performed by a trained research assistant. The rater observation of affect was collected both at the time of screening and approximately 1 month later. Each individual was observed for 5 minutes, on three occasions, using a 14-item observational measure of affect. Frequency of affective states are coded as follows: "occurs not at all"; "occurs with very little frequency (once or twice)"; "occurs with some frequency (several times)"; "occurs with moderate frequency (many times, but not continuous)"; "occurs with great frequency (almost continuously)." Items include "agitated," "crying", "emotionally labile," "smiling/laughing," and "staring blankly." Definitions of the items are included in a manual; extensive training was conducted to ensure interrater reliability. Training includes rating 10 'gold-standard' videotapes, followed by rating a sample of 10 residents against a 'gold-standard' rater who accompanies the individual to the training sessions. Interrater reliabilities were in the .80s and .90s. (Teresi et al., 1993). The scale alphas are typically in the high .60s to low .70s. (Holmes et al., 1990; Teresi, Holmes, & Monaco, 1993). The scale alphas in one recent study ranged from .66 to .71 at baseline, and from .68 to .72 at follow-up. For this sample, the alpha was somewhat lower, .58.

RESULTS

Utility of the protocol for diagnosing the communication impaired and those with severe cognitive impairment. First, it is noted that the SCID could be completed by only 104 subjects and the Hamilton by 116 subjects, restricting the use of these measures to the approximately one-third of the sample capable of sufficient degree of self-report to allow completion of the measure. The Cornell, Feeling Tone, and Diagnostic Impression Worksheet could be completed by between 215 and 268 individuals, increasing the proportion assessable by one-third or more. Turning to capability to provide clinical diagnoses, examination of the entire original sample of 319 reveals that 15.5% could not be diagnosed by psychiatrists due to a variety of reasons: refusal (6.3%), language difficulty (1%), transfer or other reasons (1.6%), illness/hospitalization (1%), severe perceptual disorder (1%), severe communication disorder (6.3%). Of the total sample, 15.4% could not be diagnosed for major and 16.3% for minor depression.

The rate of communication disorder in the sample was high. One-third (34.6%) of the sample was at Global Deterioration Scale (Reisberg, Ferris, DeLeon, & Crook, 1982) stage 7, and not testable on cognitive screening tests. Nonetheless, the majority of these individuals were able to be diagnosed. For example, 7.5% ($n = 24$) of the sample were alert, arousable, and able to follow simple commands, but were not testable on cognitive screens due to rambling, incoherent responses. Of this group, nearly all ($n = 23$) were able to be assessed for depression. Examining the next level of communication impairment, of the 16.9% ($n = 54$) who were alert/arousable, but unable to follow simple commands, 50 could be diagnosed. On the other hand, of the 10.3% ($n = 33$) who were not alert or arousable (after repeated attempts), only 36.4% ($n = 12$) were able to be diagnosed. This suggests that diagnosis is possible on the majority of nursing home residents up to the point that they are no longer able to respond. Put another way, among the nontestable, severely cognitively impaired individuals, 76.6% (85/111) were able to be diagnosed.

Associations among measures of depression and depression diagnoses. Table 9.2 shows the correlations among depression diagnoses and other measures. The correlations below the diagonal show that diagnosis of major depression is correlated highest with the psychiatric sections of the Diagnostic Impression Worksheet (.82), with the Hamilton (.69), and the Cornell Consensus (.76). Purported measures of affect have lower correlations (.38 to .51 with the FTQ subscales). Correlations above the diagonal show that, as expected, minor depression is correlated highest with the DIW psychiatric ratings of minor depression. The correlations of the depression measures, i.e., the Cornell and Hamilton, are lower than with major depression, and the affect measures correlate higher with minor than with major depression diagnosis.

Examining the convergent validity of the Cornell Consensus and the Feeling Tone Questionnaire, the Cornell correlated .63 with the psychiatrist-rated total FTQ scale and .35 with the staff-rated version, collected at a later date.

Of note is that a separate measure of observed affect correlated considerably higher (.32) with the affective scale of the FTQ than with the Response subscale of the FTQ (.13). This same observation measure correlated in the .30s with the Nurse DIW, the Hamilton, and the Cornell Informant and Resident subscales. However, it correlated only .03 with diagnosis of major and minor depression, .07 with the psychiatrist DIW for major depression, but .16 for minor. Finally, the correlation of the affect observation measure with the Cornell Consensus was only .19. Thus, the measures of major depression appear to be operating in a fashion distinct from broader measures of affective state.

Examination of the correlations in parentheses reveals that the observed affect score correlates .40 with the same measure collected at a later date, within 1 month of the former; this relatively low correlation provides further support for the conceptualization of affect as a state.

The correlations of the FTQ in parentheses are between the psychiatrist and the staff ratings collected within 11 days of the psychiatrist ratings for 65% of the subjects and within 1 month for 80% of ratings. These correlations are lower due to: (a) the time interval between ratings and (b) the different sources (research staff vs. psychiatrist). However, what is shown is that the FTQ resident response scale is most convergent (.56) and the Affect scale less convergent (.27).

While the correlation of the two affect measures (FTQ and observed affect) was generally lower (.32) than for affect with depression measures from the same source (correlations of .48 to .58 for the FTQ rated by psychiatrists and with depression diagnoses and the Cornell and Hamilton), the correlations for the Feeling Tone, collected by other sources (the research staff) with depression scales were lower (.20 to .30). Because the latter correlations may have been affected either by the time difference or the differences in source of information, it is difficult to comment definitively on the convergent and divergent validity of the affect and depression measures, using this particular set of correlations. However, taken as a whole, the results generally support the divergent validity of the depression and affect measures.

Associations among psychiatrist ratings and recognition measures. Table 9.3 presents the correlations of scale scores according to source of information. As shown, the nurse aides are more convergent than are the social workers or nurses with respect to the psychiatrist-based diagnostic scale. Of the three groups, the social workers are the most convergent with respect to the Hamilton, and the nurses are least convergent for all scales except the diagnostic scale.

TABLE 9.2 Correlations Among Diagnoses of Depression, Measures From the Diagnostic Impression Worksheet and Other Depression Scales for Major (Below the Diagonal) and Minor (Above the Diagonal) Depression. All Measures Except as Noted Below Were Compiled by a Psychiatrist

	Depression Diagnosis N=270	DIW: Psychiatrist N=268	DIW: Nurse N=258	DIW: Resident N=192	Hamilton N=116	Cornell Informant N=254	Cornell Resident N=186	Cornell Consensus N=237	Feeling Tone Questionnaire Resident Response N=212	Feeling Tone Questionnaire Resident Affect N=215	Feeling Tone Questionnaire Resident Total N=200	Observed Affect N=287
Depression Diagnosis N=267	.75	.78	.64	.71	.48	.57	.55	.64	.47 (.37)[a]	.54 (.30)	.58 (.35)	.03
DIW: Psychiatrist N=266	.82	.87	.78	.88	.73	.68	.69	.81	.51 (.44)	.58 (.27)	.63 (.39)	.16
DIW: Nurse N=205	.62	.74	.90	.67	.54	.86	.47	.76	.34 (.27)	.47 (.24)	.48 (.30)	.29
DIW: Resident N=184	.74	.80	.64	.90	.82	.68	.84	.85	.58 (.50)	.67 (.31)	.72 (.44)	.26
Hamilton N=116	.69	.67	.49	.80	1.00	.64	.87					
Cornell Informant N=254	.65	.73	.83	.62	.64	1.00	.57					
Cornell Resident N=186	.66	.69	.45	.83	.87	.57	1.00					
Cornell Consensus N=237	.76	.80	.73	.79	.84	.84	.82	1.00				
Feeling Tone Questionnaire Resident Response N=212	.38 (.30)	.37 (.32)	.24 (.22)	.48 (.39)	.52 (.49)	.36 (.29)	.58 (.43)	.52 (.38)	1.00 (.56)			
Feeling Tone Questionnaire Resident Affect N=215	.48 (.21)	.49 (.19)	.37 (.19)	.57 (.24)	.56 (.20)	.45 (.17)	.63 (.26)	.58 (.24)	.53 (.31)	1.00 (.27)		
Feeling Tone Questionnaire Resident Total N=200	.51 (.28)	.51 (.29)	.37 (.23)	.60 (.31)	.62 (.36)	.45 (.27)	.68 (.38)	.63 (.35)	.78 (.48)	.92 (.29)	1.00 (.35)	
Observed Affect N=287	.03	.07	.33	.30	.34	.28	.33	.19	.13	.32	.26	1.00 (.40)[b]

Note. Correlations are pairwise so N's vary. N's for the Depression Diagnostic Protocol range from 114 for the correlations involving the Hamilton to 270 for those involving major depression. The largest n is for the measure of observed affect (287), which is not part of the protocol. Most N's are about 200. The SCID is not included because the N was too small to permit confident estimates of the correlation coefficient. [a]Correlations in parentheses are for the FTQ completed independently by research staff within 1 to 2 months of the first administration of the measure. [b]Correlation is for the observed affect scale completed independently within 1 month of the psychiatric assessment.

TABLE 9.3 Zero-Order Correlations Among Staff Depression Recognition Scales, Direct Resident Assessment Depression Scales, and the Diagnostic Scale from the Diagnostic Information Worksheet

STAFF INFORMANT DEPRESSION RECOGNITION SCALES	RESIDENT ASSESSMENT AND DIAGNOSTIC SCALES			
	Cornell Consensus	Hamilton	Feeling Tone	Diagnostic Scale
Nurse Aide	.46 (n = 162)	.32 (n = 98)	.26 (n = 151)	.50 (n = 158)
Social Worker	.48 (n = 157)	.40 (n = 101)	.30 (n = 145)	.37 (n = 154)
Nurse	.23 (n = 181)	.29 (n = 107)	.25 (n = 168)	.37 (n = 178)

DISCUSSION

Examination of the psychometric properties of the measures that could be assessed showed adequate to good internal consistency and interrater reliability for the depression scales, the DIW psychiatrist and nurse scales, and for the DSM diagnoses. Individual items, however, varied in terms of interrater agreement. For the direct psychiatric assessment, given the relatively large number of items with maximum kappas over .60, several items achieved observed kappas that were less than desirable. However, agreement for the Worksheet psychiatric assessment as a whole was good. Less agreement was observed for items such as "feelings of inadequacy" and "feelings of self-reproach." A major problem was the low prevalence of many items, particularly those from the chart; the notes of social workers, physicians, and occupational therapists commented infrequently on depression and thus provided the least amount of data, a finding illustrated by the low maximum obtainable kappas. However, on the occasions when depressive symptoms were noted in the chart and particularly when consistent across sources, this information was helpful in making a diagnosis. Generally, information from the nurses was less reliable, both in terms of the Cornell Informant subscale and the nursing notes. Nurses were less convergent with psychiatrist ratings than were aides and social workers. However, nurses typically provided more observations about depression in the nursing notes than did social workers in the social work notes. Lawton and colleagues (1999) discuss the difficulty in obtaining reliable, valid measures of affect from nursing attendants. The current study found that, for informant-based measures, nurses were less convergent with psychiatrists than aides. However, given that nurses are likely to provide most of the informant data, as we found with the Cornell Informant subscale, there is a need to enhance the reliability and validity of such data, both by collecting multiple-source data and by providing more staff training.

While the traditional depression diagnostic protocols, namely, the Hamilton and SCID, were able to be completed on only one-third of the subjects, the new protocol was able to be completed on about three-fourths of the sample, and a diagnosis made on 84%. Among the communication-impaired and severely demented, diagnoses were possible on about three-fourths of the sample. However, among the most impaired (those who were not alert or arousable), the majority could not be diagnosed.

Correlations with other depression measures were in the expected direction. The Hamilton and Cornell depression scales correlated higher with major depression than with minor depression. The FTQ affect scale correlates highest with minor depression, indicating that the FTQ is more likely to be a measure of dysphoric states or various depressive symptoms than of the full syndrome of major depression. Evidence supporting the contention that affect and depression, as measured in this effort, represent different constructs was provided by examining the patterns of correlations.

One of the chief aims of this project was to create a protocol which would address the particular difficulties of assessing depression in demented chronic care residents. In so doing, it was necessary to take into account the following pair of conditions: the substantial overlap between the presenting signs and symptoms of depressive disorders and dementia; and the difficulty, encountered by individuals with moderate to severe dementia in providing meaningful reports of their own mood states.

The first condition, namely, the overlap between the clinical presentation of depressive and dementing disorders, was addressed in several ways. Most fundamentally, the use of multiple depression assessment instruments helped to assure that a wide range of depressive signs and symptoms would be assessed and that different conceptual frameworks would be represented. Assessing a broad range of signs and symptoms is helpful because certain constructs are more specific to depression than others; for example, mood-incongruent delusions may be found in both psychotic depression and dementia, while mood-congruent delusions are more characteristic of depression (Alexopoulos et al., 1988). The use of different conceptual frameworks in depression diagnosis is also desirable in the setting of comorbid dementia. For example, DSMs III-R and IV require for Major Depression the presence of depressed mood/affect or loss of interest/pleasure in usual activities *plus* a variety of neurovegetative and behavioral symptoms, whereas the Cornell Scale uses a broader syndromic perspective, wherein sad affect is weighted equally with the other 18 items; this alone may permit greater sensitivity among elderly demented subjects who appear less frequently than younger or cognitively intact subjects to have melancholic symptoms (Alexopoulos, Abrams, Young, & Shamoian, 1988b). The Cornell scale also uses a different time frame than the DSM, shorter but more flexible; because of the frequently transient nature of depressive symptomatology in the setting of comorbid dementia, subjects assessed using the Cornell Scale are not required to show depressive symptoms for the entire time frame of each item. Next, the Diagnostic Impression Worksheet is geared not only to the assessment of major depression diagnoses but to minor depression as well, in order to help capture the highest possible number of treatable depression syndromes, consistent with the distinction between affect and the clinical diagnosis of major depression. Individuals with minor depression may have scattered affective symptoms which, while not meeting full diagnostic criteria for the Major Depression syndrome, may nevertheless be amenable to treatment.

The second condition, the limitations imposed by dementing disorders on subjects' ability to describe their depressive symptoms, is addressed by the flexibility of the protocol in avoiding such instruments as the Hamilton Depression Rating Scale for subjects whose dementia is too far advanced to permit appropriate use of the scale. The Hamilton and SCID are skipped in such instances, and only the Feeling Tone Questionnaire, Cornell Scale for Depression in Dementia, and the Diagnostic Impression Worksheet are used; the FTQ and the Cornell Scale both rely upon observation (direct observation in the former, caregiver and direct observation in the latter) and on clinical judgment. The influence of clinical judgment is pervasive in the protocol; it is, for example, applied not only in the scoring of individual instruments such as the Cornell Scale and the Feeling Tone Questionnaire, but again for the overall results via the "final psychiatric opinion" in the DIW. Clinical judgment provides an additional "hedge" against the distortion of subject responses owing to impaired cognition. Taken together, these strategies have been designed to adapt the protocol to the widest possible spectrum of cognitive functioning, leaving, in the end, an undiagnosable group comprising mainly of subjects with impairments of attention/consciousness or those unwilling to cooperate.

The current effort also resulted in a standardized protocol for depression recognition for use among staff; another such effort was recently completed by Ryden and colleagues (Ryden et al., 1998) who developed a protocol which includes two depression screening measures, a rating of emotions, and a depression screen checklist. Clearly, such efforts are needed to help identify residents at risk for adverse outcomes associated with undetected major depressive disorder, which is highly prevalent in nursing homes and most likely, other long-term-care settings. As concluded in a recent Consensus Statement (Lebowitz et al., 1997), "Early recognition, diagnosis, and initiation of treatment of depression in older persons present opportunities for improvements in quality of life, the prevention of suffering or premature death, and the maintenance of optimal levels of function and independence for older people" (p 1189).

REFERENCES

Abrams, R. C. (1996). Assessing personality in chronic care populations. *Journal of Mental Health and Aging, 2,* 231-242.

Abrams, R. C., & Alexopoulos, G. S. (1994). Assessment of depression in dementia. *Alzheimer's Disease and Associated Disorders, 8,* 227-229.

Aldwin, C. M., & Levenson, M. R. (1994). Aging and personality assessment. In M. P Lawton & J. A. Teresi, *Annual review of gerontology and geriatrics, Vol. 14: Focus on assessment techniques* (pp. 1-22). New York: Springer Publishing.

Alexopoulos, G. S., & Abrams, R. C. (1991). Depression in Alzheimer's disease. *Psychiatric Clinics of North America, 14,* 327-339.

Alexopoulos, G. S., Abrams, R. C., Young, R. C., et al. (1988a). Cornell scale for depression in dementia. *Biological Psychiatry, 23,* 271-284.

Alexopoulos, G. S., Abrams, R. C., Young, R. C., & Shamoian, C. S. (1988b). Use of the Cornell scale in non-demented patients. *Journal of the American Geriatrics Society, 36,* 230-236.

Bartko, J. J. (1966). The intraclass correlation coefficient as a measure of reliability. *Psychological Reports, 19,* 3-11.

Bartko, J. J. (1994). General methodology II: Measures of agreement: A single procedure. *Statistics in Medicine, 13,* 737-745.

Cicchetti D. V., & Feinstein, A. R. (1990). High agreement but low kappa: II. Resolving the paradoxes. *Journal of Clinical Epidemiology, 43,* 551-558.

Cohen, J. (1960). A coefficient of agreement for nominal scales. *Educational and Psychological Measurement, 20,* 37-46.

Copeland, J. R. M., Kelleher, M. J., Kellett, J. M., Gourlay, A. J., Gurland, B. J., et al. (1976). A semi-structured clinical interview for the assessment of diagnosis and mental state in the elderly. The Geriatric Mental State: I. Development and reliability. *Psychological Medicine, 6,* 439-449.

Dunn, G. (1989). *Design and analysis of reliability studies.* New York: Oxford University Press.

Feinstein, A. R., & Cicchetti, D. V. (1990). High agreement but low kappa: I. The problems of two paradoxes. *Journal of Clinical Epidemiology, 43,* 543-549.

Fleiss, J. L. (1986). *The design and analysis of clinical experiments.* New York: Wiley and Sons.

Fleiss, J. L., & Cohen, J. (1973). The equivalence of weighted kappa and the intraclass correlation coefficient as measures of reliability. *Educational and Psychological Measurement, 33,* 613-619.

Golden, R. R., Teresi, J. A., & Gurland, B. J. (1984). Development of indicator scales for the Comprehensive Assessment and Referral evaluation Interview Schedule. *Journal of Gerontology, 39,* 138-146.

Greenwald, B., Kramer-Ginsberg, G., Kremen, N. J., et al. (1991, May). *Depression complicating dementia.* Presented at the 14th annual meeting of the American Psychoatric Association, New Orleans.

Gurland, B., Fleiss, J. L., Goldberg, K., Sharpe, L., Copeland, J. R. M., et al. (1976) A semi-structutred clinical interview for the assessment of diagnosis and mental state in the elderly. The Geriatric Mental State: II. A factor analysis. *Psychological Medicine, 6,* 451-459.

Gurland, B., Kuriansky, J., Sharpe, L., Simon, R., Stiller, P., & Birkett, P. (1977-1978). CARE: Rationale, development and reliability. *International Journal of Aging and Human Development, 8,* 9-42.

Gurland, N., Cross, P., DeFiguerido, J., Shannon, M., Mann, A., et al. (1979). A cross-national comparison of the institutionalized elderly in the cities of New York and London. *Psychological Medicine, 9,* 781-788.

Gurland, N., Golden, R., Teresi, J., & Challop, J. (1984). The SHORT-CARE: An efficient instrument for the assessment of depression, dementia, and disability. *Journal of Gerontology, 39,* 166-169.

Gurland, B., Teresi, J., McFate-Smith, W., Black, D., Hughes, G., & Edlavitch, S. (1988). The effects of treating isolated systolic hypertension on cognitive status and depression in the elderly. *Journal of the American Geriatrics Society, 36,* 1015-1022.

Hamid, P. N., & Cheng, S.-T. (1996). The development and validation of an index of emotional disposition and mood state: The Chinese Affect Scale. *Educational and Psychological Measurement, 56,* 995-1014.

Hamilton, U. (1960). A rating scale for depression. *Journal of Neurology, Neurosurgery, and Psychiatry, 23,* 56-62.

Hertzog, C., & Nesselroade, J. R. (1987). Beyond autoregressive models: Some implications of the trait-state distinction for the structural modeling of developmental change. *Child Development, 58,* 93-109.

Hockwarter, W. A., Harrison, A. W., & Amason, A. C. (1996). Testing a second-order multidimensional model of negative affectivity: A cross-validation study. *Educational and Psychological Measurement, 56,* 791-808.

Holmes, D., Teresi, J., Weiner, A., Monaco, C., Ronch, J. & Vickers, R. (1990). Characteristics of patients in special care units. *The Gerontologist, 30*(2), 178-183.

Huelsman, T. J., Nemanick, R. C., & Munz, D. C. (1998). Scales to measure four dimensions of dispositional mood: positive energy, tiredness, negative activation and relaxation. *Educational and Psychological Measurement, 58,* 804-819.

Katz, I. R., & Parmelee, P. (1996). Assessment of depression in patients with dementia. *Journal of Mental Health and Aging, 2,* 243-257.

Kay, D., Henderson, R., Scott, J., Wilson, D., Rickwood, D., & Grayson, D. (1985). Dementia and depression among the elderly living in the Hobart Community: The effect of the diagnostic criteria on the prevalence rates. *Psychological Medicine, 15,* 771-788.

Kenny, D. A., & Zautra, A. (1995). The Trait-State-Error (TSE) model for multi-wave data. *Journal of Consulting and Clinical Psychology, 63,* 52-59.

Kraemer, H. C. (1979). Ramifications of a population model for k as a coefficient. *Psychometrika, 44,* 461-472.

Lawton, M. P. (in press). Positive and negative affective states among older people in long-term care. In *Research on the Nature of Depression in the Elderly.*

Lawton, M. P., Kleban, M. H., Rajagopal, D., Dean, J., & Parmelee, P. A. (1992). The factorial generality of brief positive and negative affect measures. *Journal of Gerontology: Psychological Sciences, 47,* P228-P237.

Lawton, M. P., VanHaitsma, K., Klapper, J, Kleban, M. H., Katz, I. R., & Corn, J. (1998). A stimulation-retreat special care unit for elders with dementing illness. *International Psychogeriatrics, 10,* 379-395.

Lawton, M. P., Van Haitsma, K. S., & Klapper, J. A. (1996). Observed affect in nursing home residents. *Journal of Gerontology: Psychological Sciences, 51B,* P3-P14.

Lawton, M. P., Van Haitsma, K., Perkinson, M., & Ruckdeschel, K. (1999). Observed affect and quality of life in dementia: Further affirmations and problems. *Journal of Mental Health and Aging, 5,* 69-81.

Lawton, M. P., Winter, L., Kleban, M. H., & Ruckdeschel, K. (1999). Affect and quality of life: Objective and subjective. *Journal of Aging and Health, 11,* 169-198.

Lawton, M. P., Parmelee, P. A., Katz, I., & Nesselroade, J. (1996). Affective states in normal and depressed older people. *Journal of Gerontology: Psychological Sciences, 51B,* 309-316.

Lebowitz, B., Pearson, J. L., Schneider, L. S., Reynolds, C. F., Alexopoulos, G. S., et al. (1997). Consensus Statement: Diagnosis and treatment of depression in late life: Consensus statement update. *Journal of the American Medical Association, 278,* 1186-1190.

Mann, A., Graham, N., & Ashby, D. (1984). Psychiatric illness in residential homes for the elderly: A survey in one London borough. *Age and Ageing, 13,* 257-265.

National Institutes of Health. (1991). Diagnosis and Treatment of Depression in Late Life. Reprinted from NIH Consens. *Dev. Cont. Consensus Statement, 9,* 4-6.

Reisberg, B., Ferris, S. H., DeLeon, M. J., & Crook, T. (1982). The Global Deterioration Scale for assessment of primary degenerative dementia. *American Journal of Psychiatry, 139,* 1136-1139.

Roberts, R. E., Kaplan, G. A., Shema, S. J., & Strawbridge, W. J. (1997). Prevalence and correlates of depression in an aging cohort: The Alameda County study. *Journal of Gerontology: Social Sciences, 52B,* S252-S258.

Roesch, S. C. (1998). The factorial validity of trait positive affect scores: Confirmatory factor analyses of unidimensional and multidimensional models. *Educational and Psychological Measurement, 58,* 451-466.

Rovner, B. W., German, P. S., Brant, L., et al. (1991). Depression and mortality in nursing homes. *Journal of the American Medical Association, 265,* 993-996.

Ryden, M. B., Pearson, V., Kaas, M. J., Snyder, M., Krichbaum, K., et al. (1998, February). Assessment of depression in a population at risk. *Journal of Gerontological Nursing, 24,* 21-29.

Shue, V., Beck, C., & Lawton, M. P. (1996). Measuring affect in frail and cognitively impaired elders. *Journal of Mental Health and Aging, 2,* 259-271.

Spagnoli, A., Foresti, G., MacDonald, A., & Williams, P. (1986). Dementia and depression in Italian geriatric institutions. *International Journal of Geriatric Psychiatry, 1,* 15-23.

Spitznagel, E. L., & Helzer, J. E. (1985). A proposed solution to the base rate problem in the kappa statistic. *Archives of General Psychiatry, 42,* 725-728.

Spitzer, R., Williams, J., Gibbon, M., & First, M. (1989). Instruction Manual for the Structured Clinical Interview for DSM-III-R. *Biometrics Research.* New York State Psychiatric Institute.

Teresi, J. A., Golden, R., & Gurland, B. (1984). Concurrent and predictive validity of the indicator-scales developed for the Comprehensive Assessment and Referral Evaluation (CARE) interview. *Journal of Gerontology, 39,* 158-165.

Teresi, J., & Holmes, D. (1994). Overview of methodological issues in gerontological and geriatric measurement. In P. Lawton & J. Teresi (Eds.), *Annual review of gerontology and geriatrics: Focus on assessment techniques* (vol. 14; pp. 1-22). New York: Springer Publishing.

Teresi, J., & Holmes, D. (1997). Reporting source bias in estimating prevalence of cognitive impairment. *Journal of Clinical Epidemiology, 50,* 175-184.

Teresi, J., Holmes, D., Benenson, E., Monaco, C., Barrett, V., et al. (1993). A primary care nursing model in long-term care facilities: Evaluation of impact on affect, behavior and socialization. *The Gerontologist, 33,* 667-674.

Teresi, J., Holmes, D., & Monaco, C. (1993). An evaluation of the effects of commingling non-cognitively and cognitively impaired individuals in long-term care facilities. *The Gerontologist, 33,* 350-358.

Thompson, W. D., & Walter, S. D. (1988). A reappraisal of the kappa coefficient. *Journal of Clinical Epidemiology, 41,* 949-958.

Toner, J. A., Teresi, J. A., Gurland, B., & Tirumalasetti, F. (1999). The Feeling Tone Questionnaire: Reliability and validity of a direct patient assessment screening instrument for detection of depressive symptoms in cases of dementia. *Journal of Clinical Geropsychiatry, 5,* 63-78.

Volicer, L., Hurley, A. C., & Camberg, L. (1999). A model of psychological well-being in advanced dementia. *Journal of Mental Health and Aging, 5,* 83-94.

Watson, D., & Clark, L. A. (1984). Negative affectivity: The disposition to experience aversive emotional states. *Psychological Bulletin, 96,* 465-490.

Watson, D., & Tellegen, A. (1985). Toward a consensual structure of mood. *Psychological Bulletin, 98,* 219-235.

Acknowledgment. Funding for the study presented in this chapter was provided by the National Institute of Nursing Research NR 030508 and the New York State Department of Health. This Chapter is dedicated to the late Jacqueline Savinon-Sun who was the field coordinator of the study and who died of cancer in April 1998 at the age of 28.

10

The Memory Enhancement Program*: A New Approach to Increasing the Quality of Life for People With Mild Memory Loss

Joyce Simard

The National Institutes of Health, pharmaceutical companies and private foundations are investing millions of dollars each year toward unraveling the mysteries of Alzheimer's disease (AD). Much of this research is focused on discovering the cause or causes of AD and on developing medications that will slow or halt the progression of the disease. However, rarely in Alzheimer's care does medication, without environmental or behavioral interventions, result in significant changes in the lives of people with memory loss. To truly impact the quality of lives of individuals with AD, a broader approach to treatment is needed. Although such approaches have seldom been empirically investigated, clinical experience suggests that a variety of interventions, including elements such as pharmacological treatment, environmental support, memory enhancement, physical exercise, and involvement in social activities may act synergistically to enhance quality of life (QOL) for individuals with AD.

This chapter describes such an intervention, the Memory Enhancement Program (MEP), which has been developed for people residing in assisted living facilities

---

*A registered product of CareMatrix, Inc.

who are experiencing memory loss from early stage Alzheimer's disease or Mild Cognitive Impairment (MCI). The program is designed to empower individuals who have felt helpless about their declining mental status to take active steps in the fight against their memory loss and to improve the quality of their lives.

ASSISTED LIVING PROGRAMS

Although assisted living is a relatively new option for residential care, it has grown dramatically in the past 10 years. The assisted living market generally offers two "products:" traditional assisted living and Alzheimer's care. Alzheimer's or dementia programs represent about 30% of assisted living beds (Volpe, Brown, & Whelan, 1999). Although there are no uniform standards for these facilities, they are usually located in a secured area for residents who are at risk for wandering and include a structured program of activities. These units may also be staffed at higher levels than traditional assisted living, and staff in these units often receive special dementia care training (Grant & Sommers, 1998). The cost of these special programs is usually higher than the cost of traditional assisted living, but lower than the cost of a nursing home (Leon & Moyer, 1999).

Traditional assisted living care usually includes three meals a day, expanded nursing care as physical needs increase, leisure activities, a wellness program, and transportation to physician appointments. Although statistics vary regarding the number of people living in traditional assisted living communities who have memory problems, most administrators report that 30% to 70% of their residents exhibit memory loss beyond what is normal for an aging population. Many of these residents have MCI or very mild AD, but have not progressed to the point where they need or want to live in a secured Alzheimer's program. In these assisted living communities, a "wellness program" is typically offered to residents, however, it is usually focused on medical problems, not cognition. The program described in this chapter, the Memory Enhancement Program (MEP) was developed to fill a gap in the delivery of services to residents in traditional assisted living communities by expanding a wellness program to include assistance with mild cognitive problems. Such programs potentially enhance the quality of lives of older adults by allowing them to remain as independent as possible, while providing needed support services in an assisted living environment.

THE MEMORY ENHANCEMENT PROGRAM

Identifying Participants

Residents with mild memory problems are identified by facility staff, and they and their family are invited to a meeting with MEP staff where the program is explained to them. The program is most successful when the participants are aware that they have a problem with memory loss and are active in all aspects of the MEP. Residents who wish to participate in the program are assessed by the Wellness Director (a licensed nurse) and/or the Medical Director to determine whether they have the potential to benefit from the program. Only residents with mild cognitive impairment are recommended for the MEP program. Residents who wander or have moderate to severe cognitive impairment require special supervision that is not provided in the MEP program, and may be more appropriately served in a secure Alzheimer's unit.

The MEP links residents with a variety of services, including bio-cognitive screening, medication management, rehabilitation therapy screening, and access to research opportunities. It also provides an ongoing structured program to enhance quality of life for participants.

Bio-Cognitive Screening

The first component of the MEP is Bio-Cognitive Screening. The goal of this screening is to rule out physical causes of memory loss. The Wellness Director reviews the resident's medical record or contacts his/her physician to discuss the resident's memory problems, and to ensure that appropriate medical tests have been administered within the past year. The Wellness Director also interviews the resident, family, and staff to rule out depression, alcohol, or drug abuse as potential causes of the memory loss. A consulting pharmacist may be asked to assist with the review of medications and to make recommendations to the attending physician. Recommendations may include consideration of the use of medications for memory loss, such as donepezil or alpha-tocopherol (Rogers, Farlow, Doody, Mohs, & Friedhoff, 1998). As new drugs that may impact memory loss are introduced to the marketplace, information is passed on to residents and their families, to allow them to consider their alternatives and discuss their options with their physician.

Medication Management

Residents who are experiencing memory loss must be monitored so that they take the proper medication in the prescribed manner. This will insure that their memory loss is not due to an error in their medication regime. One of the goals in the MEP is that each resident is as independent as possible for as long as possible, therefore, each resident is assessed by the nursing staff to determine the degree of self-medication the resident is capable of achieving. Medication management may range from simple reminders by the MEP staff (usually not a nurse) to actually dispensing of medications by a licensed nurse or specially certified nursing assistant.

Rehabilitation Therapy Screening

MEP participants are referred for screening by an Occupational Therapist (OT), Physical Therapist (PT) and/or Speech-Language Pathologist (SLP). After the initial screening, the therapist may make recommendations for additional assessment and treatment. Such treatment must be approved by the resident's physician, and may be carried out within the facility where the resident lives. Often facility staff are trained to continue the program after the therapist is no longer involved with the resident. When changes in the resident's functioning occur, the therapist may be called back for further consultation.

Access to Research Opportunities

Residents and families are also provided with information on potential opportunities to participate in research in local teaching hospitals, universities, or research centers.

ONGOING MEP PROGRAMS

The MEP is scheduled for at least 5 days a week. Programs are scheduled at times that do not conflict with other activity programs in the facility, so that MEP participants are not singled out or excluded from facility-wide activities.

Memory Classes

Although individuals with AD have difficulty learning and remembering new material, studies have indicated that memory enhancement programs may help improve and maintain cognitive functioning (Quayhagen et al., 1995; Watanabe, 1996). In the MEP, memory classes are held in the morning when residents are most alert and have the energy necessary to fully participate. Lesson plans for teaching memory improvement have been developed using several programs that have been effective in teaching memory improvement in older adults (Bonner & Cousins, 1996; Caprio-Prevette & Fry, 1996; Fogler & Stern, 1994; Oswald, Rupprecht, Gunzelman & Tritt, 1996).

Physical Exercise

It has become clear in studies of the elderly that physical exercise is helpful in maintaining health (Cress et al., 1999; Hultsch, Hammer & Small, 1993), mood (Kivela et al., 1994), and cognitive function (Netz & Jacob, 1994). Studies show that exercise is a useful treatment focus with individuals with AD (Teri et al., 1998). In the MEP, physical exercise is offered at least 5 days a week for 30 minutes each session. Most exercise classes are offered as a group, however, some participants prefer to use the exercise machines or walk each day. After completing their individual exercise program each day, participants or the MEP staff records their effort on a chart to provide motivation and track their progress.

Brain Exercise

Brain exercises are scheduled each afternoon. While the morning memory class is more structured and focuses on techniques to improve memory, the afternoon brain exercises are more social, fun programs. They involve trivia, word games, crossword puzzles, etc. They challenge participants to think and use their minds to solve problems. The leader plans a variety of exercises and may repeat them to build success into the program. When these exercises are repeated, residents are able to answer correctly, building self-esteem. This component of the MEP addresses two major goals of the program, one is to exercise the brain, the other to increase socialization. One of the characteristics of mild dementia and MCI is isolation. Isolation and depression add to memory loss deficits. Several studies of mid-stage Alzheimer's patients who came together for socialization and therapeutic programming showed improvement in communication, relating to others, and involvement in activities (Pietro & Boczko, 1999; Quayhagen et al., 1995; Watanabe, 1996).

Evening Programs

The majority of residents in assisted living communities return to their rooms after the evening meal. They watch television alone and nod off to sleep very early. When residents fall asleep early in the evening and have taken several naps during the day, they may have trouble sleeping at night and may take sleeping medication that contributes to drowsiness and memory loss the following day. The MEP encourages evening activities in which residents join a game of checkers or cards, work on puzzles (one is always in process), or watch and try to out-guess contestants on one of the game shows. Food is offered (as an incentive) and the MEP staff is present to keep things moving in the evening.

Environment

The MEP living room or gathering place is a comfortable looking area where participants are welcomed to socialize with each other and the MEP staff. This area is centrally located and contains comfortable couches, chairs, tables, lamps, and television. It looks and feels like a living room in a home. A small kitchen, located close to the living room, provides space for making coffee, tea, and snacks. It is available all the time for residents to enjoy and staffed during the day and early evening. In the morning the local newspaper is delivered, the local news show is playing, and a pot of freshly brewed coffee is always available.

Stress Reduction Approaches

Research shows that continued stress creates neurological damage (Katz & Rubin, 1999). The MEP offers several services to all participants to help reduce stress. The

MEP is also individualized such that if a resident struggles with some specific stressful situation, we can work with him/her to alleviate the problem.

Personal Calendar

Staff in the MEP assist residents to create personal calendars (Figure 10.1) to ease their fear of forgetting important dates. The MEP staff talks to residents and their families

April
Joanna Smith

Sun	Mon	Tue	Wed	Thur	Fri	Sat
			1	2 2:00 PM Beauty Shop	3 10:00 AM Shopping for Daughter Amy's present with friend	4
5	6 Daughter Amy's Birthday	7	8	9 2:00 PM Beauty Shop	10 10:00 AM Aquarium Trip with Daughter Amy and Granddaughter Nicole	11
12	13 10:00 AM Dr. Brown – Eye Visit Appt.	14	15	16 2:00 PM Beauty Shop	17 10:00 AM Shopping for son Justin's present wit friend Leah	18
19	20 12:30 PM Lunch with friend Leah – Leah will pick you up at 12:30	21	22	23 2:00 PM Beauty Shop	24 1:00 PM Barbecue with son Justin and his family	25 Son Justin's Birthday
26	27 Daughter Jean's 15th Wedding Anniversary	28	29 10:00 AM Podiatrist appointment with Dr. Connor	30 2:00 PM Beauty Shop		

Mail Delivery by 3 p.m.

Figure 10.1 Sample personal calendar.

each month to find out what important dates to mark on the resident's calendar. Residents keep a copy of their monthly calendar; many residents post their calendars on their refrigerators where they see them often.

The MEP staff also maintains an appointment book for all residents. They can then help residents remember and plan in advance for important occasions like scheduling a beauty shop appointment the day before a family celebration, or reminding a resident of a scheduled shopping excursion the activity department has planned, where a birthday gift could be purchased for an upcoming birthday.

Finally, participants in the MEP are given a calendar of daily events showing the date, meal times, MEP activities, "house" activities and mail delivery times. The daily events schedule (Figure 10.2) is delivered to residents in the MEP every morning, seven days a week. Not only does this lower residents' stress, it is helpful to staff who must respond to repetitive phone calls and questions from residents.

Nutrition and Dining Service

Poor nutritional status appears to have important effects on cognitive function in older patients (Cattin, 1997; Khalsa, 1997). In the MEP, all meals offer at least one menu item that is heart and head smart. Snacks served as part of the MEP program not only taste good, but are good for participants.

When presented with the menu in the dining room at each meal, residents may have difficulty making choices. In an effort to alleviate this problem, menus are posted in the MEP so residents can view the menu before mealtime. For some residents, the MEP staff may review the menu with them and take their order for the meal. In the dining room, the resident hands the food order to the server and enjoys the meal.

Personal Maps

Another area of anxiety for some residents with memory loss is finding their way to the dining room or other common areas of the building. Individual maps can be created to help a resident negotiate a "sometimes confusing" number of floors and corridors that all look alike. Maps are designed so that "cues" are easy to identify, for instance, the way to the dining room may say turn right at the grandfather clock. Once a map is designed, the resident and a staff person follow it to make sure it is "user friendly" for the resident. Directions are laminated and carried in a pocket. This eliminates the need for asking directions or having a staff escort.

Family Involvement

Families are involved in the MEP in a variety of ways. They are given educational material on the memory classes and informed about the individual reminders that have been designed for their family member. These help families communicate with patients in ways that validate patient experience (Benjamin, 1999).

Chancellor Gardens

Thursday
April 15, 1999

TODAY'S EVENTS

TIME	ACTIVITY	LOCATION
* Review Personal Calendar *		
8:00 a.m. to 9:30 a.m.	Breakfast	Dining Room, First Floor
9:30 a.m.	Bright Ideas	Living Room
10:00 a.m.	Fitness Class	Wellness Center, 1st Floor
11:30 a.m to 1:00 p.m.	Lunch	Dining Room, First Floor
1:30 p.m.	Bingo	First Floor Dining Room
3:00 p.m.	Mind Matters	Living Room
4:00 p.m.	High Tea	Patio, First Floor
5:00 p.m. to 6:30 p.m.	Dinner	Dining Room, First Floor
7:30 p.m.	Memory Joggers & Table Games	Living Room
8:00 p.m.	Movies, Games & Snacks	Living Room

Figure 10.2 Sample calendar of daily events.

New Approaches

In their book on neurobic exercises, Katz and Rubin (1999) maintain that the brain has the ability to create new connections. They propose presenting the brain with nonroutine or unexpected experiences. The MEP has integrated this approach at least once a week when they urge participants to try breaking their routine such as brushing their teeth with a different hand or eating and drinking using the nondominant hand. Keeping a journal on food you eat, exercises, and other important events that could help a person live a healthier life, is advocated by Null in his book on "anti-aging" (Null, 1999). As new ideas on how to improve memory are published, they are reviewed and if found to be worthwhile, integrated into the MEP.

CONCLUSION

The MEP was designed to impact the QOL of people with MCI or mild dementia. As the program is implemented in assisted living facilities, we are learning that we can make a positive difference in the lives of program participants. Communities that have implemented the program report that they have seen changes in residents within several weeks. Residents who were reluctant at first to participate have reportedly become involved and are excited to be a part of the program. Residents enrolled in the MEP tend to be over 80 years of age. Many residents are physically frail, and their endurance is low. We find lesson plans have to be adjusted and simplified to help our residents understand them. We repeat the same classes often and limit them to 30 minutes. Physical exercises must be adapted and supervised for this frail population.

Thus far, the MEP has focused on people with MCI or mild dementia. We are also looking at its benefits for residents of Alzheimer's care assisted living programs, to see whether it can be adapted to improve QOL in individuals with more severe dementia. We are challenged to motivate residents who have "given up" and become apathetic, and to improve quality of life for all assisted living residents.

REFERENCES

Benjamin, B. J. (1999). Validation: A Communication alternative. In L. Volicer & L. Bloom-Charette (Eds.), *Enhancing the quality of life in advanced dementia* (pp. 107-124).

Bonner, A. P., & Cousins, S. O. (1996). Exercise and Alzheimer's disease: Benefits and barriers. *Activities, Adaptation & Aging, 20*(4).

Cattin, L. (1997). Factors associated with cognitive impairment among older Italian inpatients. *Journal of the American Geriatrics Society, 45*(11), 1324-1330.

Caprio-Prevette, M. D., & Fry, P. S. (1996). *Memory enhancement program for older adults.* Maryland, MD: Aspen Publications.

Cress, M. E., Buchner, D. M., Questad, K. A., Esselman, P. C., deLateur, B. J., & Schwartz, R. S. (1999). Exercise: Effects on physical functional performance in independent older adults. *Journal of Gerontology: Medical Science, 54*(5), M242-M248.

Fogler, J., & Stern, L. (1994). *Teaching memory improvement to adults.* Baltimore: The Johns Hopkins University Press.

Grant, L. A., & Sommers, A. R. (1998). Adapting living environments for persons with Alzheimer's disease. *Geriatrics, 53*(Suppl. 1), S61-S65.

Hultsch, D. F., Hammer, M., & Small, B. J. (1993) Age differences in cognitive performance in later life: Relationships to self-reported health and activity lifestyle. *Journals of Gerontology: Psychological Sciences, 48*(1), P1-P11.

Katz, L. C., & Rubin, M. (1999). *Keeping your brain alive.* Workman Publishing Company, Inc.

Khalsa, D. S. (1997). *Brain longevity.* New York: Warner Books Inc.

Kivela, S. L., Kongas-Saviaro, P., Kesti, E., Pahkala, K., & Laippala, P. (1994). Five-year prognosis for depression in old age. *International Psychogeriatrics, 6*(1), 69-78.

Leon, J., & Moyer, D. (1999). Potential cost savings in residential care for Alzheimer's disease patients. *The Gerontologist, 39*(4), 440-449.

Netz, Y., & Jacob, T. (1994). Exercise and the psychological state of institutionalized elderly: A review. *Perceptual and Motor Skills, 79,* 1107-1118.

Oswald, W. D., Rupprecht, R., Gunzelman, T., & Tritt, K. (1996).The SIMA-project: Effects of 1 year cognitive and psychomotor training on cognitive abilities of the elderly. *Behavioral Brain Research, 78,* 67-72.

Quayhagen, M. P., Quayhagen, M., Corbeil, R. R., Roth, P. A., & Rodgers, J. A. (1995). A dyadic remediation program for care recipients with dementia. *Nursing Research, 44*(3), 153-159.

Rogers, S. L, Farlow, M. R., Doody, R. S., Mohs, R., Friedhoff, L. D., & The Donepezil Study Group. (1998). A 24-week double blind placebo controlled trial of donepezil in patients with Alzheimer's disease. *Neurology, 50,* 136-145

Santo-Pietro, M., & Boczko, F. (1998). The Breakfast Club: Results of a study examining the effectiveness of a multi-modality group communication treatment. *Alzheimer's Disease and Related Disorders, 13*(3), 147-158.

Teri, L., McCurry, S. M., Buchner, D. M., Logsdon, R. G., LaCroix, A. Z., et al. (1998). Exercise and activity level in Alzheimer's disease: A potential treatment focus. *Journal of Rehabilitation Research and Development, 35*(4), 411-419.

Watanabe, Y. (1996). The long-term effect of day care rehabilitation on individuals with dementia. *Hokkaido Igaku Zasshi, 71*(3), 391-402.

Part V

Conclusions and Future Directions

11

A Life Greater Than the Sum of Its Sensations: Ethics, Dementia, and the Quality of Life

Bruce Jennings

The concept of "quality of life" plays an important, if somewhat vexed and controversial, role in social, scientific, clinical, and health services research on the care of patients with dementia, principally Alzheimer's disease (AD). The methodological sophistication and the ingenuity in study design that researchers in the field have brought to bear on this problem are impressive. However, in this area of research in particular, multidisciplinary dialogue and perspectives are essential. The concept of quality of life raises inherently philosophical, ethical, and even political issues that researchers cannot afford to ignore.

Unexamined philosophical conceptions may shape in the first instance the very questions researchers ask, and thus affect the answers research studies are likely to give. Moreover, ethical and political values will influence the ways in which the findings of research are received, understood, and applied in the clinical and policy arenas. Enhancing our ability to understand and to discuss the quality of life of persons with AD is one of the single most important keys to improving the quality of care and services they receive. And improving our capacity to care for persons with dementia is one of the single most important challenges facing our aging society in the next 50 years. When the notion of the quality of human life is at issue, the intellectual challenges are formidable and the social stakes are very high.

Empirical researchers interested in quality of life will find that their more theoretically minded colleagues in philosophy and ethics do, in fact, have a good deal to say on the subject. And students of AD will find that this insidious and devastating disease provides a fascinating test case for much of the philosophical literature on the concept of quality of life. In this paper, I focus on what contributions philosophy might make to our understanding of the quality of life lived with dementia, but I do so without forgetting that this is but one side of a two-way conversation. Philosophical work on the concept of quality of life also has something to learn from those who study and work with AD patients and their families.

QUALITY OF LIFE:
THE MORAL CAREER OF A CONCEPT

One school of thought in philosophy and ethics holds that the concept of quality of life should not be used at all because it is so prone to misunderstanding and so weighed down with morally objectionable connotations (Hastings Center, 1987). This objection is not so much wrong as pointless, however. The phrase "quality of life" can be eschewed, certainly, but the concept behind the words is indispensable in any domain, like health care, where we are essentially talking about matters of human well-being and where fundamental human interests and goods are at stake.

In ordinary usage the objectionable meaning that some hear behind the phrase has to do with the notion that something (life) is being evaluated that should not be evaluated. Another version of this objection holds that the very idea of quality of life entails a mistaken assessment of the value of human life. The familiar distinction between intrinsic and instrumental value will help to clarify these concerns. Something (for example, human life or biological existence) has "instrumental" value when it is valuable only for the sake of something else. Human life has "intrinsic value" when it is valuable for its own sake, when it is taken as a given and treated as an end in itself, and not merely as a means for something else. This may be because human reason dictates that we take this attitude toward the value of human beings, or because God endowed human beings with inherent dignity (McCormick, 1978). The term quality of life seems to suggest instrumental or contingent value only; it seems to suggest that life is not intrinsically worthy of respect, but can have greater or lesser value according to its circumstances. In addition to those who regard all talk about the quality of life as an affront to the inherent dignity and moral worth of the human person, no matter what his or her social or physical condition, objections to the term also come from the disability rights community. From this perspective, quality of life is part of a broader normalizing ideology in the mainstream culture and works to the detriment of persons with disabilities by perpetuating their stigmatization and discrimination against them (Taylor, 1994; Wolfensberger, 1994).

Finally, the term grates on many ears for a vaguer, but no less culturally powerful, reason. The United States, particularly the middle class, has a strikingly non-judgmental, even antijudgmental, cultural ethos (Wolfe, 1998). Apart from a core set of notions about harm to others and wrongdoing, we are made profoundly uncomfortable by appraisals of how others choose to live their lives, and we resent it deeply when others presume to judge us. The notion of quality of life seems to suggest that there is some common metric according to which two or more different lives can be compared and rated relative to one another. Americans are largely skeptical of that notion, if they have not rejected it altogether. If quality of life assessments are to be made, most people believe, they can only be made subjectively; they can and should only be made by persons for themselves, about themselves.

These are powerful and plausible arguments, but I think there is a way that the concept of quality of life can be used to enhance rather than detract from ethics. Properly understood, it can be used to strengthen the case for greater social justice and social reform on behalf of those whose quality of life is lessened more by the systems of relationship and support they inhabit than by the functional limitations of their own bodies (Cohen, 1983). If we pay closer attention to the different ways in which the concept of quality of life is used in health care, however, it is possible to make one's way successfully through this semantic minefield. For present purposes, I shall distinguish four different senses of the notion of quality of life.

QUALITY OF LIFE AS PROPERTY
OF THE INDIVIDUAL

First, the notion of quality of life is used to refer to some characteristic or state of being of the individual person. A quality of life (whether good or poor) is something one has or possesses, much as one has a physical characteristic or a personality trait. Moreover, it is a contingent characteristic, not a defining one— it is a temporary condition that can in principle change over time, or it is a characteristic that can be compensated for or ameliorated by some artificial device or by special training—and for this reason it is not essential to one's identity or one's self-esteem. As such it has no straightforward moral significance. A poor quality of life (due to ill health, loss of a job, breakdown of personal relationships, or the like) is not necessarily a sign of a person's moral failing, and it says nothing about the intrinsic value of life as such, or even about the moral value of that particular life at that particular time. Those who suffer are not generally thought to be less deserving on that account of others' care and concern. On the contrary, morality teaches that they are more deserving.

QUALITY OF LIFE AS A GOAL OF CARE

A second common meaning of quality of life defines it as a goal of care. The moral point of our dealings with one another (whether the situation be health care or some other form of relationship) is to sustain and improve the quality of life. In this sense, quality of life becomes a benchmark to guide human activity and a concept of assessment and evaluation. But notice that the evaluation here is directed primarily at the caregiver and the caregiving process, not at the recipient of care, who partakes of the quality of life achieved but is not judged by it. Moreover, the quality of life that the person enjoys may be thought of as a characteristic or property of that person, or it can be thought of as a more general state of being—an interaction, so to speak, between the person and her surrounding circumstances, including other people. Thus understood as a goal or outcome of care, an improved quality of life may be a change (for the better) in the person's symptoms or perceptions; or it may be a change in the person's relationship with his environment. Medical cure, symptom relief, psychological happiness, or social empowerment may all be goals of care as comprehended by the concept of quality of life.

QUALITY OF LIFE AS A SOCIAL SITUATION

This suggests the next sense of the concept of quality of life, namely, as something that refers to a state of interaction between an individual and his social and physical environment. Here a certain quality of life is not a property of the individual per se, but a function of that individual's form of life, his way of being in the world. Once again, thus understood a low quality of life assessment does not necessarily suggest a negative evaluation of the person or his worth; it can equally well imply a critical evaluation of the person's environment and indicate ways in which that environment could be changed, so as to enhance the quality of life according to some scale of norms such as justice, freedom, health, happiness, and the like. Far from rejecting human dignity as a moral touchstone, the concept of quality of life in this sense can be used as a critical champion of dignity, attacking circumstances that undermine it and supporting change in the person's surrounding conditions that will comport with it. In this sense, the notion of quality of life is an ecological concept, referring not to the internal properties of things but to the nature and dynamics of their interaction. Quality of life, high or low, does not reside in people, but in the space of interactions between and among people.

QUALITY OF LIFE AS THE MORAL
WORTH OF A LIFE

Finally, it must be acknowledged that the term quality of life is sometimes, perhaps often, used to refer to the moral worth or value of a person and his or her life. Pushed to its logical extreme, this understanding of the quality of life takes us to the infamous Nazi concept of "life unworthy of life," (*lebensunwertes Leben*), which was used to rationalize everything from active euthanasia of those with disabilities to the genocidal death camps (Lifton, 1986). To say that a person has no quality of life or a very low quality of life—as is often said of persons in a persistent vegetative state (PVS) or persons living in unrelieved pain and suffering, like some of the plaintiffs in the *Glucksberg* and *Quill* cases on physician assisted suicide—is, according to this usage, to say that prolonging this person's life has no moral significance, either to the person himself or to society. Indeed, one might go on to say that unless the quality of life can be improved, it is a moral duty not to prolong the person's life because to do so would be tantamount to torture (if the person can experience suffering), or to a waste of scarce resources (if the person cannot).

It is this last sense of the concept of quality of life, and this last sense only, that makes the concept prone to abuse and morally dangerous. How can a life of very poor quality possibly be respected or judged to have moral value? If the notion of "quality" refers to the moral worth of life, then the notion would seem incompatible with the idea of life's intrinsic value, and it would lead us, perhaps illicitly and improperly, into the realm of instrumental value only. But the notion of quality can be understood differently and the implications are then reversed. The notion of quality may mark the gap between the *actual* circumstances and the *possible* circumstances of an intrinsically valuable life. I need not say that Beethoven is merely a means to the end of making great music (and thus value him only instrumentally) in order to say that he would be better off with access to a piano than he would be without access to one. Nor do I have to deny his intrinsic worth (or indeed make any judgment about his moral worth whatever) if I were to make the (admittedly much more controversial) quality of life judgment that Beethoven was better off when he could hear than he was after he became deaf.

Now, these considerations do not show that one is foolish in worrying about the ways in which talk about quality of life may undermine respect for life or may be used to devalue or dehumanize persons who are, so to speak, on the receiving end of quality-of-life assessments. But they do suggest that this is a complex philosophical problem and not a straightforward definitional one. I certainly will not be able to do justice to the problem in this article. I do want to suggest, without being able to fully argue the point, that when quality of life is used as a measure of the moral worth of human beings, this is a conceptual mistake, and usually a dangerous ethical misstep as well. We might say that an account of moral worth is based on an underlying account of humanness or the human person; an account, that is, of what it is to be human. The concept of quality of life, on the other hand, is based on an account of a person's inherent capacities and external circumstances. Quality of life may tell us something about the experience, but not the moral worth of humanness, or it may tell us something about *becoming (more fully) human*, but never about the value of *being human*.

In the end, the concept of quality of life must be judged by how it is used. In the hands of those who want to deny services or rights of individuals who purportedly experience a life of low quality, the concept has little to recommend it, and much to condemn. However, the concept may also be used by those who seek a way to assess individual need and the quality of care and services so that more effective and humane care can be provided, and so that more human benefit will result from these services. When researchers who study the behavioral manifestations of AD talk about quality of life and seek ways to operationalize this concept and to study it empirically, they have in mind the goal of improving the care we provide to patients with dementia and to lessening the burden of those who care for them. In this context the concept can seem to be morally unproblematic and unambiguous, and so I believe it is. Nonetheless, it is a concept that must be used with some care and precision, for it is surrounded with ethical pitfalls, and it has the capacity to reinforce and rationalize great injustice.

PHILOSOPHICAL THEORIES OF
QUALITY OF LIFE

Philosophical theories are not comprised of well-tested and confirmed universal laws and propositions about cause and effect relationships. In philosophy the term "theory" is used more broadly to refer to a systematic, coherent account that can be used to provide a foundation for our true, but prereflective beliefs and to sort out those ideas that should be held with rational conviction from those that should be discarded. In this sense, a philosophical theory of quality of life is an account of what makes human life worth living and an attempt to single out those fundamental elements of human experience or the human condition that provide the content for such an account. In the history of philosophy there are, of course, innumerable such accounts, presented as each philosopher explicates his or her preferred account of the human good.

This is not the place to attempt a survey of this literature, but it is possible to identify a broad typology into which most of the main philosophical discussions can be subsumed (Brock, 1993; McCormick, 1978; Scanlon, 1993). This consists of three types of philosophical accounts of quality of life, which I shall refer to as: (1) hedonic theories, (2) desire or preference theories, and (3) theories of human flourishing.

HEDONIC THEORIES

These accounts identify quality of life with states of awareness, consciousness, or experience of the individual. Happiness or pleasure, however those terms are precisely to be defined, are the sine qua non of quality of life. This allows for considerable individual variation in assessing good quality of life because different things make different people happy, but it also allows for some kind of common metric (at least on the negative side) because there are seemingly universal negative states of pain or suffering or unhappiness that all (normal) persons avoid.

An interesting question, when applying this type of theory to the case of AD, is whether it is necessary for the person to realize he is happy in order to be happy. In other words, is the kind of happiness (or pleasure) that makes for a good quality of life a direct, unmediated sensation, or is it a psychic state that results from some act of self-interpretation? If it is the former, then it would seem to follow that a person locked in a cell with an electrode implanted in a pleasure center of the brain would be experiencing the highest quality of life. That conclusion, I take it, is ridiculous and counts against the theory. On the other hand, if the pleasure or happiness the theory requires involves some form of cognitive mediation and secondary interpretation, then at some point in the course of AD, when that capacity is lost, this theory will provide only a negative assessment of the patient's quality of life. But surely we want that to remain an open question, subject to empirical research, and not a closed question settled in advance by the terms of the theory.

DESIRE OR PREFERENCE THEORIES

The second type of theory defines quality of life in terms of the actual satisfaction or realization of a person's rational desires or preferences. This is a much more objective theory than the hedonic account in that a person need not be aware that his preferences are being fulfilled (or need not take pleasure in that knowledge) in order for the quality of his life to be good, it just must be the case that they are. For example, if I arrive in Chicago during a snow storm to attend a political meeting that furthers the cause of justice, my quality of life is enhanced (because my rational desire for justice is furthered) even though subjectively I may feel cold, miserable, homesick, and bored by longwinded speeches. If I skip the meeting and go to a beach in the Virgin Islands instead, my pleasurable experience may be enhanced, but my quality of life will be diminished. The underlying appeal of theories of this type is the notion that individuals have a good life when the objective state of the world conforms to what they rationally desire.

THEORIES OF HUMAN FLOURISHING

This type of philosophical theory attempts to base our understanding of the good life on an account of those functions, capacities, and excellences that are most fully and constitutively human. To the extent that we attain and master those capacities, and to the extent that we negate those conditions that would stunt or undermine those capacities, we flourish as human beings. Theories of this type also usually have a developmental component built into them, for those most fully human capacities are ones that are not mastered at birth or automatically expressed by instinct, but must be developed and nurtured by education, interaction with others, and practice over the course of a life time. To the extent, then, that the individual continues to grow and develop throughout her or his life, the quality of life is enhanced thereby.

Once again, accounts of these most fully human capacities differ among philosophers working in this tradition of theorizing, but as a generalization we can say that philosophical accounts of this type usually emphasize the human capacity to express and to experience meaning in social relationships of intimacy, friendship, and cooperation; the capacity to use reason and to develop and follow a life-plan of self-fulfillment and self-realization; the capacity for independence and self-reliance; and the human need for an appropriate social and cultural environment that provides the individual with various types of resources—material, symbolic, spiritual—necessary to live a developmentally human life and to meet both basic and secondary needs.

These brief sketches scarcely do justice to theories that are in fact very elaborate and complex. But perhaps enough of a flavor of these three common approaches to the concept of quality of life comes through to draw a few conclusions.

For understandable reasons perhaps, in the literature on quality of life and dementia the most commonly adopted philosophical perspective is the hedonic. It may seem that only this type of theory is compatible with the radically diminished cognitive capacity in AD and other dementias. Or it may be that this type of theory seems most congenial to the value relativism and the subjective approach Americans are most comfortable with in dealing with such a sensitive and potentially discriminatory concept as the quality of life, especially when applied to this most vulnerable population. Neither of these reasons seems to me to be sufficient to warrant a predominant focus on hedonic conceptions. The main problem, as I see it, however, is the tacit nature of this conceptual bias in the field. In discussions of quality of life in dementia, the relative strengths and weaknesses of these three types of philosophical theory have not been explicitly discussed, and the hedonic approach has been adopted without sufficient critical analysis.

A second conclusion to mention is that no one of these philosophical theories has completely carried the day among philosophers, and each of the three is still under development in the philosophical literature on quality of life. None of them offers a complete account; all three are essential for the purposes of both bioethics and social science.

Third, the concept of quality of life is misused, in my judgment, when it becomes a floor below which no significant societal expenditure of resources is required, and below which personal caregiving efforts may be reduced to the decent minimum. A much better way to think about quality of life is to see it as a ceiling, a potential level of functional capacity and capacity for relationship, toward which caregiving efforts should be designed to strive. The height of this ceiling will not be the same for everyone, and quality of life is not a test that you fail if you do not reach a certain height. But the important point is that quality of life should be used as a teleological concept—setting a goal to reach and a process to reach it, rather than as a prioritizing concept—setting a rank ordering for the allocation of scarce resources.

Of course, there is no one-to-one correlation between how one gives the notion of quality of life substantive content and how one employs its measurement or assessment for the purposes of health policy and health system design. Hedonic theories can be used in a teleological way, and rational desire and human flourishing theories can be used to set priorities and to allocate resources. But in the field of dementia, when discussion focuses too much on the hedonic elements of pleasant sensation and immediate experience, this very point about how quality of life notions are used in policy analysis tends not to be raised at all. Since we assume the ceiling is inevitably going to be so low, we turn our attention to not "wasting" resources on those who have already fallen below the floor.

This, then, brings me to my main contention and recommendation. Future work on the quality of life with dementia needs to adopt a more synthetic and eclectic conceptual approach, drawing on the resources offered by each of the main types of philosophical theory in this field. Most philosophers have had in mind examples and social problems far removed from the severely compromised cognitive capacities represented in dementia, to be sure. Nonetheless, life lived with dementia, even well into its later stages, can be explicated by drawing on conceptions of rational desire and even human flourishing, and it need not be assessed only in the most directly sensate, hedonic terms.

I offer this proposition partly in the spirit of a testable hypothesis. If we try to work with broader and richer notions of quality of life, as Lawton, for example, has done, we will in fact be rewarded with more insightful findings that will be helpful in guiding public policy and clinical practice (Albert et al., 1996; Burgener, 1998; Lawton, 1991, 1995; Russell, 1996). But I also argue for it because I believe the consequences of not doing it, and adhering to the hedonic approach exclusively, are unacceptable. In closing, I shall indicate briefly why that is the case.

A LIFE GREATER THAN THE SUM
OF ITS SENSATIONS

When researchers define and study quality of life in dementia there is more at stake than matters of research design. Such research inevitably has a political and a moral significance. It is with this context that I have been principally concerned in this paper, and it is in light of this context that I see at least three serious problems raised by defining quality of life in exclusively hedonic terms.

The first problem is that when we use hedonic notions of quality of life as our lens to view life lived with dementia, we run the risk of too quickly closing off aspects of semantic agency and moral personhood from persons with AD. By "semantic agency" I mean the activity of making and experiencing meaning, where meaning taps a level or circuit of communication between human beings that goes beyond unilateral sensation or sensate experience. (Perhaps I should say communication between conscious beings in order to make room for what may be transpiring in pet therapy with AD patients.) Of course, communication here does not mean verbal or even semiotic communication, for the capacity to manipulate previously learned semiotic systems may be lost with AD patients. But touch, gesture, facial expression, posture, eye contact, even control of body movements to permit prolonged physical closeness, like sitting together, can conceivably be media of semantic agency, and these are much slower to be lost than memory, speech, functional capacities for ADLs and self-care, and the rest.

By "moral personhood" I mean the notion that maintaining, sustaining, and creating relationships—connections and commitments—with the moral person is itself a duty of ethical responsibility for other individuals in the moral person's environment. If I am a moral person, I cannot rightfully be ignored, abandoned, exiled from the space of connection between selves that we call the moral community. If we come to the too easy conclusion that AD patients have lost moral personhood—have lost this status, this claim on our attention and response—then it will be all the easier to turn aside from these connections and all the easier to tolerate institutions and care-giving systems that fail to fashion, mend, and create those connections and relationships. And is this not precisely what we do so often with demented patients now in our health care institutions? And isn't this what our lack of social support to AD families makes so difficult to achieve even in the home setting?

In asking these rhetorical questions, I do not mean to say that when AD patients are seen as lacking in moral personhood they are necessarily neglected, abused, or abandoned. Nor do I mean to say that we fail to see that they are still human beings. That clearly is not so. But I do claim that the moral basis of our care giving changes. It is one thing to give care and protection out of a sense of pity, or charity, or professional duty, or even love; it is another to maintain relationship and connection with the other for as long as possible out of a sense of the moral importance of that connection per se. Caring and caregiving, after all, are not only about meeting an individual's needs or making him comfortable; they are about the recognition of the person of the other, the one being cared for, and they are about the recognition of the caregiver's own personhood therein also. I have just said the recognition of the person of the other; I should also say that caregiving and quality of life are about the preserving, conserving, sustaining, nurturing, and eliciting of that personhood as well.

Now, when we define quality of life in exclusively hedonic terms— especially when we conceptualize happiness or pleasure in terms of direct sensation rather than the secondary interpretation or mediation of first-order sensation—we effectively leave no room for semantic agency and moral personhood, whereas those constructs are at work to some extent in rational desire theories and figure very largely indeed in human flourishing theories. If we thought that an AD patient had the capacity for semantic agency or moral personhood, why would we ever be content to say that he or she has a good quality of life if her or his pleasurable sensations outnumber the painful ones? Surely we would look at the surrounding conditions that the patient is living in and ask, how can the range of her or his exercise of (remaining) capacity for semantic agency be enhanced and facilitated? How could caregivers be given a better opportunity to mend and maintain those relationships and interactions appropriate to the recognition and honoring of moral personhood? Pleasant sensations or feelings will come through the exercise of semantic agency and with the recognition of moral personhood, to be sure, but they, not the feelings per se, are the sum and substance of her or his quality of life. (Tragically, with AD we may actually have to choose between happiness and agency, for to slow the progress of the disease in its early or middle stages and to extend the period of capacity and agency is also to extend the suffering that accompanies the awareness of ongoing and impending loss. Hedonic conceptions of quality of life would not necessarily view drugs that have this effect as beneficial.)

In response to this one might well argue as follows: We don't think the AD patient has semantic agency or moral personhood because we do not know how to find evidence through behavioral observation, interviewing of caregivers, and other research designs that these capacities are present. To that the answer might be: perhaps they are not present, at least not in every individual, for AD patients are quite different in the manifestation of their disease. Still, another equally plausible answer might be: perhaps we haven't found evidence of these capacities because we haven't thought clearly and carefully enough about what we are looking for; and once we do, we will then devise techniques to observe it. The jury is still out, but I will place my bets on the second answer.

Two additional reasons why relying solely on hedonic conceptions of quality of life is a bad idea can be mentioned more briefly. One is that doing so casts substantial doubt on the currently prevailing ethical and legal approach to end-of-life care in AD. I refer to the practice of making end-of-life treatment decisions on the basis of the patient's advance directive or on the basis of what the surrogate decision maker infers would be the patient's express preference if he or she were able to make the decision (the so-called substituted judgment standard). As Dresser has argued, a contemporaneous best interest standard for decision making could well come to different conclusions about forgoing life-sustaining treatments, such as artificial nutrition and hydration, if we assess the AD patient's quality of life in hedonic terms. Counter-arguments by Dworkin and Post, among others, necessarily appeal to interests and senses of personhood that go beyond hedonic quality of life as reasons why we should honor a person's advance directive or long-standing wishes and values. (Dresser, 1986; Dresser & Robertson, 1989; Dworkin, 1993; Post, 1995). Dworkin, for instance, makes a distinction between what he calls "experiential interests" and "critical interests," the former being those things that a person experiences as enhancing his or her good and the latter those things that rationally, objectively do enhance a person's good whether he or she is aware of it or not. (This distinction parallels the gap between hedonic conceptions of quality of life, on the one hand, and rational desire and human flourishing accounts, on the other.) A person with AD may have lost all experiential interest in her previous values, beliefs, and instructions—because she has forgotten them or can no longer understand what they mean—but it does not follow that her critical interests in these things have been lost, or that their significance for the person's quality of life has been erased. And it is on the basis of a person's critical interests that both quality of life and the obligations of caregivers toward the person must be assessed; experiential interests (or hedonic quality of life) alone are important but insufficient.

Moreover, as new drugs for AD that promise some therapeutic benefit enter the research process at last, the ethical and legal validity of surrogate consent for participation in research studies will become an increasingly important issue. I can see no reason why Dresser's argument about forgoing life-sustaining treatment would not also apply to participation in research that would have more than negligible risk or would entail hedonic discomfort with no offsetting benefit to the individual research subject. If we want to allow family members to consent to participation in research studies, or if we want to encourage individuals in the early stages of disease who retain decision-making capacity to execute advance directives concerning research participation, then we are going to have to appeal to something beyond the hedonic existence of persons with AD, and we are going to have to find a way to argue that the quality of their lives is enhanced, not diminished, by respecting their desire to participate in research.

Finally, as a tool of quality of care and health services research applied to health policy, the hedonic conception of quality of life sets the bar too low for policy makers. Except in the final stages of disease, when hospice care is ethically and medically appropriate, I would argue against a purely "palliative" model of care only in long-term care for AD (Solomon & Jennings, 1998). Instead, some appropriately modified version of a "rehabilitative" model is the appropriate standard for policy reform. By rehabilitation I do not mean the restoration of functional capacity, but rather the structuring of the environment of caregiving so that the meaning-making and relational human powers of the self may be sustained as long as possible; in different forms as neurological function deteriorates, to be sure, but as long as possible in some form nonetheless.

As my generation ages into the first few decades of the next century, I do not want to send a message to young policy makers that it is enough merely to provide a shelter where I can be kept pleasantly senile, as important as comfort and safety are. If Alzheimer's disease is destined to be the last chapter in the story of my life, I want those pages to have more of a plot, and more of a character than that. I can't bring that about by myself now, no matter how much I save or how much long-term-care insurance I buy; and I won't be able to protect my own quality-of-life interests then. But the people and the institutions that care for me could do so. Will they have the resources, and the social investment, and the proper understanding of the goals of care? They will if our nation can muster the moral courage and the political will to honor its fathers and its mothers.

REFERENCES

Albert, S. M., Del Castillo-Castaneda, C., Sano, M., Jacobs, D. M., Marder, K., Bell, K., Bylsma, F., Lafleche, G., Brandt, J., Albert, M., & Stern, Y. (1996). Quality of life in patients with Alzheimer's disease as reported by patient proxies. *Journal of the American Geriatrics Society, 44*, 1342-1347.

Brock, D. (1993). Quality of life measures in health care and medical ethics. In M.C. Nussbaum & A. Sen (Eds.), *The quality of life.* New York: Cambridge University Press.

Burgener, S. C. (1998). Quality of life in late stage dementia. In L. Volicer & A. Hurley (Eds.), *Hospice care for patients with advanced progressive dementia.* New York: Springer Publishing

Cohen, C. (1983). 'Quality of Life' and the analogy with the Nazis. *Journal of Medicine and Philosophy,8*(2), 113-135.

Dresser, R. S. (1986). Life, death and incompetent patients: Conceptual infirmities and hidden values in the law. *Arizona Law Review, 28*, 373-405.

Dresser, R. S., & Robertson, J. A. (1989). Quality of life and non-treatment decisions for incompetent patients: A critique of the orthodox approach. *Law, Medicine, and Health Care, 17*, 234-244.

Dworkin, R. (1993). *Life's dominion.* New York: Knopf.

Hastings Center (1987). *Guidelines on the termination of life-sustaining treatment and the care of the dying.* Bloomington, IN: Indiana University Press.

Lawton, M. P. (1991). A multidimensional view of quality of life in frail elders.In J. E. Birren, J. E. Lubben, J. C. Rowe, & D. W. Deutchman (Eds.), *The concept and measurement of quality of life in the frail elderly.* New York: Academic Press.

Lawton, M. P. (1995). Quality of life in Alzheimer's disease. *Alzheimer's disease and associated disorders, 8* (Suppl. 3), 138-150.

Lifton, R. J. (1986). *Nazi doctors.* New York: Basic Books.

McCormick, R. (1978, February). The quality of life, the sanctity of life. *Hastings Center Report, 8*, 30-36.

Post, S. (1995). *The moral challenge of Alzheimer's disease.* Baltimore, MD: Johns Hopkins University Press.

Russell, C. K. (1996). Passion and heretics: Meaning in life and quality of life of persons with dementia. *Journal of the American Geriatrics Society, 44*,1400-1401.

Scanlon, T. (1993). Value, desire, and quality of life. In M.C. Nussbaum & A. Sen (Eds.), *The quality of life.* New York: Cambridge University Press.

Solomon, M. Z., & Jennings, B. (1998). Palliative care for Alzheimer patients: Implications for institutions, caregivers, and families. In L. Volicer and A. Hurley (Eds.), *Hospice care for patients with advanced progressive dementia.* New York: Springer Publishing Company.

Taylor, S. (1994). In support of research on quality of life, but against QOL. In D. Goode (Ed.), *Quality of Life for persons with disabilities: International perspectives and issues.* Cambridge, MA: Brookline Books.

Wolfe, A. (1998). *One nation, after all.* New York: Viking Penguin.

Wolfensberger, W. (1994). Let's hang up "quality of life" as a hopeless term. In D. Goode (Ed.), *Quality of life for persons with disabilities: International perspectives and issues.* Cambridge, MA: Brookline Books.

12

Conclusion

Quality Of Life: Future Directions

Peter J. Whitehouse

As the work of the authors of this book demonstrates, the science of quality of life (QOL) in dementia is flourishing. In this concluding summary, we will review these accomplishments and point to future areas of needed work. However, we will also raise some questions about the limitations of our current approaches. We are early in the evolution of this area of inquiry in dementia and should reflect broadly on the implications of our current approaches and possible future expansions. We believe the stakes are high. Scholarship in quality of life sits at the interface of the two cultures of science and humanities. How we explore quality of life in dementia could serve as a paradigm case for observing and influencing the changing relationship between science and society.

The history of scientific study of quality of life in dementia is brief. Initial papers were published in the late 1980s. Even today many of the developments, particularly in instrumentation, are awaiting publication. For example, the paper by Selai and colleagues in this volume may be the first paper to elicit QOL domains from patients with mild dementia. The reasons for the delay in studying quality of life in dementia have been reviewed elsewhere (Whitehouse & Rabins, 1992). Probably the most important factor was the recognition that patients' participation in discussions of their quality of life is limited by the dementia. Impairments of memory, language, and particularly insight and judgment make it difficult for patients to answer questions about QOL in the past.

The healthcare system has increased its focus on patient (consumer) partici-pation. This trend has influenced positively the desire to incorporate the voice of demented patients in discussions about their care. The face of Auguste D., the first patient with Alzheimer's disease (AD), has frequently replaced Alois Alzheimer as the initial slide in general talks about AD (Whitehouse et al., 1998). Perhaps this substitution symbolizes this refocus of attention to the person affected by the disease rather than the professional who studies it.

The principal area of development in QOL studies in dementia has been in the assessment. Three complementary approaches have been adopted. First, one can observe individuals and make some judgments about the quality of their lives. If a person appears agitated or distressed in some way, one can make a reasonable assumption that quality of life is lowered. The second approach is to ask the caregiver about the patient and to make judgments on behalf of the individual affected by dementia. Finally, there is the opportunity to use self-ratings in which patients themselves are asked questions about their quality of life. Approaches in this area tested by Brod, Logsdon, and Selai have demon-strated that mildly affected patients can reliably participate in discussions about their own quality of life; some moderately affected patients also appear able to report on QOL.

Each of these approaches has strengths and weaknesses. The use of observer ratings excludes the opportunity for a subjective sense of well-being to be communicated by the patients themselves. These approaches are best for severely demented patients with limited communication abilities. The use of ratings from other people is clearly limited by the fact that caregivers have different notions of quality of life and may distort their assessments of the care recipient's quality of life because of aspects of their own caregiving experi-ence. Logsdon and Selai, for example, both report that caregiver depression was highly correlated with caregivers' reports of patient QOL.

The use of self-rating scales allows the voice of the patient into the dialogue, but, as mentioned, is potentially limited by the extent of cognitive impairment. Almost every type of cognitive impairment in dementia could affect either actual quality of life or the ability to assess QOL. Most obviously, some patients with AD have essentially no insight into their condition and may, in fact, not report that they suffer from any memory problems at all. If the disease is denied for either psychiatric or neurological reasons, how can we believe a patient's assessment of the impact of the disease on quality of life? Some patients will have difficulty remembering pleasant events in the past, and thus, this will color their judgments of QOL. Some patients have problems with executive function, so their judgments may be unreliable. Finally, certain patients may have profound language problems, making it difficult for them to communicate with others about their own QOL. Additional studies to establish how the varying patterns of neuropsychological disabilities affect the patients' ability to participate in judgments of their own quality of life need to be performed. Teresi and colleagues in this volume have gone some way in this effort by developing a protocol to identify depression among such patients.

One specific aspect of QOL that needs further elaboration is expectation. How we judge our quality of life is dependent on what we expect to accomplish in life, and in the case of dementia what we expect interventions to accomplish. Professionals modify these expectations through individual patient contact and by participating in community educational programs. Are our expectations about the value of biological approaches unrealistic? Is the cure for AD really just around the next scientific corner?

Although it now seems well established that quality of life deserves consideration as a separate category for assessment, quality of life is clearly multi-dimensional. We need to continue to ask the question whether quality of life is more than the sum of its individual parts (see Jennings's paper, this volume). Two particularly important components are function and affect, as stressed by the chapters contributed by Albert, Lawton, and Sano. All would agree that quality of life is more than competence in the activities of daily living. But agreement is less strong when it comes to incorporating functional status into QOL models (see the different approaches of Brod and Albert, for example) or what, beyond function, should be included as QOL domains. Volicer and colleagues take this issue up in a dementia-specific model of patient well-being.

Another area of needed research is the effect of co-morbidity on quality of life in dementia. Teresi and colleagues examine this issue in the case of depression. Frequently associated psychiatric and behavioral symptoms can impair quality of life. However, patients with dementia are at risk for many other factors that can affect quality of life, including other medical illnesses and psychosocial traumas. These individuals are often elderly and will suffer from illnesses and losses common to this stage of life. Moreover, the caregiver also shares in the experience of the disease. How the quality of life of patients and caregivers interact needs further investigation, though findings presented by Selai and Logedon already show that caregiver reports of patient QOL are affected by caregiver mental health.

Cross-cultural studies of QOL will also be useful to enrich our understanding of the diversity of human experience. Such studies may be within or among countries. Of course, careful attention to translation (and cultural equivalence) of assessment instruments will be key. The International Working Group for Harmonization of Dementia Drug Guidelines (Whitehouse, 1997) is exploring such issues through its Cultural and Translation Committees.

Special attention will need to be placed on the quality of life at the end of life, or what might be called the quality of death. How do we treat severely demented, uncommunicative patients (Post & Whitehouse, 1992; Whitehouse et al., 1996)? Do we use medications to improve cognition or slow progression at the end of life? What is the appropriate use of physical restraints, antibiotics, and even feeding tubes? These will be questions that will increasingly dominate discussions concerning this phase of the disease (Post & Whitehouse, 1998).

Hospice care is increasingly being viewed as appropriate for patients with terminal AD (Volicer & Hurley, 1998). In the Netherlands, consideration is being given as to when it would be appropriate to conduct euthanasia on individuals with dementia. Thus, quality of life in the terminal phases of the disease will be a critical part of the study of quality of life in the future.

Combined studies of costs and quality of life will also need to continue. A few cost-utility studies are being reported (Whitehouse, 1998; see also Sano and colleagues, this issue). Modeling techniques are being used to assess values or utility weights for various outcomes. These approaches allow the calculation of quality-adjusted life years (a measure not just of how long you live but how well you live for a given length of time). In cost-utility analyses, the costs associated with an intervention and the impact of that intervention on these utility weights can be compared. Thus, in a world in which increasing attention is being paid to the large expenditures for health care, particularly for the elderly, keeping quality of life in the discussion will be important. One way of doing this is in the equations of cost-utility analysis.

However, there are dangers to increasing the medicalization or economization of quality of life. Both the medical models, with the use of assessment instruments and quantification, and the economic models of comparing quality of life to costs are too narrow. Yes, quality of life is, in some sense, the quantitative summation of a variety of different variables. Yes, quality of life can be compared to costs in the sense that we all make judgments about the value of certain life activities in relationship to their costs. However, there are broader ethical and humanistic aspects to quality of life that cannot be ignored. We can celebrate the science of quality of life, but recognize that quality of life goes beyond our ability to study it scientifically. In fact, the study of quality of life may be a perfect example of where, in order to place something into a scientific or economic framework, we may distort it considerably.

Alzheimer's is a disease that affects the very personhood of the individual (Whitehouse and Deal, 1995). Although it is too strong to say that there is a loss of self, there are clearly alterations in the personal attributes of the individual (Deal and Whitehouse, 2000). Some might say that the patient with dementia is less than fully human. Clearly, as the disease progresses from the day after diagnosis to the day before death, the change in the human being caused by the dementia itself and also by the label "being demented" is profound. Quality of life discussions could be used to argue for the limited value of someone affected by dementia. Clearly, an individual who is severely demented, unable to recognize family and caregivers, and unable to feed himself is a human being with severe limitations. Through an individual's advanced directive or through policy, the patient or society may decide to limit the care we can offer those individuals. However, this should be done with care and deliberation, and not with a simplistic process of labeling the demented as less than human.

Other conceptions of quality of life from a broader philosophical perspective are also important. Jennings, this volume, mentions the notion of human flourishing. Simard, in the QOL-oriented approach to integrated care for people with mild cognitive impairment described in this volume, offers one program designed to encourage such flourishing. We are all trying to seek out the good life in ways that are personal and yet responsive to the community in which we live. Our conceptions of quality of life are developmental and vary from adolescence to old age. Part of this evolution of the human person involves dimensions which seem difficult to incorporate within the scientific framework. Scientific studies have demonstrated the importance of spiritual beliefs and religion to health. Yet, in the assessment of quality of life, we frequently exclude these dimensions of spirituality. AD is clearly a disorder that affects quality of life not only in a health-related way but in other ways as well. Thus, if we are to fully understand how quality of life is affected by dementia, we need to examine it in its broadest contexts. Brod's inclusion of "aesthetic sense" and Rabins's inclusion of "awareness of self" as QOL domains speak to the broader context of QOL assessment.

The dangers of medicalization of dementia are not only evident in the ways in which we conceptualize quality of life, but also in how we conceptualize the disease as a whole. Academic medicine views AD as a condition needing a cure. The discovery of genes that cause the disorder and drugs that help to modest degrees only serve to validate our notion that this is a biological condition to be treated. However, AD is a very common condition that many societies believe is a normal part of aging. Clearly, some intellectual changes affect most people as they age. It cannot be scientifically disproved that all of us would get AD if we live long enough. Thus, a biopsychosocial concept of disease with all of its cultural underpinnings will serve us better than a purely biological model.

AD is one of many diseases from which we may die. Unrealistic goals for the treatment of any disease near the end of life are not helpful to overall quality of life. Thus, the study of quality of life in dementia raises issues that have broad social ramifications. Dementia is one of the critical diseases for the next century (Ballenger & Whitehouse, 1998). Science will continue to affect quality of life for patients and caregivers, but so too will the revolution in healthcare systems and evolution of what it means to be a human being.

The medicalization of health puts too much emphasis on the prevention of death. AD opens our eyes yet again, and in a different way, to the fact that we must all die somewhere, sometime, and of something. It is particularly when we reflect on these latter stages of life that spiritual and religious beliefs seem to surface.

REFERENCES

Ballenger, J. F., & Whitehouse, P. J. (1998). The body as cultural text. Review of nerves and narratives: A cultural history of hysteria in nineteenth-century British prose. *Medical Humanities Review, 12*(1), 96-99.

Deal, W. E., & Whitehouse, P. J. (2000). Concepts of personhood in Alzheimer's disease: Considering Japanese notions of the relational self. In S. O. Long. (ed.), *Caring for the elderly in Japan and the US.* New York: Routledge.

Post, S. G., & Whitehouse, P. J. (1992). Dementia and the life-prolonging technologies used: An ethical question. *Alzheimer Disease and Associated Disorders, 6,* 3-6, 1992. (Commentary)

Post, S. G., & Whitehouse, P. J. (1998). Emerging antidementia drugs: A preliminary ethical view. *Journal of the American Geriatric Society, 46,* 784-787.

Volicer, L. & Hurley, A. (1998). *Hospice care for persons with Advanced Progressive Dementia.* New York: Springer Publishing Co.

Whitehouse, P.J. (1997). The international working group for harmonization of dementia drug guidelines: Past, present, and future. *Alzheimer Disease and Associated Disorders, 11,* (Suppl 3), 2-5.

Whitehouse, P. J. (1998a). Chapter on future drug development for Alzheimer's disease. In J. Growdon & M. Rossor (Eds.), *The blue books of practical neurology series on the dementias.* Woburn, MA: Butterworth Heinemann.

Whitehouse, P. J. (1998b). Measurements of Quality of Life in Dementia. In Wimo, Jonsson, C. Karlsson, & B. Windblad (Eds.), *Health economics of dementia* (pp. 403-417). John Wiley & Sons Ltd. Chichester United Kingdom.

Whitehouse, P. J., & Deal, W. E. (1995). Situated beyond modernity: Lessons for Alzheimer's disease research. *Journal of the American Geriatrics Society, 43,* 1314-1315.

Whitehouse, P. J., Maurer, K., & Ballenger J. F. (1998). The concept of Alzheimer's Disease: Past, present, and future (Meeting Report). *Neuroscience News 1*(4), 39-40.

Whitehouse, P. J., Post, S. G., & Sachs, M. A. (1996). Dementia care at the end of life: Empirical research an international collaboration. *Alzheimer Disease and Associated Disorders, 10*(1), 3-4.

Whitehouse, P. J., & Rabins, P. V.(1992). Quality of life and dementia. *Alzheimer Disease and Associated Disorders, 6,* 135-138.

Index

Page numbers in *italic* indicate illustrations; those followed by t refer to tables.

Springer Publishing Company

Hospice Care for Patients with Advanced Progressive Dementia

Ladislav Volicer, MD, PhD
Ann Hurley, RN, DSNc

"A worthy guide to all those who seek better care for the worst stages of dementia."
—**Joanne Lynne,** MD, MA, MS
Director, Center to Improve the Care of the Dying

"[This book] is distinguished by its humane approach to demented patients as persons worthy of medically expert care even as it is mindful of the need for person-centered palliative care in the later stages of this tragic and mortal disease. This is an essential, unique, and long overdue contribution."

—**Steve Miles,** MD
Soros Faculty Scholar, Project Death in America
Geriatric Medicine, St. Paul Ramsey Medical Center
Center for Bioethics, University of Minnesota

This volume demonstrates how hospice care leads to improved quality of life for patients with terminal dementia and their families.

Much of the information is based on the successful 10-year experience of the E. N. Rogers Memorial Hospital, where the first palliative care program for the management of patients with advanced dementia was developed.

The book discusses Alzheimer's and other progressive dementias and reviews the clinical problems encountered, including infections, eating difficulties, and behavioral problems. It addresses how to implement hospice care programs for these patients and the ethical aspects involved.

This volume is of importance to nurses, physicians, and social workers involved in hospice or home care of patients at the terminal stage of dementia.

Springer Series on Ethics, Law and Aging
1998   305pp.   0-8261-1162-9   hard   www.springerpub.com

536 Broadway, New York, NY 10012-3955 • (212) 431-4370 • Fax (212) 941-7842

Advances in the Diagnosis and Treatment of Alzheimer's Disease

Vinod Kumar, MD, MRC, Psych.
Carl Eisdorfer, MD, PhD, Editors

"Kumar and Eisdorfer have succeeded in bringing together a group of leading experts for this comprehensive and timely volume. Clinicians, students, and investigators with an interest in Alzheimer's disease will find this book to be an important addition to their libraries."
—Gary W. Small, MD

Professor of Psychiatry & Biobehavioral Sciences
Director, UCLA Center on Aging

"Noted Alzheimer's experts provide a thorough update of current knowledge. In addition to covering general issues (epidemiology, etiology and neuropathogenesis, neurobiology, genetics), they discuss diagnostic (e.g., neuropsychological assessment, neuroimaging methods) and treatment approaches (both pharmacological and nonpharmacological—the latter addressing care of families with a relative with dementia, and community care)."

—Bulletin of the Menninger Clinic

Vinod Kumar and Carl Eisdorfer present the latest research in the assessment and treatment of Alzheimer's Disease. The contributors address important new methods of assessment, including neuropsychological assessment, neuroimaging, and biological testing. Other topics of this volume include: • the use of noncholinergic drugs for improving memory • mental health and behavioral issues such as paranoia, depression and agitation • family and community caregiving • an update of ethical and medicolegal debates.

Springer Series on Psychiatry

1998   428pp.   0-8261-1167-X   www.springerpub.com

536 Broadway, New York, NY 10012-3955 • (212) 431-4370 • Fax (212) 941-7842